Inclusive Green Growth
The Pathway to Sustainable Development

Inclusive Green Growth

The Pathway to Sustainable Development

THE WORLD BANK
Washington, D.C.

Contents

Boxes

Figures

Tables

Foreword

Inclusive green growth is *the* pathway to sustainable development.

Over the past 20 years economic growth has lifted more than 660 million people out of poverty and has raised the income levels of millions more, but growth has too often come at the expense of the environment. A variety of market, policy, and institutional failures mean that the earth's natural capital tends to be used in ways that are economically inefficient and wasteful, without sufficient reckoning of the true social costs of resource depletion and without adequate reinvestment in other forms of wealth. These failures threaten the long-term sustainability of growth and progress made on social welfare. Moreover, despite the gains from growth, 1.3 billion people still do not have access to electricity, 2.6 billion still have no access to sanitation, and 900 million lack safe, clean drinking water. Growth has not been inclusive enough.

This report argues that sustained growth is necessary to achieve the urgent development needs of the world's poor and that there is substantial scope for growing cleaner without growing slower. Green growth is necessary, efficient, and affordable. It is the only way to reconcile the rapid growth required to bring developing countries to the level of prosperity to which they aspire with the needs of the more than 1 billion people still living in poverty and the imperative of a better managed environment.

Indeed, green growth is a vital tool for achieving sustainable development. But sustainable development has three pillars: economic, environmental, and social sustainability. We cannot presume that green growth is inherently inclusive. Green growth policies must be carefully designed to maximize benefits for, and minimize costs to, the poor and most vulnerable, and policies and actions with irreversible negative impacts must be avoided.

Green growth also requires improved indicators to monitor economic performance. National accounting indicators like GDP measure only short-term economic growth, whereas indicators like comprehensive wealth—including natural capital—help us determine if growth is sustainable in the long run.

The Conference on Environment and Development, held in Rio in 1992, focused on inclusion and the environment but failed to mention growth. In the lead up to Rio+20, we are reminded that, in 1987, Gro Harlem Brundtland, then Prime Minister of Norway, framed the call for governments to change their approach to growth: *"What is needed now is a new era of economic growth— growth that is forceful and at the same time socially and environmentally sustainable."*

Today, more than ever, we must pay attention to the triple bottom line. Inclusive growth must be green. Green growth must be inclusive.

Rachel Kyte
Vice President
Sustainable Development Network
The World Bank

Acknowledgments

This report was written by a team led by Marianne Fay and Stéphane Hallegatte and composed of Marjorie-Anne Bromhead, Alex Bowen, Michael Chaitkin, Mark Dutz, Atsushi Iimi, Urvashi Narain, and David Tréguer. Significant contributions were made by Antonio Estache, Adrian Fozzard, Kirk Hamilton, Tim Kelly, Masami Kojima, Andreas Kopp, Somik Lall, Eduardo Ley, Marcelino Madrigal, Diego Rodriguez, Siddharth Sharma, and Adrien Vogt-Schilb.

Geoffrey Heal acted as adviser to the report, in addition to being a key contributor to developing the analytical framework.

This report benefited from extensive discussions with Milan Brahmbhatt. We gratefully acknowledge the comments and advice provided by our peer reviewers: Rosina Bierbaum, Richard Damania, Uwe Deichmann, Vivien Foster, Jean-Charles Hourcade, Mike Toman, David Popp, Thomas Sterner, Jeff Vincent, and Zhang Yongsheng. Other useful inputs and suggestions were provided by Zoubida Allaoua, Edward Andersen, Jock Anderson, Ruben Bibas, Dan Biller, James Brumby, Christophe Crepin, Jacqueline Devine, Casper Edmonds, Louis-Gaëtan Giraudet, Céline Guivarch, Bernard Hoekman, Guy Hutton, Vijay Jagannathan, Nalin Kishor, Franck Lecocq, Robert Lempert, Robin Mearns, Aurélie Méjean, Christopher Neal, Junko Narimatsu, Elisa Portale, Valentin Przyluski, Riikka Rajalahti, Apurva Sanghi, Randeep Sudan, Nancy Vandycke, Xiaodong Wang, and Monika Weber-Fahr.

Finally, the report drew on background papers produced for the inaugural conference of the Green Growth Knowledge Platform (available at http://www.greengrowth knowledge.org) by Brian Copeland; Stefan Dercon; Jaime de Melo; Tony Gomez-Ibañez; Winston Harrington, Richard Morgenstern, and Daniel Velez-Lopez; Larry Karp and Megan Stevenson; Howard Kunreuther and Erwann Michel-Kerjan; David Popp; Guido Porto; Andreas Schäfer; Sjak Smulders and Cees Withagen; Jeff Vincent; and Elke Weber and Eric Johnson.

The report was edited by Barbara Karni and Laura Wallace.

This report was sponsored by the Sustainable Development Network of the World Bank under the leadership of Inger Andersen and Rachel Kyte.

Abbreviations

$	US$ unless otherwise indicated
AMMA	African Monsoon Multidisciplinary Analyses
ANS	adjusted net savings
CO_2	carbon dioxide
CO_2-eq	carbon dioxide equivalent
COMTRADE	Commodity Trade Statistics database
ESCO	energy service company
ESTD	early-stage technology development
ETS	Emissions Trading System
EU	European Union
GDP	gross domestic product
GGKP	Green Growth Knowledge Platform
GRP	Green Rating Project (India)
Gt	gigatons
HPS	Husk Power Systems
IEUA	Inland Empire Utility Agency
IFI	international financial institution
ITQ	individual transferable quota
ITS	Intelligent Transport Systems
MCA4Climate	Multi-Criteria Analysis for Climate
MDG	Millennium Development Goal
NO_x	nitrogen oxides
OECD	Organisation for Economic Co-operation and Development
PES	payments for environmental services
PERP	performance evaluation and ratings program
PM10	particulate matter up to 10 micrometers in size

PNK	Putri Naga Komodo (Indonesia)
ppm	parts per million
PPP	purchasing power parity
PROPER	Program for Pollution Control, Evaluation, and Rating (Indonesia)
PV	photovoltaic
R&D	research and development
REDD	Reducing Emissions from Deforestation and Forest Degradation
RSPO	Roundtable on Sustainable Palm Oil
SME	small and medium enterprise
SO_2	sulfur dioxide
TAC	total allowable catch
UNEP	United Nations Environment Programme
UWMP	Regional Urban Water Management Plan
VC	venture capital
WAVES	Wealth Accounting and Valuing Ecosystem Services

Overview

Key Messages

- *Greening growth is necessary, efficient, and affordable.* It is critical to achieving sustainable development and mostly amounts to good growth policies.
- *Obstacles to greening growth are political and behavioral inertia and a lack of financing instruments*—not the cost of green policies as commonly thought.
- *Green growth should focus on what needs to be done in the next five to 10 years* to avoid getting locked into unsustainable paths and to generate immediate, local benefits.

- *The way forward requires a blend of economics, political science, and social psychology*—smart solutions to tackle political economy constraints, overcome deeply entrenched behaviors and social norms, and develop the needed financing tools.
- *There is no single green growth model.* Green growth strategies will vary across countries, reflecting local contexts and preferences—but all countries, rich and poor, have opportunities to make their growth greener and more inclusive without slowing it.

Our current growth patterns are not just unsustainable; they are also deeply inefficient. As a result, they stand in the way of sustainable development and its objectives of social, environmental, and economic sustainability (figure O.1). The past 20 years have shown that the economic and social goals are not only highly compatible, but also largely complementary. Growth drives poverty reduction (though the extent to which it does so depends on the degree of inequality). And improved social outcomes, such as better health and education and greater equality of opportunity, are good

FIGURE O.1   The three pillars of sustainable development

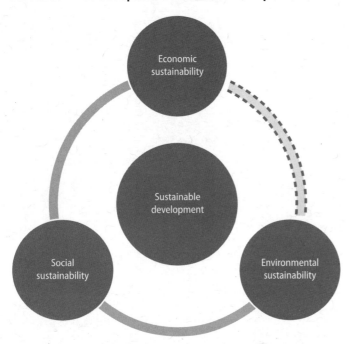

Note: Economic and social sustainability, on the one hand, and social and environmental sustainability, on the other, have been found to be not only compatible, but also largely complementary. Not so with economic and environmental sustainability, as growth has come largely at the expense of the environment—hence, the dotted line on this figure—which is why green growth aims to ensure that economic and environmental sustainability are compatible.

damage. As such, efforts to foster green growth must focus on what is required in the next five to 10 years to sustain robust growth, while avoiding locking economies into unsustainable patterns, preventing irreversible environmental damage, and reducing the potential for regret.

Moreover, rapid action is needed to keep the costs of greening growth manageable and avoid irreversible losses. This urgency applies to developing and developed countries alike:

- Developing countries—which will account for the vast majority of global growth in income, infrastructure, and population in the coming decades—need to choose whether to build right or risk facing costly policy reversals in the future.
- High-income countries—which, with 16 percent of world population, still account for more than 75 percent of global consumption and 41 percent of global emissions of carbon dioxide (CO_2)—must act according to their responsibility. Most important are changes in the patterns of consumption and production that boost demand for green technologies. This is essential to stimulate technological innovation and the scale of production necessary for prices to drop and green technologies to become competitive. Thus, Germany's aggressive solar feed-in tariff was critical in boosting global demand for solar panels, thereby reducing their cost.

As to *how* to make growth greener, textbooks going back at least to the 1950s offer the basic instruments, with environmental taxation, norms, and regulations being the main tools of a green growth strategy. Today, technology is making it easier to implement these measures and monitor their impacts. However, making these measures work is complex in real-world settings plagued by governance failures, market failures, and entrenched interests and behaviors. It requires complementary policies, including public investments, innovation and industrial policies, education and training, labor market reforms, and communication. Making matters worse is the urgency with which

for growth. Not so with the economic and environmental pillars: for the past 250 years, growth has come largely at the expense of the environment. And environmental damages are reaching a scale at which they are beginning to threaten both growth prospects and the progress achieved in social indicators.

What can be done to turn this situation around? We argue that what is needed is green growth—that is, growth that is efficient in its use of natural resources, clean in that it minimizes pollution and environmental impacts, and resilient in that it accounts for natural hazards and the role of environmental management and natural capital in preventing physical disasters. And this growth needs to be inclusive.

Inclusive green growth is not a new paradigm. Rather, it aims to operationalize sustainable development by reconciling developing countries' urgent need for rapid growth and poverty alleviation with the need to avoid irreversible and costly environmental these policies must be designed and implemented, especially in the face of enormous uncertainty about the future climate and technology.

Although we have much theoretical and empirical knowledge to draw on, green growth raises challenging questions, especially when it comes to the developing world. For example, how can developing countries avoid locking in unsustainable and inefficient socioeconomic systems? Will technology allow developing countries to pursue a less environmentally damaging development path than industrial countries did? What is the best way to manage growth with scarce fiscal resources and limited planning and technical know-how? Is green growth just an aspirational goal—desirable from an environmental and ethical point of view, but unattainable given competing economic needs?

At heart, these are questions of economics, which is why the report takes an economic approach—using the standard tools of mainstream growth and environmental economics—with some forays into what social psychology can tell us about the determinants of human behavior. Chapter 1 examines whether green growth is, in fact, feasible and the implications for welfare—the ultimate goal of economic policy. It argues that our current system is inefficient, thereby offering opportunities for cleaner (and not necessarily slower) growth. And it identifies the flaws in the "grow now, clean up later" argument.

The next two chapters tackle the crosscutting issues of market and governance failures. Chapter 2 looks at the range of tools that can be marshaled to change behavior with respect to environmental and natural resources—tools that aim to improve social welfare through greener growth. These include effective market signals, properly framed and judiciously used information, and rules and regulations. Chapter 3 explores the need to navigate between market and governance failures through the careful use of innovation and industrial policies, such as research and development (R&D) subsidies for drought-resistant crops, national strategies for electric cars, and efforts to create

new green industries (such as China's promotion of solar photovoltaic production).

The subsequent three chapters focus on human, natural, and physical capital and their roles in a greener production function. Chapter 4 tackles the debate on whether green growth will create jobs, with political leaders keen to promote the idea of green jobs to reduce high unemployment levels. It finds that, while there is surely potential to create green jobs, the net impact is what matters, and that will depend largely on the nature of the policy chosen and the soundness of labor markets and the business environment. Importantly, evidence on past regulation suggests that fears about massive job losses are misplaced.

Chapter 5 reviews what we know about managing natural capital. Depending on the type of resource (such as extractable or cultivated renewable), the tools include defining property rights, helping firms to move up the value chain, managing trade-offs between higher growth and greener outcomes, and incorporating the economic values of services in policy decisions.

Chapter 6 explores why infrastructure is at the core of inclusive green growth policies, underscoring the high potential for both regret (given the tremendous inertia built into infrastructure investments) and benefits (given the need for massive increases in infrastructure services in developing countries).

Chapter 7 filters the key lessons through a political economy lens and provides a framework for building an inclusive green growth strategy—in light of the technical tools available, the need to maximize local and immediate benefits while minimizing lock-in, and the uncertainties about the future climate and technologies.

What are the overall messages of the report?

First, *inclusive green growth is necessary, efficient, and affordable*. It is necessary because sustainable development cannot be achieved without it. It is efficient in that addressing the market and governance failures that plague our economic systems will create plenty of scope for growing cleaner without necessarily growing slower. The best example is the $1 trillion to $1.2 trillion currently being spent on environmentally harmful subsidies for fossil fuel, agriculture, water, and fisheries. Green growth is affordable because many green policies pay for themselves directly, and the others make economic sense once externalities are priced and ecosystem services are valued.

Second, *greening growth is constrained by social and political inertia and by a lack of financing instruments—not affordability, as is commonly believed.* Entrenched behavior, special interests, and the complicated political economy of reform explain why measures that amount to good growth policies have not yet been implemented. Also, many green growth measures require increased up-front capital. Yet the debate on financing remains focused on who pays what, rather than on how to finance economically (let alone socially) profitable investments.

Third, *greening growth should be carefully sequenced—not occur in one fell swoop—with priority going to what needs to be done in the next 5 to 10 years, both to avoid getting locked into unsustainable paths and to offer immediate, local benefits.* Those benefits will help to reduce the cost of the transition and facilitate the political economy of reform. Urban forms that are created today will affect city structures and housing and transport options for decades or even centuries. With urban populations in developing countries set to increase by 1.5 billion over the next 20 years, there is a window of opportunity to affect urban patterns at low cost.

Fourth, *the search for solutions needs to shift from a search for more financial resources (difficult anyway amid today's fiscal woes) to "getting smart":*

- Smart about learning the lessons of complex reforms to tackle difficult political economy questions, given that many green policies trade immediate costs for later benefits or redistribute benefits from one group to another. Notable successes include trade reforms across the world, reform of fish-

eries in Namibia, reform of the Common Agricultural Policy in the European Union (EU), and progress on fossil fuel subsidies in the Islamic Republic of Iran, where care was taken to manage the losers and publicize the benefits.

- Smart about changing the behavior of consumers and firms and the view of societies about what constitutes social success and acceptable behavior. This entails combining economic incentives with well-framed information and the marketing techniques that public health specialists (or car salesmen) commonly use.

- Smart about developing the appropriate financing tools for the private sector, especially small firms, for local governments (China's cities are developing in a sprawling fashion in part because land sales at their peripheries are an important source of revenue for city governments; World Bank and DRC 2012), and for national governments, which are sometimes so fiscally constrained that they have to choose the investment with the lowest up-front cost (such as a thermal power plant) over one that may be less expensive in the medium term (such as a hydroelectric plant in a country with abundant water resources).

Fifth, *there is no single green growth model.* Inclusive green growth strategies will vary across countries, reflecting local contexts, preferences, and resources, but all countries—rich and poor—have opportunities to green their growth without slowing it.

Greening growth is necessary, efficient, and affordable

Necessary: Making development sustainable requires inclusive green growth

Growth—even measured with such an imperfect metric as gross domestic product (GDP)—is now recognized as a critical driver of poverty reduction (figure O.2, panel a; Ferreira and Ravallion 2009). It has resulted in an 80 percent increase in GDP per capita in developing countries over the past 20 years, despite substantial increases in population. Living standards have improved for many (figure O.2, panels b and c), with more than 660 million rising out of poverty and remarkable progress being made in literacy, education, life expectancy, malnutrition, and infant, child, and maternal mortality. And while China drove much of global poverty reduction, other countries that experienced growth also saw poverty decline rapidly. Ghana, for example, grew much faster than the African average and managed to reduce its poverty rate from 51 to 30 percent between 1990 and 2005 (World Bank 2011c).

Moreover, growth need not cause income inequality. The famous Kuznets curve argument, which posits that inequality first increases and then decreases with income, is not supported by the evidence. Inequality has increased substantially in recent decades in China, but also in the United States and most of Europe. And it has declined in much of Latin America (Milanovic 2010). Some countries reduce inequality as they grow; others let it increase. Policies matter.

Thus, the links between the economic and social pillars of sustainable development are generally self-reinforcing. But the story is not so simple when it comes to the economic and environmental pillars. Economic growth causes environmental degradation—or has for much of the past 250 years—driven by market failures and inefficient policies. As with inequality, overall environmental performance does not first get worse and then improve with income—no Kuznets curve here either. Of course, some local and visible environmental public goods do worsen at first and eventually improve with income—typically local air quality. But this is not true of local pollutants with invisible or long-term impacts (such as the accumulation of pesticides and toxic chemicals in land and water) or global pollutants (such as greenhouse gases in the atmosphere). These often get worse with higher income (figure O.3).

Against this backdrop, some observers, mostly in high-income countries, have argued

FIGURE O.2   As incomes increase . . .

a. . . . Poverty recedes (poverty headcount and GDP per capita)

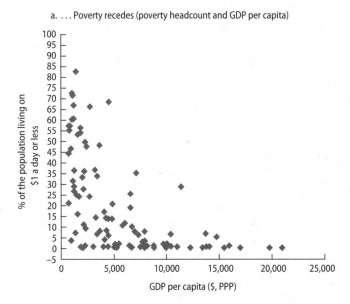

b. . . . Literacy rises (female literacy rate and GDP per capita, 2009)

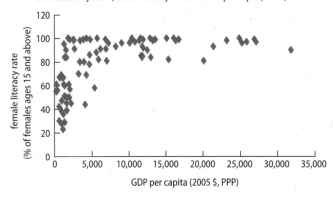

c. . . . Child mortality falls (mortality rate for children under five and GDP per capita, 2010)

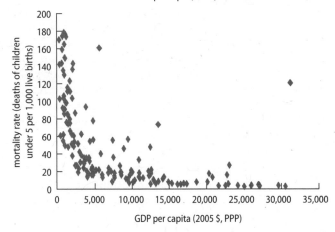

Source: For panel a, Ferreira and Ravallion 2009; for panels b and c, World Bank 2011c.

FIGURE O.3 As incomes increase . . .

a. . . . Local and visible pollutants tend to decline (PM10 concentration and income per capita, 2008)

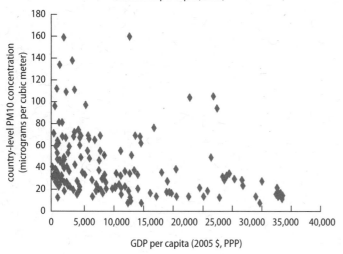

b. . . . Global pollutants, such as CO_2 emissions, tend to increase (CO_2 emissions and income per capita, 2008)

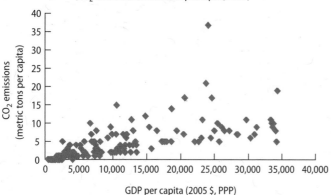

Source: For both panels, World Bank 2011c.

against the need for more growth, suggesting that what is needed instead is a redistribution of wealth (Marglin 2010; Victor 2008). They point to the happiness literature, which suggests that above a country average of $10,000 to $15,000 per capita, further growth does not translate into greater well-being (Easterlin 1995; Layard 2005).

While this argument has value, it remains more relevant for high-income countries, where average annual incomes hover around $36,000. Developing countries—with average income of around $3,500 per capita—are still far from the point at which more wealth

will bring decreasing returns to well-being. In fact, in low-income countries, average income is only about $500 (World Bank 2011c).[1] A redistribution of world income across rich and poor countries—even if it were politically feasible—would leave all with an income of about $8,000 per person per year.

Further, even after the rapid growth of the past decade, some 1.3 billion people do not have access to electricity, 900 million do not have access to clean water, 2.6 billion lack access to improved sanitation, and around 800 million rural dwellers do not have access to an all-weather road and are cut off from the world in the rainy season (Fay and others 2010; IEA 2011). Even with the rapid decline in the share of people living in poverty, close to 1 billion could still be living on $1.25 per day in 2015. With continued growth at about the same speed as during the past 20 years, developing countries would account for about half of the world's income and consumption (but close to 90 percent of the world population) by 2050.

Continued rapid population growth in several developing regions further complicates matters. Current projections are that the world will reach some 9 billion people by 2050. This implies that even more rapid growth is needed to tackle poverty, and more aggressive social policies are needed to ensure that children, especially girls, and mothers receive the care, nutrition, schooling, and employment opportunities they need. And, of course, this demographic challenge puts further stresses on the environment, particularly because much of the rapid population growth is happening in environmentally fragile locations, notably in Africa.

Thus, growth is a necessary, legitimate, and appropriate pursuit for the developing world, but so is a clean and safe environment. Without ambitious policies, growth will continue to degrade the environment and deplete resources critical to the welfare of current and future generations. And what about the argument that ambitious policies would be too costly and destroy jobs? The evidence reviewed in this report suggests that there is plenty of room to green growth without slowing it.

Efficient: Current patterns of growth are not only unsustainable, but also wasteful

There is mounting evidence that our patterns of growth and consumption are unsustainable at the scale required by our current and projected population. Much of this, however, is owing to inefficient production and consumption and poor management of natural resources.

Unsustainable

Population and income growth and the resulting increase in demand for food have driven the expansion of agricultural production around the world.[2] Intensification and productivity increases have helped to limit ecosystem loss in many countries, but poorly managed intensification has also exacerbated agrochemical and water pollution, soil exhaustion, and salinity. Extensive farming, driven by large-scale expansion in some regions and poverty-level subsistence agriculture in others, has contributed to land degradation and deforestation; forest losses averaged 5.2 million hectares annually between 2000 and 2010, mostly in tropical—and, hence, more intensely biologically diverse—regions (FAO 2010). By 2008 one quarter of the world's land surface was degraded as a result of soil erosion, salinization, nutrient depletion, and desertification (Bai and others 2008).

Income and population growth have also stretched water supplies. Water withdrawals have tripled in the past 50 years, leading to water scarcity and groundwater depletion (World Bank 2007b). Withdrawals are projected to increase in developing countries by another 50 percent by 2025, by which time roughly 5.5 billion people—two thirds of the projected global population—will live in areas facing moderate-to-severe water stress (UNESCO and WWAP 2006).

Growth has similarly strained ecosystems, with roughly 60 percent of ecosystem services now of lower quality than 50 years ago (MEA 2005). Additionally, the current rate of species extinction, stemming mainly from habitat loss and degradation, is 100 to 1,000 times higher than before humans walked the planet (Pimm and others 1995). In 2008, 875 species became extinct, and more than 17,000 others are at high risk (IUCN 2009).

Carbon dioxide emissions are accumulating in the atmosphere, approaching a level that will make it impossible to maintain global mean temperature below 2°C in excess of the preindustrial level, even though the probability of irreversible environmental changes is increasing with temperature (for example, rapid ice loss in Greenland and forest dieback in the Amazon). Carbon dioxide is also affecting the world's oceans. Because of global warming, we have already committed to high probabilities of coral bleaching and mortality by the late twenty-first century, which will significantly harm reef ecosystems (World Bank 2010d). The concurrent acidification of oceans, which absorb about one quarter of the excess carbon dioxide in the atmosphere, is threatening marine food webs and could undermine the global fishing industry and food security (Laffoley and Baxter 2009).

Lastly, energy prices are likely to be high in the future, because oil resources that are easy and cheap to extract and use have already been extracted, and the world is now turning toward fossil fuels that are more expensive—and more damaging to the environment—such as shale gas, tar sands, oil from deep offshore wells, or even liquefied coal. Without significant changes in energy policy, the amount of resources the world economy will have to dedicate to fossil fuel extraction and energy production is likely to increase substantially, making higher energy efficiency even more desirable in the future than it is today.

Wasteful

The environment can be thought of as natural capital that is often inefficiently managed, with many precious resources wasted. Investing in natural capital—just like investing in human or physical capital—is therefore good growth policy. The value of the services provided by well-managed ecosystems is illustrated by the impact of reforestation and watershed restoration programs. In China's Loess plateau, such programs were associated with a near doubling of household incomes as a result of higher-value agricultural production as well as reduced frequency of landslides and flooding and increased resilience to drought (figure O.4; World Bank 2005b).

This inefficiency stems partly from the fact that many natural resources are common property, so consumption by one person precludes consumption by another, and it is hard to exclude potential users. Open-access regimes for common property create incentives to use up such resources as quickly as possible. Open access fisheries are a classic example in which catch per fisher and per vessel has been declining steadily because of overfishing, and continued depletion threatens the livelihood of more than 100 million people and the food security of many more.

Subsidies exacerbate common property problems, yet substantial resources are allocated to environmentally harmful price support schemes (box O.1). Global subsidies to fisheries are estimated at $10 billion to $30 billion and are partly to blame for the sixfold increase in the fleet capacity index between 1970 and 2005 (World Bank and FAO 2009).[3] In Mexico, subsidies for energy used in irrigation, amounting to around 1 percent of GDP, are exacerbating excessive groundwater withdrawals and the depletion of key aquifers. India suffers from the same problem in addition to spending some 2 percent of GDP on a fertilizer subsidy overly weighted in favor of nitrogen; the resulting use of fertilizer is causing serious pollution problems.

Production and consumption processes are often wasteful, too. This is particularly obvious in the energy sector. Existing energy efficiency technologies can cost-effectively reduce energy use in new buildings by at least 30 percent. In fact, making new buildings in China more energy efficient would reduce energy costs by more than 50 percent, while increasing construction costs by only 10 percent. Waste also plagues food production. Some 15 to 30 percent of food produced in developing countries is lost before it reaches the market due to poor storage and transport facilities. In high-income countries, meanwhile, one third of food is wasted through losses in supermarkets and homes and "plate-waste" (Foresight 2011).

The possibility of solving market and governance failures opens the way to policies that have both economic and environmental benefits and is at the heart of green growth strategies. (In that respect, greening growth is first and foremost based on good growth policies.) These market and governance failures have long been understood,

FIGURE O.4   The Loess plateau, before and after the watershed restoration program

Source: For the left-hand image, Till Niermann, March 25, 1987, http://en.wikipedia.org/wiki/File:Loess_landscape_china.jpg; for the right-hand image, http://digitalmedia.worldbank.org/slideshows/china1005/.

BOX O.1 What is the aggregate economic support to the (over)use of natural capital? $1 trillion to $1.2 trillion annually

A compilation of estimates by international organizations of aggregate support for the use of natural capital suggests an approximate total of $1 trillion to $1.2 trillion, consistent with McKinsey's estimate of $1.1 trillion (McKinsey and Company 2011). This support includes the following:

- *Fossil fuel subsidies: $455 billion–$485 billion.* This includes subsidies to fossil fuel production or use in Organisation for Economic Co-operation and Development (OECD) countries ($45 billion to $75 billion a year between 2005 and 2010) and consumption in developing economies ($409 billion in 2010; IEA 2011).
- *Water subsidies: $200 billion–$300 billion.* This represents subsidies to groundwater extraction or irrigation infrastructure—estimated as the difference between the market value of water and the part of costs covered by tariffs. Limited data are available, but Myers and Kent (2001) estimate water sector subsidies at $230 billion in 2000 and McKinsey (2011) cites estimates of $200 billion to $300 billion.
- *Fishery subsidies: $10 billion to $30 billion.* This encompasses a wide variety of instruments such as

fuel price supports, grants, concessional credit and insurance, and direct payments to industry. Estimates range from $10 billion per year (World Bank and FAO 2009) to $27 billion per year (UNEP 2011).
- *Transfers to agriculture: $370 billion.* This represents total support to the agriculture sector in OECD countries (OECD 2011a) and includes different types of instruments, some environmentally harmful, such as market price supports, but some not, such as payments decoupled from production levels.

While these estimates suffer from errors of inclusion (some of the OECD countries' agricultural subsidies that were included are not environmentally harmful) and exclusion (they do not include developing countries' subsidies to agriculture, estimated by the OECD at about $200 billion for the few emerging economies for which data were available) and are therefore neither precise nor exhaustive, they do suggest that substantial resources go to environmentally harmful subsidies.

and their persistence suggests that the difficulty of correcting them should not be underestimated.

Affordable: Much of green growth pays for itself, and an innovative private sector keeps costs in check

Environmental policies should, in principle, improve social welfare and economic efficiency by reducing excessive pollution and other environmental bads. Nevertheless, such policies clearly have costs. They can hit taxpayers who have to pay the bill (for subsidies to renewable energy or public spending on green R&D) or producers and consumers if the policies mandate the use of more expensive or less productive technologies (such as renewable energy resources that are more

costly than fossil fuel). Environmental policies alter relative prices and therefore change the structure of demand, requiring costly adjustments in the structure of production. Demand may decrease in sectors that have high capacity (coal production) and increase in sectors that have limited capacity (public transport). As a result, efficiency may fall, at least during an adjustment phase, jobs may be lost, and the poor may suffer if compensatory measures are not adopted.

Moreover, the up-front capital requirements are high. The energy investments needed globally to achieve greenhouse gas concentration of 450 parts per million (ppm) carbon dioxide equivalent (CO_2-eq; the level needed to maintain a 50 percent chance of not exceeding global warming of 2°C above preindustrial temperatures) could amount to

FIGURE O.5   Up-front investment costs for energy supply and energy efficiency could be substantial

(additional investment needed in the energy sector, both in energy supply and demand, in 2030 to reach a 450 ppm and a 550 ppm CO$_2$-eq objective, according to four global models)

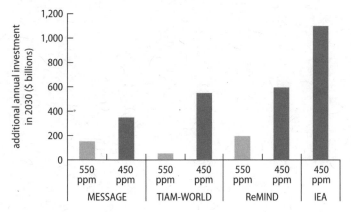

Source: More information on these models can be found in the following sources: on MESSAGE, van Vliet and others 2012; on ReMIND, Luderer and others 2012; on TIAM-WORLD, Loulou and Labriet 2008; on IEA, IEA 2011.
Note: IEA (2011) does not provide estimates for a 550 ppm scenario.

between $350 billion and $1.1 trillion per year by 2030 (figure O.5). A 550 ppm target appears much easier to achieve, requiring some $50 billion–$200 billion of additional investments per year, but an additional $75 billion to $100 billion would still be needed to adapt to climate change (World Bank 2010d). Adding needed investments in water and land to energy, annual investments of $900 billion to $1,700 billion could be needed over and above business-as-usual requirements (McKinsey and Company 2011).

But many of these capital investments will be recouped through subsequent savings, so the net financial costs will be much lower. For example, the high capital cost of wind and solar energy or hydropower is offset by their low operating costs. Globally $1 spent on energy efficiency saves $2 through investments in new supply, with the savings even greater in developing countries (World Bank 2010d). As a result, the World Bank estimates that more than half the measures needed to decarbonize the energy systems of developing countries would eventually pay for themselves, bringing the financial costs down to

between $140 billion and $175 billion per year in 2030 or perhaps half a percentage point of developing countries' GDP (World Bank 2010d). In East Asia, the estimated additional net financing required for a sustainable energy path is $80 billion, not much more than the $70 billion the region currently spends on fossil fuel subsidies (Wang and others 2010; IEA 2008).

Furthermore, determining affordability is about more than a financial ledger. Green policies can contribute to growth (box O.2) and boost a nation's overall wealth. And they help to reduce the damage done by environmental degradation, which is costly for an economy: equivalent to 8 percent of GDP across a sample of countries representing 40 percent of the developing world's population (figure O.6). As a result, benefits may well outweigh the costs (implying a negative net economic cost). $900 billion to $1,700 billion of green investments in land, water, and energy could yield economic returns of around $3 trillion per year, rising to $3.7 trillion with carbon at $30 per ton and no energy, agricultural, or water subsidies (McKinsey and Company 2011).

Thanks to such benefits, the net costs of greening growth appear manageable, although affordability will, of course, depend on the speed and ambition of the greening (as illustrated by the difference between the 450 ppm and 550 ppm targets) and on the design of policies. But the worse the environmental degradation and existing inefficiency, the greater the potential benefits to be obtained from green policies.

At the firm level, the cost of environmental regulation to firms is typically modest, with costs lower than expected thanks to the ability of firms to adapt and innovate (chapter 3). As a result, there is no evidence that environmental regulation systematically hurts profitability. While studies from the 1980s and 1990s found negative impacts, more recent papers find more positive results, partly because they allow a few years for firms to adapt and partly perhaps because we have become better at designing environmental regulations that promote efficiency gains

BOX O.2   The many ways in which green policies can contribute to growth

Green policies and practices can contribute to growth through three channels (see chapter 1). First, *they can help to increase the amount of natural, physical, and human capital available*: Better-managed soil is more productive. Well-managed natural risks result in lower capital losses from natural disasters (Hallegatte 2011). Healthier environments result in more productive workers: a recent California study shows a strong impact of air quality on the productivity of farm workers (Graff Zivin and Neidell 2011).

Second, *they can promote efficiency*. For instance, imposing environmental taxes (taxing "bads") and removing distortionary subsidies creates fiscal space for governments to lower labor taxes or subsidize green public "goods" such as public transport or renewable energy. In London, congestion taxes, besides reducing traffic, helped to finance investments in the aging public transport system, thereby increasing effectiveness of the price signal by reducing the costs or "disutility" associated with switching from single-car use to public transport (Transport for London 2008). And many firms—including large multinationals such as Hewlett Packard, Cisco, Clorox, and FedEx—are finding that embracing sustainability has improved the bottom line in part by promoting greater efficiency (Nidumolu and others 2009).

Third, *green policies stimulate innovation*. Study after study reports that well-designed environmental regulations stimulate innovation by firms, as measured by R&D spending or patents (see chapter 3). Surveys of firms in the European Union identify existing or future environmental regulation as the main driver for the adoption of incremental innovations. Similarly, international sustainability standards can help local firms to upgrade their environmental practices, a form of catch-up innovation. In developing countries, green policies can also encourage the adaptation and adoption of greener technologies that have been developed elsewhere.

Finally, *green policies also accrue non-growth gains to welfare*. They can reduce inequality through job creation and poverty alleviation, and they can reduce output volatility by increasing resilience to environmental and economic shocks, like natural disasters or spikes in commodity prices. A modeling exercise suggests that half of the cost of climate policies to limit greenhouse gas concentration at 550 ppm could be paid for by less vulnerability to oil scarcity (Rozenberg and others 2010).

(Ambec and others 2011). Further, where revenues from environmental taxes are used to reduce taxes on labor and income, the impact on GDP is likely to be neutral or positive, as found in an analysis of seven EU countries (Andersen and others 2007, cited in Ambec and others 2011).

Other ex-post analyses confirm this conclusion. The EU Emissions Trading System has no negative impact on net imports in the aluminum, steel, and cement sectors (Ellerman and others 2010; Quirion 2011; Sartor 2012) or on the performance of German firms in general (Anger and Oberndorfer 2008). Meanwhile, the climate levy on U.K. firms seems to affect energy efficiency, but not economic performance and firm exit (Martin and others 2009).

Refineries located in Los Angeles significantly increased productivity in the late 1980s and early 1990s, a time of dramatically expanded regulation in California and decreasing refinery productivity in the rest of the United States. Interviews with plant managers suggest productivity increases resulted from a careful redesign of production processes to comply with the new regulations (Berman and Bui 2001 and others). Similarly, the productivity of the Mexican food-processing industry increased with stronger environmental regulations (Alpay and others 2002, cited in Ambec and others 2011).

Moreover, there is no evidence that environmental policies have led to an exodus of firms to "pollution havens" (locations with lax environmental policies). Tighter environmental regulation may cause firms to relocate, but they will choose locations that are more attractive overall, as pollution abatement costs represent a small share of production costs for most industries (Copeland

FIGURE O.6 **Reducing environmental degradation would provide substantial economic benefits**

(cost of enviromental degradation expressed as percentage of GDP equivalent)

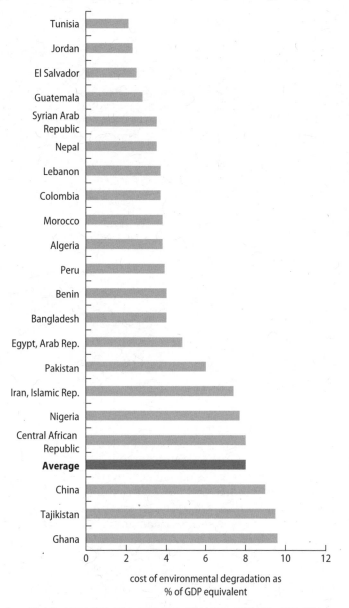

cost of environmental degradation as
% of GDP equivalent

Source: World Bank 2004, 2005a, 2006a, 2006b, 2006c, 2006d, 2006e, 2006f, 2007a, 2007b, 2007c, 2008, 2009, 2010a, 2010b, 2010c, 2011a, World Bank and DRC 2012.

2012). Factors such as availability of capital, labor abundance, location, institutions, and agglomeration effects are more important than environmental policy in determining the location choice and competitiveness of firms.

But obstacles are plentiful, and green growth is no substitute for good inclusive growth policies

If green growth is necessary, efficient, and affordable, what is impeding it? Across countries and income levels, a mix of governance and market failures, complex political economy, entrenched interests and behaviors, and financing constraints are significant obstacles. Further, despite much rhetoric to the effect, green growth is no panacea and will not substitute for a good business environment and the reforms that are needed to promote growth and protect the poor.

When first-best recommendations meet second-best situations

Much of green growth is about good growth policies—addressing market failures and "getting the price right" by introducing environmental taxation, pricing environmental externalities (such as carbon pricing), creating tradable property rights, and reducing inappropriate subsidies. These measures are critical for enabling the private sector to undertake needed investments and innovations and for getting consumers to internalize the true costs of their behavior. But as with all good economic policy making, textbook policy recommendations, however appropriate, must be applied with insights into behaviors, political economy, and governance and market failures. This is an enormous challenge for a variety of reasons.

First, *getting prices right may be difficult because of political or social acceptability issues.* The benefits are usually diffuse and uncertain, while the costs (the burden of the price increase) are immediate, visible, and often concentrated on a vocal minority. This is why price changes can be achieved only when political economy issues are managed with appropriate complementary policies.

Second, *getting prices right may not be sufficient because other market imperfections can prevent prices from being the silver bullet of environmental policies.* These market imperfections include the following:

- *Low price elasticity.* The ability of prices to trigger changes in behavior and technology is sometimes limited by substitution possibilities: the responsiveness of drivers to higher fuel prices is low in the absence of alternative means of transportation. The ability of firms in the renewable energy sector to respond to incentives will depend on whether transmission lines are built between centers of consumption and production. In these cases, price-based policies may have to be complemented with direct infrastructure investments (such as public transportation and transmission lines) and other policy actions, like changes in urban planning or in norms and regulations. But if substitution capacity is limited by alternatives, their provision may increase the economy's efficiency and boost income or promote economic growth, making the price increase more politically acceptable.

- *Missing markets or institutions.* Specific institutional measures may be required to transform the "right price" into the right incentive. Where tenants are paying energy bills, for instance, owners and developers have little incentive to "build right" or to invest in more energy-efficient appliances unless they can recoup their investments through higher rents or sales price. This "principal-agent" problem can be tackled through information (such as energy efficiency labels for homes), specific schemes to finance investments in energy efficiency, or norms (such as compulsory retrofit when homes are sold).

- *Lack of credibility and predictability of price signals.* Governments cannot commit to maintaining environmental price instruments over the long term, which puts them in a poor position to encourage firms to undertake long-term, risky investments (notably in R&D and long-lived infrastructure).

- *Coordination failures and knowledge externalities.* Prices are ill-suited to address the "classic" market failures usually invoked to justify innovation and industrial policies. Think about electric cars whose development requires coordination between elec-

tricity providers, city planners, battery producers, and car manufacturers.

Third, *inertia and biases in behavior are such that many efficiency measures that might pay for themselves are not implemented.* Household responses to higher energy prices are often disappointing, and firms do not always exploit all opportunities to improve efficiency (Gillingham and others 2009; Allcott and Mullainathan 2010). Energy savings of 20–25 percent could be achieved through improved industrial processes in high-income and emerging economies (World Bank 2010d).

Fourth, *financing tools to tackle up-front investments are inadequate.* Take the case of solar, wind, or hydroelectric energy, which is characterized by much higher capital costs than fossil-based energy, but extremely low operating costs, or energy efficiency that requires up-front investments in new equipment or add-ons whose costs are then recouped over time through energy savings. Even with agriculture or fisheries, a shift to more sustainable practices typically results in lower returns and investments in early years that are then offset by higher returns in the future. The need for up-front financing can be a binding constraint for developing-country governments (especially local ones with limited access to capital markets and a small tax base) and the private sector (especially small and medium enterprises). Few countries have a well-developed banking sector, let alone energy service companies that specialize in financing investments in energy efficiency.

No substitute for good growth policy: The private sector needs an enabling environment

Green growth strategies are growth strategies with the additional goal of fostering a better environment. As such, they cannot substitute for good growth policies: environmental measures are unlikely to offset distorted labor markets, illiquid financial systems, or poor business environments.

FIGURE O.7   Developing countries may have substantial unexploited potential in green exports

(green and close-to-green exports as a share of total exports from developing countries, 2000–10)

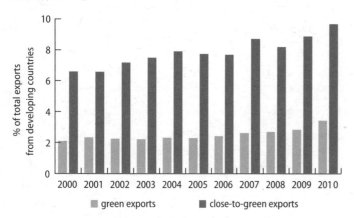

Source: Dutz and Sharma 2012, based on data from the Commodity Trade Statistics database (COMTRADE) and a six-digit proximity matrix based on COMTRADE.
Note: Close-to-green exports are exports of goods that are not "green" but require similar skills—in the way growing apples requires the same set of skills as growing pears so that a country that is good at the former is likely to be good at the latter.

A case in point is "green jobs," a topic that has attracted substantial attention following the recent global financial crisis. Advocates stress that, in a situation of high unemployment, a green fiscal stimulus could effectively address recession-induced unemployment and set the stage for cleaner post-recession growth patterns. The argument is attractive: although green projects may not be the most labor intensive or "shovel ready," they have the added advantage of carrying environmental benefits. That said, a fiscal stimulus—green or not—is effective only if unemployment is linked to insufficient demand rather than to structural issues (such as lack of skilled workers or a poor investment climate).

Beyond stimulus effects, some countries—including Brazil, China, Germany, Japan, the Republic of Korea, and Morocco—are looking at green growth as a potential source of longer-term growth through which to create new markets. And even though not every country can become the world leader in solar panels or wind turbines, developing countries may have substantial unexploited potential in green exports (figure O.7). Many developing countries have natural endowments that

create a potential comparative advantage in green activities (such as water resources and hydropower potential or insolation and solar power potential). Realizing this potential could generate jobs and exports, thereby boosting growth and output.

But green policies cannot address structural constraints to growth and employment creation, at least if deployed alone. They will not be effective at creating green jobs where labor markets are distorted and regulations discourage small business development. They will not offset an unattractive business environment. And where the labor force's skills are inappropriate for developing a competitive manufacturing sector, environmental policies can hardly replace education. Thus, a recent study of South Africa concludes that, while the idea of developing green industries (such as solar power) is appealing, it has little chance of succeeding unless structural problems such as regulatory obstacles to the creation of small enterprises and the lack of skilled workers are addressed (World Bank 2011b).

Skill shortages already appear to be impeding the greening of growth. In China and India, rural electrification programs are suffering from a lack of skilled workers. Reasons for these shortages include a scarcity of scientists and engineers, the poor reputation and limited attractiveness of some sectors important for the green transition such as waste management, and a limited number of teachers and trainers in environmental services (ILO and CEDEFOP 2011).

In countries where the business environment is not conducive to investment and growth, better economic policies must be the first step. Lessons from trade liberalization are telling: where labor mobility is limited by skills and regulations and where investments in the sectors that benefit from trade liberalization are impaired by inappropriate policies, both workers and the private sector take longer to adjust. The benefits from more trade take longer to materialize, and adjustment costs are much higher. Similarly, economic benefits from green policies are more likely to be large and immediate if economic policies are conducive to change and favor the development of more environmentally friendly and more productive activities.

The poor and vulnerable need social protection

While there is a general presumption that the poor suffer most from environmental degradation and its impact, this need not imply that they would benefit automatically from green growth policies. For example, removing fossil fuel subsidies would clearly reduce the poor's purchasing power unless compensated for by other measures.

But subsidies are often regressive and can be replaced by better-targeted transfers at a fraction of the cost (figure O.8). By one estimate, the cost to the budget of transferring $1 to the poorest 20 percent of the population via gasoline subsidies is $33 (Arze del Granado and others 2010). Similarly, consumption subsidies for water and electricity can usefully be replaced by connection subsidies that are invariably better targeted, as the

poor account for the majority of those without access to basic services.

In sum, hopes that green growth will single-handedly solve countries' employment, competitiveness, or poverty problems are probably as unfounded as the fear that environmental policies will lead to massive loss of jobs or competitiveness. Adjustment costs may vary across industries because some sectors are inherently more innovative than others and tend to adapt better. Better regulation—particularly if supported by training, R&D support, and the recycling of environmental taxes into other tax cuts—will help to minimize these adjustment costs and maximize benefits. Also needed are steps to protect the poor from the potential downsides of green policies and to ensure that they benefit fully from the likely upsides.

The way forward: Good and inclusive growth policies tailored to real-world challenges

So greening growth requires good growth policies adapted to political economy realities and entrenched behaviors. It entails reforms in the patterns of pricing, regulation, and public investment that trigger resistance. It requires complex changes in behaviors and social norms because, even with efficiency gains and new technology, it is unlikely that middle-class consumers (whether in rich or in poor countries) can stick to current consumption patterns. And it requires knowing when to go for the politically expedient rather than the economically optimal, carefully deploying social marketing tools and making financial tools available.

Complicating matters is the fact that opportunities to green growth at a manageable cost are not evenly distributed over time. This creates urgency for some, though not all, green policies and is one of several arguments for why "grow dirty and clean up later" is not a good option even for poor countries (box O.3).

What follows is a three-prong strategy for tackling entrenched interests and behaviors, financing constraints, and the risk of lock-in.

FIGURE O.8   Fossil fuel subsidies benefit primarily the rich

(fossil fuel subsidy allocation, by income quintile, average across 20 countries, various years)

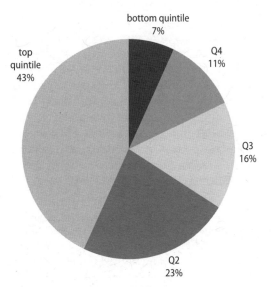

Source: Arze del Granado and others 2010.

BOX O.3   Why "grow dirty and clean up later" is misleading

Many argue that poor countries should focus on satisfying human needs before attending to nature, especially given their relatively small environmental footprint. This argument is misleading for several reasons.

First, not all environmental goods are superior goods whose share in total consumption increases with income. Individuals who struggle to feed and house themselves may not see biodiversity protection and climate change mitigation as priorities, but local environmental goods affect their daily lives, with significant impact on income and welfare. The lack of solid waste disposal, for example, is not merely an environmental issue. By clogging drains, it leads to health hazards and flooding, with serious economic and human consequences:

- In Haiti, poor solid waste disposal is to blame for the resurgence of diseases such as dengue and for vulnerability to storms.
- In India, better solid waste disposal systems were a principal recommendation of the fact-finding committee established to investigate the causes of the 2005 Mumbai floods, which caused almost $2 billion in damages and killed an estimated 500 people.

Similarly, mismanaging water resources impairs people's ability to grow crops and feed their families. Where natural assets like soil quality, water, and standing forests serve as critical inputs into economic production, good environmental policies enhance income generation and poverty alleviation.

Second, it may be impossible or prohibitively expensive to clean up later. The loss of many environmental assets—most obviously biodiversity—is irreversible. This is also the case with climate. Because greenhouse gases reside in the atmosphere for a long time, each emitted molecule will influence the climate over decades (for methane), centuries (for CO_2), or longer. Irreversibility may also occur because of economic and technological lock-in. A lot of infrastructure is long lived, and today's choices will be hard to reverse. Urban forms are largely determined when city populations are increasing rapidly and most buildings and transport systems are being built. The consequences of development based on a low-density, individual-vehicle transportation model are largely irreversible, as evidenced by the current struggles of U.S. urban planners to densify and develop public transport systems.

Prong 1: Tailored strategies that maximize local and immediate benefits and avoid lock-in

Green growth policies require governments to do a better job of managing both market and governance failures. This is obvious in any discussion of green innovation or industrial policies, but also of the regulatory and market ("good growth") reforms that are needed, some of which are complex. Even sophisticated administrations may struggle with market-based instruments, as experience with the European Trading System has demonstrated (Betz and Sato 2006). Optimal solutions will differ across countries with varying degrees of institutional capacity, transparency, accountability, and civil society capacity. Therefore, green growth strategies need to be tailored to a country's circumstances, and "best practices" should be imported with caution.

Maximize local and immediate benefits. In addition to being tailored to local circumstances, strategies need to address the political economy of reform. Green growth strategies should aim to minimize transition costs by offsetting them to the extent possible, with visible and immediate benefits. This implies designing policies to maximize short-term, local benefits, such as increased efficiency and productivity, safety and resilience, job creation, and poverty alleviation.

Avoid lock-in. Governments cannot make all of the changes needed at once: they have limited resources and limited implementation capacity to devote to complex problems; they also have limited political capital to defend

TABLE O.1   Some guiding principles for establishing green growth strategies

		Local and immediate benefits	
		LOWER (Trade-offs exist between short-and long-term or local and global benefits)	**HIGHER** (Policies provide local and immediate benefits)
Inertia and/or risk of lock-in and irreversibility	**LOWER** (action is less urgent)	• Lower-carbon, higher-cost energy supply • Carbon pricing • Stricter wastewater regulation	• Drinking water and sanitation, solid waste management • Lower-carbon, lower-cost energy supply • Loss reduction in electricity supply • Energy demand management • Small-scale multipurpose water reservoirs
	HIGHER (action is urgent)	• Reduced deforestation • Coastal zone and natural area protection • Fisheries catch management	• Land use planning • Public urban transport • Family planning • Sustainable intensification in agriculture • Large-scale multipurpose water reservoirs

policies against interest groups and political opposition. A focus on the sectors and interventions that are most urgent—that is, those that can help to prevent irreversibility or reduce inertia—is thus called for.

Table O.1 illustrates the implications for priority setting of emphasizing local and immediate benefits and urgency. While lower-carbon energy from renewable sources is highly desirable, it is easier to build renewable plants later (even if this requires retiring thermal power plants) than to try and reverse poor land-use planning that has resulted in sprawling cities. Good land-use planning and urban public transport can provide short-term benefits—for instance, by reducing congestion and exposure to disasters and by favoring denser and more energy-efficient development. Table O.1 provides general statements on a few green policies; this analysis needs to be carried out at regional, national, and local scales to take into account specific contexts (see, for instance, an application to the Mediterranean countries in CMI 2012).

Developing countries (especially low-income countries) should prioritize policies that (a) have a negative or zero economic cost thanks to synergies with development (such as developing hydropower where appropriate, implementing effective urban plans, or scaling up family planning policies to manage population pressures and improve health and education outcomes), (b) have a positive economic cost but large direct welfare impacts (that is, when they target local environmental goods such as local air pollution or natural risks), or (c) are financed from external resources (including through carbon trading).

Actively manage the political economy of reform. Managing the political economy of reform also entails measures that target those segments of the population that would otherwise oppose reforms. For example, in 2010 the Islamic Republic of Iran increased domestic energy prices by up to 20 times, reducing fossil fuel subsidies by some $50 billion–$60 billion. It offset them with $30 billion in cash transfers that benefited 80 percent of its population, thereby addressing the fact that opposition to the reform of such subsidies usually comes from the middle class. The combination of cash transfers with a well-orchestrated public relations campaign was critical to the success of the reform (Guillaume and others 2011).

Understanding the sources of resistance to a reform helps to design the reform process in a way that minimizes this resistance (box O.4). Sound information about winners and

BOX O.4   Morocco: The importance of political economy

A sound understanding of the winners and losers of possible green growth strategies helps policy makers find ways to address tough economic reforms—as Morocco has recently learned in its quest to overhaul a universal subsidy system that rewards fossil fuel consumption. By gaining insights into the political economy of reform, Morocco is now poised to reform its energy subsidy, which would sharply reduce fiscal costs and facilitate a greener growth path.

The problems with the energy subsidy are multiple. Its fiscal impact reached 5.5 percent of GDP in 2011, absorbing roughly 17 percent of the total investment budget. It undercuts Morocco's ambitious mitigation goals by keeping the price of fossil-based energy products low, thus making renewable and efficiency investments less competitive. And it is regressive, with the wealthy benefitting the most.

So why has Morocco hesitated to reform the subsidy? A big reason is that the subsidy reform was believed to be unpopular, although the government had never done a survey to ascertain just how unpopular, among which segments of society, and whether alternatives could motivate changes. For that reason, the World Bank offered to conduct such a poll in 2010 using a nationally representative sample of 1,600 households.

The results are astonishing: more than 70 percent of the population was unaware of the existence of energy subsidies. Thus, the vast majority of buyers of 12 liter cooking gas bottles—a product as widespread as bread—did not know that the real market price was more than DH 100 ($14) instead of the standard retail price of DH 40 ($5.6). In addition, a large majority opposed the idea of reducing subsidies—although this majority decreased once offered a well-targeted social program, and fell even further when the program was explained in detail. In the end, it was the wealthy that remained the group most opposed to reform.

This simple exercise in revealing political awareness and preferences helped the previous government develop a communication strategy over the medium term, starting from informing the population of the existence of the subsidy system and explaining its disadvantages. A communication campaign ensued in the first months of 2011, and the government elected in November 2011 now has energy subsidy reform at the top of its agenda.

Box text contributed by Andrea Liverani.

---

losers enables an information campaign to be tailored to potential critics.

One way of improving public decisions and determining priorities is to inform decision makers of the value of the services provided by natural ecosystems, so that this value can be compared directly with the economic costs and benefits of their decisions. Indeed, most environmental assets do not have widely accepted prices either for their intrinsic value or for the services they provide (such as flood protection). As a result, decisions that involve a trade-off between economic interests and natural assets (such as building a road through a rain forest) are difficult to assess.

Green accounting extends beyond the valuation of natural assets and focuses on a country's stock of natural and other assets (its wealth) rather than on a flow measure like GDP. By doing so, it helps to identify situations in which economic growth does not create wealth (because natural assets are consumed more rapidly than other assets are created) and is not sustainable. For instance, a green accounting exercise suggests that China's growth would be much lower than its official GDP growth of nearly 10 percent a year if environmental depletion and degradation were included. Indeed, calculations put China's adjusted net national income growth at about 5.5 percent a year (World Bank and DRC 2012).

Prong 2: Measures that promote and incentivize smart decision making

Even though the information provided by green accounting can help inform and balance the debates on political choices and public investments, it does not constitute an incentive for firms and individuals. To influence their behavior, additional measures are required, and it is here that governments can play a critical role by ensuring that market incentives promote green behavior on the part of firms and individuals.

Getting the prices right will influence consumer demand as well as firms' choice of production processes (for example, higher energy prices will make firms use more energy-efficient technologies to minimize their production costs) and products (to respond to consumer demand that changes with relative prices). But it will also make them innovate, develop, and implement new technologies and processes.

Getting prices right also has a central role in shaping the built-up structure of cities. Land developers respond to price signals so that higher land prices lead to higher density—enhancing productivity spillovers and the supply of affordable housing and managing demand for transport. When "official" land prices do not reflect demand and are depressed at the urban periphery, sprawl or suburbanization likely will be excessive.

But market incentives will not suffice. For green policies to succeed, governments will need all of the arrows in the public policy quiver.

Informing and nudging to influence individuals and address behavioral biases

Behavioral biases limit the impact of market incentives and complicate the design of environmental policies. For example, one explanation for the large unexploited potential that exists in energy efficiency springs from the "cognitive myopia" that prevents individuals from accurately weighing future benefits against immediate costs. Also, individuals measure gains and losses with respect to a reference point and weigh losses more than gains (Tversky and Kahneman 1992); as a result, they tend to consider the cost of new environmental policy as a loss and to disregard environmental damages avoided. People are biased toward the status quo, tend to choose the default option, and have an aversion to ambiguity, resulting in a tendency

to delay decision making related to complex problems such as climate change (Tversky and Shafir 1992). At the same time, people like to "do the right thing" and are heavily influenced by social norms.

As a result, how messages are framed, what values are appealed to, and how the needed efforts are presented are critical. When given the choice of voluntarily paying for a carbon offset for an airline ticket, some 60 percent of Americans will do so regardless of political affiliation. When the offset is referred to as a carbon tax, support falls from 60 to 25 percent among Republicans (Hardisty and others 2010). More generally, framing green policies as a way to reach an ambitious and positive social goal (such as becoming carbon neutral by 2050 or becoming a leader in solar technologies) makes them more acceptable (and less prone to reversal at the next change of government) than if they are perceived as a constraint to economic development.

Another approach showing promising results is tweaking "choice architectures" to "nudge" people to make better decisions for the environment or other desirable outcomes without restricting their freedom of choice (Thaler and Sunstein 2008). To count as a nudge, the intervention must be easy and cheap, but not constitute a mandate. Changing the default options—without changing the options themselves—can be an efficient way to promote greener behaviors. In two cases where the default option offered by the electricity provider was a cleaner but more expensive one, fewer than 5 percent of customers requested a shift to a cheaper, but less green, source of electricity (Picherta and Katsikopoulos 2008).

Policies that unleash the power of the private sector

Firms have a major role to play in providing solutions to green growth. Through their capacity to innovate and adjust their production processes, firms are key to keeping the cost of green policy in check. This means that governments need to influence the behavior of firms by providing appropriate incentives and regulations in addition to the right economic incentives.

Use information. Besides prices, firms are subject to pressures from their customers, stakeholders, and investors, and this pressure can be used to green their behavior. Promoting transparency and access to information on environmental impacts can create social pressure to reduce these impacts. A 1996 amendment to the U.S. Safe Drinking Water Act requiring community drinking water systems to report regulatory violations publicly has been sufficient to reduce the incidence of subsequent violations, even in the absence of additional financial incentives.

In China, Indonesia, the Philippines, and Vietnam, performance evaluation and ratings programs that reported emissions data and assessed plants' environmental performance helped a large number of plants initially rated as "noncompliant" to rise to "compliant" (in contrast, plants rated as "flagrant violators" and "compliant" stayed in those categories). One reason these programs work is that they provide the information needed for civil society and legal and political systems to act to reduce pollution. But it also works because they attract the attention of managers to efficiency-increasing opportunities, which can be implemented at low or even negative cost.

Impose where it makes sense. Market and price instruments are sometimes difficult to implement or to enforce, they lack predictability and credibility over the long term, and they may be inefficient when economic actors do not take them fully into account, such as not fully valuing fuel economy when buying a car (Greene 2010). This is why it is sometimes easier to implement norms and regulations, as is done by Australia, Canada, China, the European Union, Japan, Korea, and the United States for car fuel efficiency standards (An and others 2007).

Use innovation and industrial policy, but with caution. Prices are notoriously limited instruments for transforming economies or triggering investments with long-term or uncertain payoffs. Since they depend on government actions, they have long-term credibility and predictability issues. They also cannot address the "classic" market failures that are usually invoked to justify innovation or industrial policies: increasing returns and knowledge externalities in new industries, information asymmetries, capital market imperfections, and the coordination needed across different sectors to permit a technological transition. As a result, most countries resort to some form of innovation and industrial policies in their growth strategies.

Such policies need to be used with care and tailored to the country context. Today, frontier innovation and basic R&D are highly concentrated in high-income countries and a few large emerging economies. High-income countries have a critical responsibility to step up their efforts on green innovation and its deployment as well as to take new technologies to scale through demand-side policies. Failure to do so will severely compromise the ability of developing countries to pursue green growth.

In lower-income countries, capacity is often not sufficient for frontier innovation; what is needed are policies to support the adaptation and dissemination of existing technologies. These technologies have been developed and tested in richer countries, making their support through trade, dissemination, and industrial policies less risky than the development of new technologies. The best way to accelerate technology diffusion is to reduce trade barriers. In China, photovoltaic panel fabrication technologies were introduced mainly through the import of manufacturing equipment from Europe. Also critical are policies to increase adaptation and adoption capacity through education and training as well as trade and industrial policies (such as local content requirements).

Moreover, several developing countries are pursuing green industrial policies—biofuels in Brazil and solar energy in China and Morocco. Lessons from past successes and failures of standard industrial policies are clear: governments should subject firms to competition, have clear sunset clauses, and focus on well-identified market failures, spillover, or latent comparative advantages (for example, solar potential in North Africa). But most green industries will require some type of policy support, making a market test more complex to design (is a technology not competitive because the government is not pricing the externality correctly or because the technology is not the most competitive available?) and making it even more imperative for government to navigate carefully the twin risks of policy and market failures. Typically, environmental policy (such as a carbon tax) should address the environmental externality, while the standard tools of innovation and industrial policies are used to address knowledge externalities and other market failures such as economies of scale and coordination failures.

Prong 3: Innovative financing tools that tackle higher up-front financing needs

Even when environmental or green infrastructure policies and investments pay for themselves, they can involve significant up-front costs and require specific financial tools. Innovative financing is therefore urgently needed, especially where gains from better environmental management cannot immediately be monetized.

Resources are available but remain small relative to need, so they need to be leveraged. With respect to climate change mitigation, recent estimates suggest that a package of public sources (including a redirection of subsidies currently destined for fossil fuels), multilateral development bank flows, and carbon offset flows could leverage some $200 billion to $400 billion in 2020 in additional private flows (MDB Working Group on Climate Finance 2011). This is close to the expected investment needed to reach a 550 ppm CO_2-eq target, but about half of what is needed to reach a 450 ppm CO_2-eq target. As for the biodiversity market, offset and compensation programs officially amount to some $2.4 billion to $4 billion per year, but may be much bigger, given that most of the existing markets are not transparent or analyzed enough to estimate their size (Madsen and others 2011).

Increasing the role of the private sector is critical. Many of the needed investments could benefit from public-private partnerships. Private participation in infrastructure has grown at a steady pace (13 percent a year) over the past 20 years but remains concentrated in a few middle-income countries and a few sectors, namely, telecom and, to a lesser extent, energy (World Bank and PPIAF 2012). New investments in renewable energy are largely private (some $143 billion of the $211 billion invested in renewables in 2010), but 82 percent of private renewable energy investments that take place in developing countries occur in Brazil, China, and India (UNEP and Bloomberg New Energy Finance 2011). Yet the need for innovation, efficiency, and "smart investments" (smart grids, smart transportation, and smart houses) makes the role of the private sector even more critical in green growth policies than it already is in traditional infrastructure finance.

Three weaknesses hold back private financing of infrastructure—green or not (MDB Working Group on Infrastructure 2011):

- The scarcity of resources to prepare projects and bring them to a stage at which they are "bankable" (that is, attractive to private sectors). Developing-country governments—at least those with limited experience with public-private partnerships—are often reluctant to borrow to prepare uncertain projects, while private investors are unwilling to invest in preparing a project they may have to bid for and not win.
- The mismatch between the tenor of the funds available, with the preference of investors for short-term funds and the needs of infrastructure for long-term funds (15–25 years). Few countries have well-developed capital markets or banking institutions able to transform short-term deposits into long-term products, and not enough refinancing tool options are available.
- The challenge of cost recovery. The ability to charge at full cost is behind the massive expansion in telecom services, but few other infrastructure sectors are able to do so, although where they have, investors have come, as they did in Colombia's water sector. Solutions include measures to price

infrastructure services close to cost recovery, while ensuring affordability for low-income households.

Another weakness springs from the additional policy risk created by the fact that the profitability of green investments is often dependent on public policies (such as feed-in tariffs or environmental taxation). Thus, Spain's retroactive reductions in solar feed-in tariffs, Germany's and France's decisions to reduce the amount of support for future projects, and the lack of progress on a U.S. energy bill all combined to depress the private sector's appetite for renewable energy investments in 2010. As a result, clean energy share prices dipped, reflecting investor concerns, despite continued strong government support for renewable energy in China (UNEP and Bloomberg New Energy Finance 2011).

Renewable energy and energy efficiency illustrate the need for innovative public financing instruments (World Bank forthcoming b). Renewable energy is capital intensive with a long payback period and may face the technology risks associated with emerging technologies (such as concentrated solar) or unique resource risks (drilling for geothermal). Energy efficiency suffers from the fact that most local banks rely on balance sheet financing, rather than project-based financing that is based on the cash flow generated by the investments. The result is that the customers most in need of financing (small businesses and households) are typically deemed not creditworthy. And energy efficiency investments tend to be small, with high transaction costs, so that banks may not find them attractive in the absence of dedicated credit lines to increase confidence and capacity and instruments to aggregate small deals.

Furthermore, access to financing is particularly problematic for small and medium enterprises (SMEs), which account for a large share (60 percent in many countries) of pollution and resource use. Some 65 to 72 percent of all SMEs (between 240 million and 315 million firms) lack access to credit, with a particularly daunting picture in Asia and Africa (Global Partnership for Financial Inclusion 2011). Even in the more sophisticated markets, most firms find it tough to get credit for investments aimed at business activities other than expansion.

How can these obstacles to green investments be overcome? The public sector, international financial institutions (IFIs), and bilateral donors can help by providing funds for project preparation as well as concessional elements for pioneer investments. Such support can go a long way toward changing risk-return profiles and giving investors more confidence in the long-term viability of their projects.

More generally, well-designed public finance mechanisms help to mobilize private investments in energy efficiency and renewable energy (World Bank forthcoming b). In the case of renewable energy and energy efficiency, the following tends to have the greatest leverage:

- Credit lines or guarantee instruments to engage private banks. The experience of the International Finance Corporation is telling: between 1997 and 2011 some $65 million in concessional funding, primarily for risk-sharing facilities, generated $680 million in sustainable energy finance investments (IFC 2011).
- "Fund of funds" under which the government invests a relatively small amount of long-term capital in a range of private, professionally managed funds that then invest in clean energy or energy efficiency
- Public funds to reduce interest rates for consumer financing, typically through financial institutions or utilities.

In addition, energy service companies (ESCOs), which provide clients with energy auditing, propose energy-savings measures, and financing, can help consolidate multiple small transactions. ESCOs as an industry often require public support to establish: in China, it took more than a decade of support by the government and the World Bank before the ESCOs grew to a $1 billion industry in 2007 (World Bank 2010d).

TABLE O.2   Financing mechanisms need to be tailored to the maturity of the local financial sector
(context-dependent financing tools for clean energy in East Asia and the Pacific)

Indicator	Level of financial sector development		
	Low	Medium	High
Country income level	Low income (e.g., Lao PDR)	Middle income (e.g., Thailand)	Upper middle income (e.g., Malaysia)
Banking services	Basic banks	Full-range banks	Universal banks
Non-bank financial services	None	• Government bonds • Equity	• Government and corporate bonds • Equity • Alternatives (private equity, venture capital)
Interest rate	Administrative setting	Largely market based	Fully market based
Access to finance for SMEs	Limited	Partial	Readily available
Availability of long-term financing	Limited (up to 1 year)	Partial (up to 7 years)	Full (up to 15 years)
Risk management	Weak	Adequate	Robust
Appropriate clean energy financing instruments	• **Lines of credit (liquidity support)** • **Concessional financing** • **Dedicated debt funds**	• **Lines of credit (demonstration)** • **Partial risk guarantee**	• **Lines of credit (demonstration)** • **Partial risk guarantee** • **Equity funds** • **Consumer financing**

Source: World Bank forthcoming b.

Overall, the relevant mix of financing instruments will depend on the market barriers (access to credit, transaction cost, or perception of risk), market segments (SMEs, large developers, or polluters), and local context (such as the maturity of the local financial sector) in which they seek to operate (table O.2).

In addition, payments for environmental services (PES)—whereby farmers and landowners are compensated for maintaining their land's ability to provide ecosystem services (such as the regulation of water flows, water purification, control of soil erosion, and habitats for wildlife)—are promising, but underutilized. Fortunately, efforts to develop REDD+ are helping to develop PES schemes.[4] In addition, in developing countries, policy makers have tried to design PES programs to benefit the poor. But whether these schemes in fact benefit the poor depends on the nature of the scheme. Brazil appears to have been successful in this regard, building on its experience in developing social safety nets for the poor (box O.5).

Conclusions

In sum, this report approaches green growth from a pragmatic point of view. The current model is not just unsustainable, it is inefficient. Improving it is good economics, so let's fix market failures, internalize externalities, assign property rights, improve governance, and influence behaviors. But making green growth happen and ensuring it is inclusive will also require an acute understanding of political economy and social psychology.

As such, this report speaks primarily to those who fear that greening growth may be too expensive, may be too ambitious at an early stage of development, or should concern only high-income countries. To them, the report makes a clear case that greening growth is neither unaffordable nor technically out of reach, there are plenty of

---

BOX O.5   "Green" cash transfers are helping poor communities in the Brazilian Amazon

An innovative addition to the Brazilian *Bolsa Família* (family allowance) conditional cash transfer program—the world's largest and one of the best regarded in terms of coverage and targeting—is being implemented for communities living inside protected areas in the Amazon region.

The *Bolsa Floresta* (forest allowance) rewards traditional communities for their commitment to stop deforestation by distributing payments for ecosystem services to families, communities, and family associations. In order to be eligible to receive the grants, families must enroll their children in school, sign a zero deforestation commitment, and attend a two-day training program on environmental awareness. Each eligible family receives a monthly stipend of R$50 ($30), paid to the mother. Community associations can also be eligible to receive payments of up to R$4,000 ($2,500) to support sustainable income generation activities, such as honey production, fish farming, and sustainable forest management.

Investments for administrative support to community associations make up 10 percent of the total paid to families during the year. *Bolsa Floresta* is being implemented by the State Government of Amazonas and the Fundação Amazônia Sustentável (Sustainable Amazonia Foundation). The funds are generated by the interest on an endowment initially established with contributions from the state government and private donors. Deforestation is monitored on a yearly basis by the Amazonas State Secretariat for the Environment and Sustainable Development through satellite imagery analyzed by independent institutions. The program currently benefits 7,614 families in 15 protected areas, covering around 10 million hectares of forests. The State of Amazonas has succeeded in halving the deforestation rate over the past five years.

Box text contributed by Adriana Moreira.

BOX O.6   Joining forces: A common platform to move forward on greening our economies and growth processes

How does the World Bank's definition of green growth as economic growth that is environmentally sustainable compare to those advocated in recent major reports on green growth? The OECD defines green growth as "fostering economic growth and development, while ensuring that natural assets continue to provide the resources and environmental services on which our well-being relies" (OECD 2011b). The United Nations Environment Programme (UNEP) defines a green economy as "one that results in improved human well-being and social equity, while significantly reducing environmental risks and ecological scarcities" (UNEP 2011). Like the approach promoted in this report, these definitions are consistent with sustainable development as an ultimate objective and with green growth or a green economy as a means to reconcile its economic and environmental pillars, without ignoring social aspects.

So while the three reports differ in their focus and target audience, they are fully consistent in their broad vision and policy advice. This common vision is being developed further in the context of the Green Growth Knowledge Platform (GGKP), a partnership of the three institutions and the Global Green Growth Institute. The GGKP—launched in January 2012—is a global network of researchers and development experts seeking to identify and address major knowledge gaps in green growth theory and practice. Through widespread consultation and world-class research, the GGKP aims to provide practitioners and policy makers with better tools to foster economic growth and implement sustainable development (http://www.greengrowthknowledge.org).

immediate benefits and a poor country can reap economic benefit from better environmental management. And although high-income countries, which still account for 75 percent of global consumption and a disproportionate share of environmental degradation, absolutely have to implement ambitious environmental measures, all countries will gain from starting early.

Greening growth need not entail slower growth and is affordable. However, achieving a green economy overnight probably is not. The costs of greening growth will depend on the degree of ambition. Rapidly and dramatically decreasing our impact on the planet would be quite costly. So, too, would delaying action for too long. Dramatic shifts would entail much slower growth at least in the medium run, and avoiding a brutal transition is the main incentive to start acting as early as possible.

This report adds to the chorus started by the Organisation for Economic Co-operation and Development and United Nations Environment Programme (UNEP) in recent reports supporting the idea that inclusive green growth is good economics and good development policy (box O.6). While we are still far from being able to price ecosystem services properly, they clearly are valuable. As such, neglecting natural capital, like neglecting human and physical capital, is simply bad management, bad economics, and bad for growth.

Notes

1. The equivalent amount using purchasing power parity (PPP) that allows for better cross-country comparisons of purchasing power is $6,000 PPP for all developing countries and $1,300 PPP in low-income countries.
2. This section is based on World Bank (forthcoming a).
3. The fleet capacity index is the relationship between the capacity of a fishing fleet to catch a particular quantity of fish and the quantity of fish that it actually catches.
4. Reducing Emissions from Deforestation and Forest Degradation (REDD) is an effort to create a financial value for the carbon stored in forests, offering incentives for developing coun-

tries to reduce emissions from forested lands and invest in low-carbon paths to sustainable development. REDD+ goes beyond deforestation and forest degradation and includes the role of conservation, sustainable management of forests, and enhancement of forest carbon stocks (http://www.un-redd.org/).

References

Allcott, H., and S. Mullainathan. 2010. "Behavior and Energy Policy." *Science* 327 (5970): 1204–05.

Alpay, E., S. Buccola, and J. Kerkvliet. 2002. "Productivity Growth and Environmental Regulation in Mexican and U.S. Food Manufacturing." *American Journal of Agricultural Economics* 84 (4): 887–901.

Ambec, S., M. A. Cohen, S. Elgie, and P. Lanoie. 2011. "The Porter Hypothesis at 20: Can Environmental Regulation Enhance Innovation and Competitiveness?" Resources for the Future Discussion Paper 11-01, Washington, DC.

An, F., D. Gordon, H. He, D. Kodjak, and D. Rutherford. 2007. "Passenger Vehicle Greenhouse Gas and Fuel Economy Standards: A Global Update." International Council on Clean Transportation, Washington, DC.

Andersen, M. S., T. Barker, E. Christie, P. Ekins, J. F. Gerald, J. Jilkova, S. Junankar, M. Landesmann, H. Pollitt, R. Salmons, S. Scott, and S. Speck, eds. 2007. "Competitiveness Effects of Environmental Tax Reforms (COMETR)." Final report to the European Commission, DG Research, and DG TAXUD (Summary Report), National Environmental Research Institute, University of Aarhus.

Anger, N., and U. Oberndorfer. 2008. "Firm Performance and Employment in the EU Emissions Trading Scheme: An Empirical Assessment for Germany." *Energy Policy* 36 (1): 12–22.

Arze del Granado, J., D. Coady, and R. Gillingham. 2010. "The Unequal Benefits of Fuel Subsidies: A Review of Evidence for Developing Countries." IMF WP/10/02, International Monetary Fund, Washington, DC.

Bai, Z. G., D. L. Dent, L. Olsson, and M. E. Schaepman. 2008. "Proxy Global Assessment of Land Degradation." *Soil Use and Management* 24 (September): 223–34.

Berman, E., and L. T. M. Bui. 2001. "Environmental Regulation and Productivity: Evidence from Oil Refineries." *Review of Economics and Statistics* 83 (3): 498–510.

Betz, R., and M. Sato. 2006. "Emissions Trading: Lessons Learnt from the First Phase of the EU ETS and Prospects for the Second Phase." *Climate Policy* 6 (4): 351–59.

CMI (Center for Mediterranean Integration). 2012. "Toward Green Growth in Mediterranean Countries: Implementing Policies to Enhance the Productivity of Natural Assets." CMI, Marseille.

Copeland, B. R. 2012. "International Trade and Green Growth." Paper presented at the Green Growth Knowledge Platform inaugural conference, Mexico City, January 12–13.

Dutz, M. A., and S. Sharma. 2012. "Green Growth, Technology, and Innovation." Policy Research Working Paper 5932, World Bank, Washington, DC.

Easterlin, R. A. 1995. "Will Raising the Income of All Increase the Happiness of All?" *Journal of Economic Behaviour and Organization* 27: 35–47.

Ellerman, A. D., F. Convery, and C. de Perthuis. 2010. *Pricing Carbon.* Cambridge, U.K.: Cambridge University Press.

FAO (Food and Agriculture Organization of the United Nations). 2010. "Global Forest Resources Assessment 2010: Main Report." FAO Forestry Paper 163, FAO, Rome.

Fay, M., A. Iimi, and B. Perrissin-Fabert. 2010. "Financing Greener and Climate Resilient Infrastructure in Developing Countries: Challenges and Opportunities." *EIB Papers* 15 (2): 35–59.

Ferreira, F. H. G., and M. Ravallion. 2009. "Poverty and Inequality: The Global Context." In *Oxford Handbook of Economic Inequality,* ed. B. Nolan, W. Salverda, and T. Smeeding, ch. 24. Oxford: Oxford University Press.

Foresight. 2011. *The Future of Food and Farming: Final Project Report.* London: Government Office for Science.

Gillingham, K., R. Newell, and K. Palmer. 2009. "Energy Efficiency Economics and Policy." *Annual Review of Resource Economics* 1: 597–619.

Global Partnership for Financial Inclusion. 2011. "Report to the Leaders of the G20." G20, Cannes. http://www.mofa.go.jp/policy/economy/g20_summit/2011/pdfs/annex06.pdf.

Graff Zivin, J. S., and M. J. Neidell. 2011. "The Impact of Pollution on Worker Productivity." NBER Working Paper 17004, National Bureau of Economic Research, Cambridge, MA.

Greene, D. L. 2010. "How Consumers Value Fuel Economy: A Literature Review." EPA–420–R–10–008, U.S. Environmental Protection Agency, Washington, DC.

Guillaume, D., R. Zytek, and M. R. Farzin. 2011. "Iran: The Chronicles of the Subsidy Reform." IMF Working Paper WP 11/167, International Monetary Fund, Washington, DC.

Hallegatte, S. 2011. "How Economic Growth and Rational Decisions Can Make Disaster Losses Grow Faster Than Wealth." Policy Research Working Paper 5617, World Bank, Washington, DC.

Hardisty, D. H., E. J. Johnson, and E. U. Weber. 2010. "A Dirty Word or a Dirty World? Attribute Framing, Political Affiliation, and Query Theory." *Psychological Science* 21 (1): 86–92.

IEA (International Energy Agency). 2008. *World Energy Outlook.* Paris: IEA.

———. 2011. *World Energy Outlook.* Paris: IEA.

IFC (International Finance Corporation). 2011. "Sustainable Energy Finance: Innovative Concessional Finance with Financial Intermediaries." IFC, Washington, DC.

ILO (International Labour Organization) and CEDEFOP (European Centre for the Development of Vocational Training). 2011. *Skills for Green Jobs: A Global View.* Geneva: ILO.

IUCN (International Union for Conservation of Nature). 2009. *Extinction Crisis Continues Apace.* Gland: IUCN. http://www.iucn.org/knowledge/news/?4143/Extinction-crisis-continues-apace.

Laffoley, D. d'A., and J. M. Baxter, eds. 2009. "Ocean Acidification: The Facts; A Special Introductory Guide for Policy Advisers and Decision Makers." Ocean Acidification Reference User Group, European Project on Ocean Acidification.

Layard, R. 2005. *Happiness: Lessons from a New Science.* London: Penguin Press.

Loulou, R., and M. Labriet. 2008. "ETSAP-TIAM: The TIMES Integrated Assessment Model Part I: Model Structure." *Computational Management Science* 5 (1, special issue: Managing Energy and the Environment): 41–66.

Luderer, G., R. Pietzcker, E. Kriegler, M. Haller, and N. Bauer. 2012. "Asia's Role in Mitigating Climate Change: A Technology and Sector Specific Analysis with ReMIND-R." Preprint.

Madsen, B., N. Carroll, D. Kandy, and G. Bennett. 2011. "Update: State of Biodiversity Markets." Forest Trends, Washington, DC.

Marglin, S. 2010. "What's Wrong with Unlimited Growth?" Department of Economics, Harvard University, Cambridge, MA.

Martin, R., U. J. Wagner, and L. B. de Preux. 2009. "The Impacts of the Climate Change Levy on Business: Evidence from Microdata." CEP Discussion Paper, Centre for Economic Performance, London School of Economics, London, U.K.

McKinsey and Company. 2011. "Resource Revolution: Meeting the World's Energy, Materials, Food, and Water Needs." McKinsey Global Institute.

MDB (Multilateral Development Banks) Working Group on Climate Finance. 2011. "Mobilizing Climate Finance" Paper prepared at the request of G20 Finance Ministers. http://climate change.worldbank.org/content/mobilizing-climate-finance.

MDB (Multilateral Development Banks) Working Group on Infrastructure. 2011. "Supporting Infrastructure in Developing Countries." Paper submitted to the G20.

MEA (Millennium Ecosystem Assessment). 2005. *Ecosystems and Human Well-being: Synthesis.* Washington, DC: Island Press.

Milanovic, B. 2010. "Global Inequality Recalculated and Updated: The Effect of New PPP Estimates on Global Inequality and 2005 Estimates." *Journal of Economic Inequality.* DOI 10.1007/s10888-010-9155-y.

Myers, N., and J. Kent. 2001. "Perverse Subsidies: How Tax Dollars Can Undercut the Environment and the Economy." International Institute for Sustainable Development, Winnipeg.

Nidumolu, R., C. K. Prahalad, and M. R. Rangaswami. 2009. "Why Sustainability Is Now the Key Driver of Innovation." *Harvard Business Review* 87 (9, September): 56–64.

OECD (Organisation for Economic Co-operation and Development). 2011a. *Agricultural Policy Monitoring and Evaluation 2011.* Paris: OECD.

———. 2011b. *Towards Green Growth.* Paris: OECD.

Picherta, D., and K. V. Katsikopoulos. 2008. "Green Defaults: Information Presentation and Pro-Environmental Behaviour." *Journal of Environmental Psychology* 28: 63–73.

Pimm, S. L., G. J. Russell, J. L. Gittleman, and T. M. Brooks. 1995. "The Future of Biodiversity." *Science* 269 (5222): 347–50.

Quirion, P. 2011. "Les quotas échangeables d'émission de gaz à effet de serre: Éléments d'analyse économique." Mémoire d'Habilitation à diriger les recherches, Ecole des Hautes Études en Sciences Sociales, Paris.

Rozenberg, J., S. Hallegatte, A. Vogt-Schilb, O. Sassi, C. Guivarch, H. Waisman, and J-C Hourcade. 2010. "Climate Policies as a Hedge against the Uncertainty on Future Oil Supply: A Letter." *Climatic Change Letters* 101 (3): 663–69.

Sartor, O. 2012. "Carbon Leakage in the Primary Aluminium Sector: What Evidence after 6½ Years of the EU ETS?" CDC Climat Research Working Paper 2012-12, Caisse des Dépots, Toulouse.

Thaler, R., and C. Sunstein. 2008. *Nudge.* New Haven, CT: Yale University Press.

Transport for London. 2008. "Central London Congestion Charging Impacts Monitoring: Sixth Annual Report, July 2008." Mayor of London, London. http://www.tfl.gov.uk/assets/downloads/sixth-annual-impacts-monitoring-report-2008-07.pdf.

Tversky, A., and D. Kahneman. 1992. "Advances in Prospect Theory: Cumulative Representation of Uncertainty." *Journal of Risk and Uncertainty* 5: 297–323.

Tversky, A., and E. Shafir. 1992. "The Disjunction Effect in Choice under Uncertainty." *Psychological Science* 3 (5): 305–09.

UNEP (United Nations Environment Programme). 2011. *Towards a Green Economy: Pathways to Sustainable Development and Poverty Eradication.* Geneva: UNEP. http://www.unep.org/greeneconomy.

UNEP (United Nations Environment Programme) and Bloomberg New Energy Finance. 2011. *Global Trends in Renewable Energy Investment 2011.* Nairobi: UNEP.

UNESCO (United Nations Educational Scientific and Cultural Organization) and WWAP (World Water Assessment Program). 2006. "Water: A Shared Responsibility." United Nations World Water Development Report 2, UNESCO, Paris. http://www.unesco.org/water/wwap/wwdr/wwdr2/table_contents .shtml.

Van Vliet, O., K. Volker, D. McCollum, S. Pachauri, Y. Nagai, S. Rao, and K. Riahi. Forthcoming 2012. "Synergies in the Asian Energy System: Climate Change, Energy Security, Energy Access and Air Pollution." *Energy Economics*, in press. Published online February 14, 2012.

Victor, P. A. 2008. *Managing without Growth: Slower by Design, Not Disaster.* Cheltenham, U.K.: Edward Elgar.

Wang, X., N. Berrah, S. Mathur, and F. Vinuya. 2010. *Winds of Change: East Asia's Sustainable Energy Future.* Washington, DC: World Bank.

World Bank. 2004. "Tunisia Country Environmental Analysis (1992.2003)." Report 25966-TN, World Bank, Washington, DC.

———. 2005a. "Arab Republic of Egypt Country Environmental Analysis (1992.2002)." Report 31993-EG, World Bank, Washington, DC.

———. 2005b. "China: Second Loess Plateau Watershed Rehabilitation Project." Implementation Completion and Results Report 34612, World Bank, Washington, DC.

———. 2006a. "Republic of Bangladesh Country Environmental Analysis." Report 36945-BD, World Bank, Washington, DC.

———. 2006b. "Republic of Colombia: Mitigating Environmental Degradation to Foster Growth and Reduce Inequality." Report 36345-CO, World Bank, Washington, DC.

———. 2006c. "Republic of El Salvador Country Environmental Analysis: Improving Environmental Management to Address Trade Liberalization and Infrastructure Expansion." Report 35226-SV, World Bank, Washington, DC.

———. 2006d. "Republic of Guatemala Country Environmental Analysis: Addressing the Environmental Aspects of Trade and Infrastructure Expansion." Report 36459-GT, World Bank, Washington, DC.

———. 2006e. "Nigeria Rapid Country Environmental Analysis (CEA)." World Bank, Washington, DC.

———. 2006f. "Pakistan Country Environmental Analysis." Report 36946-PK, World Bank, Washington, DC.

———. 2007a. "Ghana Country Environmental Analysis." Report 36985-GH, World Bank, Washington, DC.

———. 2007b. "Nepal Country Environmental Analysis: Strengthening Institutions and Management Systems for Enhanced Environmental Governance." Report 38984-NP, World Bank, Washington, DC.

———. 2007c. "Republic of Peru Environmental Sustainability: A Key to Poverty Reduction in Peru." Report 40190-PE, World Bank, Washington, DC.

———. 2008. "Tajikistan Country Environmental Analysis." Report 43465-TJ, World Bank, Washington, DC.

———. 2009. "Hashemite Kingdom of Jordan Country Environmental Analysis." Report 47829-JO, World Bank, Washington, DC.

———. 2010a. "Central African Republic Country Environmental Analysis: Environmental Management for Sustainable Growth." World Bank, Washington, DC.

———. 2010b. "The Cost of Environmental Degradation Case Studies from the Middle East and North Africa." Report 56295, World Bank, Washington, DC.

———. 2010c. "République du Bénin Analyse Environnementale Pays." Report 58190-BJ, World Bank, Washington, DC.

———. 2010d. *World Development Report: Development and Climate Change*. Washington, DC: World Bank.

———. 2011a. "Republic of Lebanon Country Environmental Analysis." Report 62266-LB, World Bank, Washington, DC.

———. 2011b. "South Africa: Economic Update; Focus on Green Growth." World Bank, Washington, DC.

———. 2011c. World Development Indicators. Washington, DC: World Bank.

———. Forthcoming a. *How Environment Sustains Development: The World Bank Group Environment Strategy; Toward a Green, Clean, and Resilient World for All*. Washington, DC: World Bank.

———. Forthcoming b. *Maximizing Leverage of Public Funds to Unlock Commercial Financing for Clean Energy in East Asia*. Washington, DC: World Bank.

World Bank and DRC (Development Research Center of the State Council, China). 2012. "Seizing the Opportunity of Green Development in China." Supporting Report 3 for *China 2030: Building a Modern Harmonious, and Creative High-Income Society*. Washington, DC: World Bank. http://www-wds.worldbank.org/external/default/WDSContentServer/WDSP/IB/2012/02/28/000356161_20120228001303/Rendered/PDF/671790WP0P127500China020300complete.pdf.

World Bank and FAO (Food and Agriculture Organization). 2009. "The Sunken Billions: The Economic Justification for Fisheries Reform." World Bank, Washington, DC; Food and Agricultural Organization, Rome.

World Bank and PPIAF (Public-Private Infrastructure Advisory Facility). 2012. Private Participation in Infrastructure Database. World Bank, Washington, DC. http://ppi.worldbank .org/.

An Analytical Framework for Inclusive Green Growth | 1

Key Messages

- It is inefficient either to pursue growth and only later worry about its environmental consequences, or to promote environmental sustainability and subsequently worry about its growth implications.
- The analytical case for green growth is strong: green policies can indeed contribute to economic growth over the short term, if they are designed in an appropriate framework.
- Green policies can contribute to growth through four effects: an input effect (increasing production factors), an efficiency effect (bringing production closer to the production frontier), a stimulus effect (stimulating the economy in times of crisis), and an innovation effect (accelerating development and adoption of technologies).
- Green policies can also contribute to welfare through direct environmental benefits, through distributional effects (including poverty reduction and job creation), and through increased resilience to shocks (including natural disasters and commodity price volatility). Welfare impacts will be greater if efforts are made to make green policies inclusive.

China grew at about 10 percent a year over the past 30 years, transforming it from a poor country to the world's second-largest economy. Yet, the Chinese government is now reconsidering the strategy that permitted this economic miracle in the hope of greening its development process (World Bank and DRC 2012). Two factors motivate this possible change in approach. First, the cost of environmental degradation, estimated at 9 percent of gross domestic product (GDP), is threatening both economic competitiveness and welfare. As a result, China's population is demanding a cleaner and safer environment. Second, China is looking for new sources of growth, supported by innovation and higher value added production, and wants to be an early

---

This chapter is based on Hallegatte and others (2011).

mover in the race toward greener production processes and products.

China is not the only such country. Brazil, Indonesia, Mexico, Morocco, and Tunisia are greening their growth process or looking to use green industries as sources of growth. Ethiopia is developing a green growth strategy. Kenya is investing heavily in geo-thermal power. And many other countries are hoping to better balance the environment and the economic imperative of rapid growth.

The reality is that the world needs green growth, and it needs it now. But what exactly does "green growth" mean? Green growth can be thought of as economic growth that is environmentally sustainable. More spe-cifically, it aims to operationalize sustainable development by enabling developing countries to achieve robust growth without locking themselves into unsustainable patterns. The World Bank's environmental strategy defines green growth as growth that is efficient, clean, and resilient—efficient in its use of natural resources, clean in that it minimizes pollution and environmental impacts, and resilient in that it accounts for natural hazards and the role of environmental management and natu-ral capital in preventing physical disasters.

Importantly, green growth is not inher-ently inclusive. Its outcome will likely be good for the poor, but specific policies are needed to ensure that the poor are not excluded from benefits and are not harmed in the transition. The welfare impacts of green policies will be greater if efforts are made to make the poli-cies inclusive.

Greening growth is essential to achieving sustainable development and its objectives of social, economic, and environmental sus-tainability (figure 1.1). Economic growth and social achievements are widely recognized as complementary, but growth and environ-mental sustainability are often perceived as antithetical. Greening growth would recon-cile the need for environmental sustainabil-ity with that for economic growth and social improvement.

Fortunately, many policies provide both environmental and economic benefits. Informal settlements can pose economic,

environmental, and social problems. Utili-ties often refuse to serve them and insecure property rights discourage residents from investing in establishing connections to water or electricity networks. Creating functioning land markets with secure land tenure helps informal settlers access solid waste removal, sanitation and drainage, and drinking water. It also increases welfare and labor produc-tivity, both directly and indirectly, by giving such settlers greater access to credit and by allowing them to invest in small businesses, thereby increasing aggregate output. One example of the environmental benefits of a green growth policy is the World Bank– financed water quality and pollution control project around the Lake of Guarapiranga in Brazil. Urban renewal and slum upgrad-ing were critical to improving water quality, which in turn provided a reliable water sup-ply source for the city of São Paulo.

Most green growth policies are environ-mental policies in the sense that their primary objective is to preserve the environment. But not all of them are. Policies that improve energy security or reduce urban congestion, for example, may yield substantial environ-mental benefits even if doing so is not their primary objective.

Many observers have argued that environ-mental issues will "solve themselves" with economic development. This chapter exam-ines the flaws in the "grow now, clean up later" argument and discusses what growth theory and evidence reveal about the com-patibility of environmentally sustainable policies and growth. It investigates whether green growth is in fact feasible—beginning with the analytical case for green growth before reviewing the implications for welfare, the ultimate goal of economic policy—and explores how to identify trade-offs and syn-ergies implied by a green growth strategy.

Why not grow now and clean up later?

The "grow now, clean up later" argument is based on the idea that environmental quality first deteriorates with growth and then improves—an environmental Kuznets curve.[1] In this framework, the environment eventually improves as national income rises because the environment is a "superior good" (a good whose consumption increases more than proportionately with income).[2] The framework implies that poor people care less about the environment than wealthier people, give priority to consumption over environmental quality, and act upon these preferences. Once basic needs have been met, this argument goes, people place greater weight on the environment, leading to investments in environmental protection and clean-up that increase environmental quality, assuming appropriate collective action proves possible. Economic growth will therefore automatically lead countries to environmental protection.

There are serious flaws in this argument. First, *a distinction needs to be made between environmental impacts that affect welfare through income and consumption and those that affect welfare through the amenity value of environmental assets.* In urban areas, poor households that struggle to feed and house themselves will indeed place a lower priority on the amenities provided by a park than wealthier households might. However, they care deeply about the absence of solid waste management and its results—dengue epidemics, clogged urban drains, and the destruction of their homes and small businesses by floods. In rural areas, protecting forests to prevent the extinction of rare animals may not be a priority for households that struggle to feed themselves (unless of course the poor can share in the benefits from wildlife protection). But the same households are likely to care about protecting soil quality and managing water flows, which allow them to grow crops.

Second, *even when poor communities care about the environment, they may not have the "voice" to make their concerns heard.* Policies implemented in developing countries may be more representative of the preferences of the elite than of the poor or may reflect institutional constraints, such as those imposed by poorly defined property rights (as in open access resources).

FIGURE 1.1 **The three pillars of sustainable development**

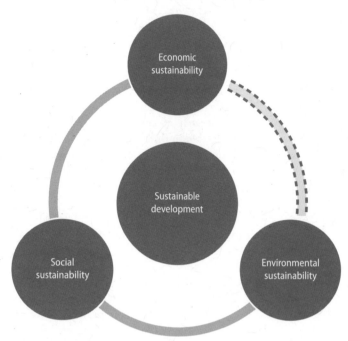

Note: Economic and social sustainability, on the one hand, and social and environmental sustainability, on the other, have been found to be not only compatible, but also largely complementary. Not so with economic and environmental sustainability, as growth has come largely at the expense of the environment—hence, the dotted line on this figure—which is why green growth aims to ensure that economic and environmental sustainability are compatible.

Third, *it is difficult to infer preferences about collective goods from individual behavior.* Cities offer many more jobs and opportunities than rural areas but also much higher levels of local pollution. The fact that people move from rural areas to cities does not mean they would not prefer slightly fewer opportunities and higher environmental quality. Their preferences are not completely revealed by the binary choice of "moving or not moving to the city," because they do not have a continuum of choices of increasing opportunities and decreasing environmental quality.

Fourth, *because the influence of environmental quality and welfare is often indirect, people may not link environmental problems (such as water or soil quality) to the health problems they confront.*[3] Better information, not just higher incomes, may be needed if individuals are to demand higher environmental quality at earlier stages of development. Even developed countries are only beginning to address the complex issue of the environmental damages of pesticides and chemicals.

Fifth, *although some dimensions of environmental quality improve with average income, many others do not.* Local environmental issues with short-term, highly visible manifestations (such as local air and some types of water pollution) are usually resolved spontaneously as countries develop. In contrast, global public goods with long-term consequences (such as climate change or biodiversity) and local environmental issues with complex and less visible consequences can keep getting worse (box 1.1).

The case of Costa Rica illustrates the contrast between local, visible pollutants and global ones. In 1978, when per capita GDP was about $2,200, emissions of nitrogen oxides (NO_x) and sulfur dioxide (SO_2) peaked, before leveling off and then declining slightly. Over the same period, however, carbon dioxide (CO_2) emissions continued to rise (figure 1.2).

Delaying action can be costly

Making the "grow now and clean up later" argument even less palatable is the fact that it may simply be too costly to do so. Indeed, it may be more economical to reduce or prevent pollution at an early stage of growth than to incur the higher clean-up costs at later stages, even when future costs and benefits are discounted. Acting early is critical when the choice of technology and infrastructure can "lock in" high-carbon or polluting lifestyles or economic structures. This issue is particularly relevant in developing countries, where most of the infrastructure will be built in the next few decades.

As for climate change, a variety of experts have studied the optimal timing of action (Nordhaus 1992; Wigley and others 1996). Prematurely depreciating investments can be costly if climate change turns out to be less threatening than expected or if the discount rate used to calculate future losses is too low. But early action may well result in savings. Lecocq and others (1998) find that in the absence of perfect foresight, specific policies regarding green infrastructure and long-lived capital must be adopted early to achieve mitigation objectives at a lower cost. Jaccard and Rivers (2007) show that early action is preferable in long-lived

---

BOX 1.1   Persistent concerns about local pollution in high-income countries

Complex and "invisible" local environmental issues do not necessarily improve with income. In countries like France, efforts to understand the transfer of pesticides to the environment (mostly water bodies) began only some 20 years ago, under the pressure of a European Union Directive regulating drinking water (Aubertot and others 2005). Soil contamination is harder to monitor and can lead to severe long-term environmental and health hazards, as the example of the insecticide chlordecone illustrates.

Chlordecone, which was banned only recently, was used extensively in the French West Indies for more than 30 years, exposing the population to severe health hazards (Multignier and others 2010). The chemical remains in the soil for decades,

polluting water and agricultural productions, and contains known carcinogenics (Aubertot and others 2005; Multignier and others 2010).

In the United States, the Safe Drinking Water Act regulates only 91 contaminants, despite the fact that more than 60,000 chemicals are used within the country's borders. Scientists have examined many of these chemicals and have identified hundreds associated with a risk of cancer and other diseases at small concentrations in drinking water, according to an analysis of government records by the *New York Times* (Duhigg 2009). The implication is that millions of Americans are exposed to water that does not meet safety standards meant to protect against cancer or other serious diseases.

FIGURE 1.2   Global pollutants and local, visible ones follow different paths
(relationship between GDP and emissions in Costa Rica, 1970–2009)

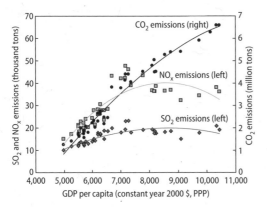

Source: Based on data from the International Energy Agency, the Joint Research Center, and World Development Indicators.

capital sectors, such as infrastructure and urbanization, even if marginal costs are higher there. Denser cities have lower CO_2 emissions from transportation (figure 1.3). But Gusdorf and others (2008) find that influencing the shape and density of cities ("changing urban forms") to make them less energy consuming is extremely costly. Developing countries would therefore do well to prevent their cities from growing in a low-density manner dependent on automobiles if their target for the end of the 21st century is to have high-density, energy-efficient cities.

One measure of the importance of early action is provided by Davis and others (2010), who estimate that without early scrapping, existing energy infrastructure commits us to warming of about 1.3°C above preindustrial temperatures. Introducing other types of infrastructure (including the capital that constrains the demand for transport, such as distant suburbs) and non-CO_2 gases, Guivarch and Hallegatte (2011) estimate this "commitment" at 1.7°C. These results imply that keeping the increase in global warming below 2°C (the internationally recognized objective of climate policies [World Bank 2009]) requires that almost all new infrastructure be designed with climate change in mind

and that urgent action be taken on long-lived infrastructure. In the absence of such action, physical capital will have to be replaced earlier, at great cost.

Another argument for early action has to do with the fact that the needed technologies will not become affordable unless there is sufficient demand to deploy them to scale. Countries or firms may be tempted to wait for better and less expensive technologies to become available. But these technologies will be developed only if serious commitments to pollution reduction are made (Goulder and Mathai 2000; Manne and Richels 2004; Sue Wing 2006). Early action is thus justified by the technological changes that action would induce. Developing these technologies is a critical role of high-income countries and the main reason why they need to act quickly on issues such as climate change.

And even worse, some damages cannot be reversed. In such cases, investments in environmental quality protection can be necessary in the short term. In Kenya, for example, traditional forests are being destroyed. Replanting can restore the country's water tower and other functions, but most biodiversity losses are probably irreversible (Chapin and others 2000).

Climate change itself may be irreversible. This irreversibility is a clear incentive for early action, as the consequences of warming exceeding 2°C are highly uncertain and potentially severe (Ambrosi and others 2003; Ha-Duong and others 1997; World Bank 2009). The 2°C objective, for example, is achievable only if significant emission reductions can be made before 2030 (Meinshausen and others 2009; O'Neill and others 2009).

If growing dirty now and cleaning up later is not an option, then what is needed are joint green and growth policies. It is inefficient to pursue growth and then worry about its environmental consequences or to promote environmental sustainability and then worry about its growth implications. But the possibility to green growth has been questioned. The next section provides a framework to investigate the potential for greening growth without slowing it.

FIGURE 1.3   The denser the city, the lower the transportation emissions
(relationship between urban density and per capita emissions)

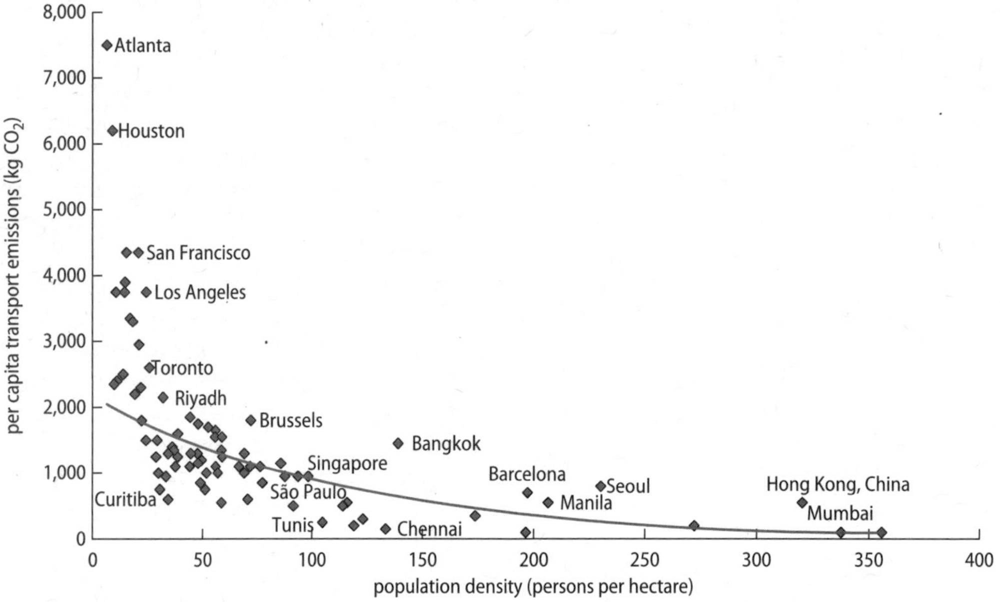

Source: Kenworthy and Laube 2001.

Is green growth really possible? The analytical basis

Modern growth theory dates back to 1956, when Robert Solow put forward a formal model that suggested that growth in output—GDP—comes from increases in physical capital, labor, and productivity (box 1.2). In this model, physical capital increases thanks to investment. Labor increases as a result of population growth, greater labor force participation, and better health and education. And productivity increases thanks to technological change—which can stem from investments in education and research and development (R&D), economies of scale, and learning by doing.

What is missing in this model, however, is the notion that economic production depends directly on the stock of natural resources and the quality of the environment—that is, that the environment is a factor in the production function. This notion has been around at least since Malthus ([1798] 1965), but it was not until the early 1970s that classical growth theory was modified to embrace the environment—referred to as

"natural capital"—as a factor of production (Dasgupta and Heal 1974; Nordhaus 1974; Solow 1974).[4] If the environment is considered as productive capital, it makes sense to invest in it, and environmental policies can be considered as investment.

In this "greener" framework, environmental policies increase economic output directly by improving environmental conditions (for example, better forestry management reduces soil erosion, leading to more productive agriculture). Failure to manage the environment results in the depreciation and destruction of natural capital, with direct adverse impacts on output. Cleaning up the environment also increases human well-being directly, by improving air and water quality and reducing exposure to natural hazards, although these benefits are not necessarily captured by conventional (GDP) statistics.

Whether investing in the environment increases only the level of production or also its rate of growth is likely to depend on the context in which the investment is made. Where credit constraints limit output growth, investing in the environment will accelerate

---

BOX 1.2 An economic framework for green growth

Classical growth theory (Solow 1956) assumes that output (Y) is produced using technology (A), physical capital (K), and labor (L). The relationship can be written as follows:

$$Y = f(A, K, L).$$

Growth in output results from increases in production factors (physical capital and labor) and productivity, which rises as a result of technological change, including changes in organization and practices. In this approach, the environment plays no productive role.

The idea that economic production depends directly on the stock of natural resources and the quality of the environment—that is, that the environment is an argument in the production function—has been around at least since Malthus (1798). It was further developed in the environmental economics literature that took off in the early 1970s. In this approach, the environment becomes "natural capital," an input in economic production and growth. The production function can thus be rewritten as follows:

$$Y = f(A, K, L, E),$$

where E represents the environment (natural capital).

To analyze the effect of green growth policies, however, growth models need to be modified to incorporate market failures and the fact that the economy is not at its optimal equilibrium. A first modification replaces the production function with the production frontier—the maximum production level possible with the available technology, physical capital, labor, and environment, assuming maximum efficiency. Actual production is given by

$$Y = \psi f(A, K, L, E),$$

where ψ (a value between 0 and 1) measures the efficiency of the production process.

A second modification introduces P_E, which can be thought of as the effort dedicated to environmental policies:

$$Y = \psi(P_E) f[A(P_E), K(P_E), L(P_E), E(P_E)].$$

In this case, environmental policies can create synergies with economic output by increasing productive capital (K, L, and E), improving efficiency ψ, and accelerating technological change by increasing A.

Ultimately, it is welfare that matters, not output. This means that the model needs to account for the impact of output on welfare (or utility, U). As investment does not increase welfare directly, utility can be modeled as depending only on the current level of consumption, C, plus the direct effect of the environment, E:

$$U = u(C, E).$$

In practice, environmental policies can affect utility directly (positively or negatively), with effects that are not mediated by aggregate consumption or the state of the environment such as distributional impacts or increased resilience. The utility function can thus be written as follows:

$$U = u(C, E, P_E).$$

Distribution (how total consumption is distributed across individuals) and volatility (how total consumption is distributed over time) affect welfare and can be influenced directly by environmental policies. Everything else equal, many people favor stable consumption patterns and lower consumption inequality; the utility function can thus include an aversion for risk and inequality.

Sources: Hallegatte and others 2011 and World Bank.

---

growth, because a higher production level increases income and savings. Where growth is limited by investment opportunities, it will fail to boost growth, because institutions are not in place to allow investors to benefit from their investment revenues. Where people are engaged in low-return activities, a limited increase in the production level may improve welfare but will not spur economic growth, because these economic activities do not generate sufficient returns to allow households to save and accumulate assets.

A key question in this framework is the extent to which production factors are complements or substitutes. If they are complements (or weak substitutes), protecting the environment is necessary to maintain economic production. If they are substitutes, in principle, increased investment in physical or human capital or technological change can compensate for damage to the environment. In fact, the ability to do so appears limited.[5] Food production requires soil and water, even if technology and increased labor intensity can reduce the quantities needed. The low elasticity of substitution between natural capital and other inputs implies that a small percentage increase in natural capital can free large percentage quantities of other inputs.[6]

While direct economic benefits from environmental policies occur mainly over the long term, green policies can also contribute to short-term economic growth because the world's economies perform far from their optimum levels. Indeed, many market failures hurt both the environment (by reducing the effective supply of natural capital) and the economy (by causing an extremely inefficient use of natural resources). Correcting these market failures, although sometimes costly, can increase efficiency and yield benefits that go beyond the environment. An example is urban congestion, which not only causes air pollution but also reduces the productivity and economies of scope cities provide. The reality is that the use and management of "natural capital" are plagued by extensive market failures, such as unpriced externalities and poorly defined property rights.

The problem for analysts is that models of economic growth usually fail to capture environmental contributions, partly because they generally ignore the role of natural capital and partly because they assume a world with no market failures. As the potential for green policies to accelerate income growth arises from market failures, such models cannot be used to assess the impact of such policies.

A real-world framework for green growth

To be useful for analyzing the effect of green growth policies, a broader framework is needed that is modified to account for market failures and other suboptimalities, such as the following:

- Knowledge spillovers and economies of scale that lead to underinvestment in R&D
- Underutilization of physical capital or labor, for temporary (crisis) or structural reasons
- Behavioral biases, such as the inability to make decisions about low-probability events (Camerer and Kunreuther 1989; Tversky and Shafir 1992)
- Other market failures, such as principal-agent issues, information asymmetry in capital markets, and coordination failures.

Actual economic output depends on the "production frontier" (the maximum production level possible with the available technology, physical capital, labor, and environment, assuming maximum efficiency) and on efficiency (how close the real-world production system actually is to the production frontier).

Green growth policies can thus be seen as policies that move the economy away from suboptimalities and increase efficiency—and hence contribute to short-term growth—while protecting the environment. Suboptimalities often persist because removing them is complex or requires large upfront investments. Assessing the possibility to correct these market failures requires devoting attention to their causes, to institutional and political obstacles, and to transaction costs.

How do environmental policies increase conventionally measured GDP? They do so through four channels linked to input, efficiency, stimulus, and innovation effects. Figure 1.4 illustrates each of these effects.

Input effect

The input channel works by increasing the quantity of natural, human (labor), and physical capital (arrow i in figure 1.4). Specifically, green policies can achieve the following:

- Increase natural capital through better management of scarce resources. Individual transferable fishing quotas, for example,

FIGURE 1.4   Green policies hold the potential to sharply boost output

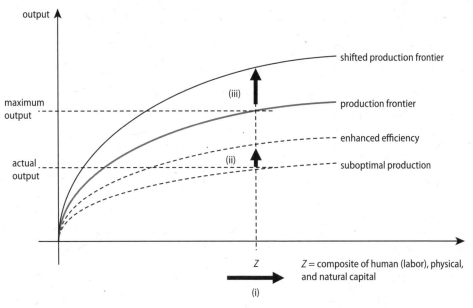

Note: Arrow (i) represents increase in factors of production. Arrow (ii) represents enhanced efficiency and stimulus effect. Arrow (iii) represents shift in production frontier.

help maintain and even increase fisheries and thus the economic activity that depends on them (box 1.3).

- Increase labor by improving health (Hanna 2011). Better environmental policies can decrease atmospheric pollution in cities, reduce the severity and incidence of respiratory diseases, increase labor effectiveness, and reduce days lost to illness. A study on the link between air pollution and labor productivity on farms in California shows that a decrease in ozone concentrations of 10 parts per billion (for an average value of 50 parts per billion) increased worker productivity by 4.2 percent (Graff Zivin and Neidell 2011).
- Increase physical capital by better managing natural risks, which in turn leads to lower capital losses from natural disasters (Hallegatte and others 2007). Protecting mangroves, for instance, not only protects biodiversity, it can also improve the resilience of coastal zones to hurricanes and storm surges, thereby

reducing economic losses caused by coastal floods.

Efficiency effect

The efficiency channel works by increasing productivity, through correcting market failures and influencing behaviors, and by enhancing the efficiency of resource use (arrow ii in figure 1.4). One example is energy efficiency. Many firms and households fail to make cost-effective energy-efficiency investments—probably because of market failures and behavioral biases (Gillingham and others 2009). Improving the insulation of new buildings is often cost-effective, but firms and households often fail to do so because of a lack of information and the fact that building and housing prices do not adequately reflect differences in heating costs. Environmental policies that aim to reduce energy consumption and carbon emissions may correct these market

---

BOX 1.3   Using individual transferable quotas to revitalize fisheries

Lack of property rights in the sea has led to over-fishing—in some cases with devastating results. The use of individual transferable quotas (ITQs) can correct this market failure, increasing both output and employment in the fishing industry.

ITQs operate by setting a cap on the total allowable catch (TAC). The cap is set at a level that is consistent with the long-term survival of the species (that is, less than the rate of growth of the fish stock). Once a TAC is set, it is divided into individual quotas, the amounts that particular boats or skippers can catch. Only quota owners are allowed to fish. If the TAC changes from year to year, the number of tons represented by the quota also changes, but the fraction of the TAC assigned to individuals does not. These quotas are transferable: they can be sold, given, or bequeathed to others. (A related approach is that of "catch shares," under which each boat or owner is entitled to a share of the TAC but the shares are not transferable.)

The value of the ITQ depends on the productivity of a fishery—1 percent of a thriving and productive fishery with large fish stocks is worth far more than 1 percent of an almost-extinct fishery. The ITQ

system thus provides an incentive for quota owners (fishers) to invest in the long-run health of their fishery. The quotas generally represent a substantial share of fishers' wealth; if they overexploit the fishery, they thus risk impoverishing themselves. Under this system, they have an incentive to leave fish in the water to breed and generate future catch, an incentive they otherwise lack. ITQs align the interests of fishers and the fishery, generally improving both the health of the fishery and the profits of the men and women who depend on it.

Are ITQs making a difference? In studies of more than 11,000 fisheries, 121 of which had instituted ITQs, Costello and others (2008) and Heal and Schlenker (2008) find a substantial increase in catch within a few years of the implementation of ITQs and a significant decrease in the chance of a fishery collapsing once it is managed as an ITQ. On average, within 17 years of implementing an ITQ, the catch at fisheries with ITQs rose by a factor of five, with yields of some fisheries rising by a factor of 200. The institution of ITQs allows fisheries to prosper, generating better livelihoods for the people who work in them and more food for the world as a whole.

---

failures or influence these behaviors, leading to less environmental damage and to a more efficient economy, with a higher growth potential.

Stimulus effect

The stimulus channel can occur during an economic recession, when capacity utilization and employment are low (also arrow ii in figure 1.4). Large investments in green infrastructure increase demand, potentially increasing employment over the short term (Zenghelis 2011). Underemployment is not always related to demand, however; it can be structural, especially in developing countries.[7] In this case, a stimulus may prove costly and do little to increase employment.

Innovation effect

Environmental policies can shift the production frontier (increasing the potential output the economy can produce) by accelerating the development and dissemination of innovation and creating knowledge spillovers (arrow iii in figure 1.4).[8] Given that investments in knowledge tend to be lower than desirable in the absence of public intervention, policies that encourage green technologies can thus usefully increase R&D (Acemoglu and others 2012; Fischer and Newell 2008; Gerlagh 2006; Otto and Reilly 2008).[9] (The opposite effect is also possible, as research on green technologies could crowd out research on other productivity-increasing technologies [Popp and others 2009].) The innovation effect is illustrated by investments in R&D on photovoltaic power motivated by the desire to mitigate greenhouse gas emissions. Success could make photovoltaics competitive with fossil fuels, increase the supply of electric power, and reduce the cost of providing electric power to remote off-grid communities (see chapter 6).

At the same time, the costs associated with environmental efforts create a trade-off between environmental protection and economic production. For example, environmental efforts may have the following effects:

- Reduced productivity, by causing producers to use more expensive or less productive technologies or by crowding out R&D in nonenvironmental domains.
- Early retirement of physical capital based on polluting technologies (Grubb and others 1995; Jaccard and Rivers 2007). This effect can be represented as a decrease in capital or an increase in capital depreciation. In addition to the direct cost, the increase in investment needed to replace retired capital reduces consumption—and thus welfare—at least over the short term.
- Increases in the pricing of some goods and services, altering relative prices. By changing the structure of demand, environmental policies may reduce the ability of the structure of production to meet demand. For example, policies may reduce demand in some sectors that have a high production capacity (such as road transport) and may increase demand in sectors that have more limited production capacity (such as public transportation). This effect can be measured as lower efficiency.

These costs, and their assessment, depend on the definition of economic output. In a green accounting framework that includes valuation of ecosystem services, a reduction in economic productivity because of environmental regulations can be more than compensated for by a reduction in externalities—through, for example, the preservation of ecosystem services (a topic explored in chapter 2).

What about welfare?

Ultimately, however, what matters is welfare, not output. The next step, therefore, is to broaden the framework to take into account the impact of the environment on welfare (or utility), which can be positive or negative. Welfare can be assessed by viewing utility as depending on the current level of consumption and the direct effect of the environment (through its health effects and amenity value).

Welfare also depends on income distribution and employment. As such, analysts must take into account the fact that environmental policies may affect different social groups or regions differently. These policies may create jobs for some types of workers in some regions and eliminate jobs for other types of workers in other regions. Because women tend to be more dependent on common property resources and more vulnerable to the impacts of natural resource degradation than men (Foa 2009), environmental protection and green policies can also help improve gender equality, with many economic and social co-benefits. These distributive effects have both social and political economy implications that may require the implementation of complementary policies to compensate losers (see chapter 2). If compensatory financial transfers are possible at zero cost and labor markets are perfect, efficiency can be separated from equity. If such transfers are impossible or costly and labor markets are imperfect, it is necessary to pursue efficiency and equity simultaneously, which may require setting more modest goals (Goulder and Parry 2008).

Analysts must also factor in the fact that environmental policies can increase or decrease volatility. These policies can create shocks in the economy and can distort intertemporal trade-offs. But they can also reduce potential risks to growth by increasing resilience to environmental

---

BOX 1.4 Reducing vulnerability to oil shocks by increasing energy efficiency

The vulnerability of the world economy to oil shocks has diminished since the 1970s (Nordhaus 2007). Possible explanations for this decline include the decrease in the average oil intensity of world GDP; the increased flexibility of labor markets (in particular wages), so that pass-through inflation is less likely for a given monetary policy; a change in the nature of oil shocks (the 1973 and 1979 shocks followed supply disruptions; the 2008 shock resulted from increased demand from emerging markets); and improved confidence in monetary policy, which stabilized inflationary expectations as a result of nearly three decades of low and stable inflation (Blanchard and Gali 2010; Gregorio and others 2007).

Specific energy security policies drove the decrease in GDP oil intensity. In some countries, higher taxes on gasoline consumption reduced oil consumption. In others, norms and regulations reduced energy consumption by cars, industries, and the residential sector.

Over the longer term, climate policies may have similar results: by driving technological change and investment away from oil-intensive patterns, these policies reduce oil consumption and vulnerability to oil shocks (Rozenberg and others 2010). Climate policies can thus reduce vulnerability to oil scarcity and uncertainty over oil reserves. In particular, such policies might reduce the obsolescence of capital in case of large changes in energy prices. Cities that are denser, less dependent on individual vehicles, and less energy consuming are also less vulnerable to volatility in oil prices (Gusdorf and Hallegatte 2007). Climate policies and other policies aiming at higher efficiency in the use of natural resources can thus increase the security and resilience of the economy.

---

shocks (such as natural disasters) or economic shocks (such as oil shocks or spikes in commodity prices) (box 1.4).[10] In so doing, they can stabilize output and consumption, increasing welfare if risk aversion is accounted for.

Trade-offs and synergies between green policies and growth

Armed with this framework for green growth, how do policy makers weigh the trade-offs between the costs (possible reductions in investments, income, and consumption) and benefits (possible improvements on the environmental, social, and economic fronts)? Given that the net impact varies depending on the policy considered, the context, and the time horizon,[11] a start is classifying the potential benefits of green growth policies, as done in table 1.1. In a green growth context, any new policy should be examined for ways to maximize the potential for short-term benefits while minimizing the costs.

Measuring the net impacts of green growth policies also requires capturing suboptimal conditions caused by market or government failures or nonrational behaviors. Models based on first-best assumptions (perfect markets, rational expectations, and so forth) can assess the costs of these policies in a perfect world; they cannot be used to estimate their benefits.

The balance between costs and benefits will be affected by how they are defined. In a narrow economic framework, a policy to protect a mangrove forest has an economic opportunity cost (because it prevents shrimp farming or tourism development, for example) and no direct benefit. In contrast, in a framework that includes the valuation of ecosystem services, the policy also has economic benefits, including protection against coastal storms, the creation or maintenance of a breeding ground for fisheries, and the availability of wood for the local community. The "green accounting" approach incorporates the valuation of ecosystem services into national accounts, thereby providing a much

TABLE 1.1 Potential benefits of green growth policies

Type of benefit	Impact on welfare	Channels through which policy affects welfare
Environmental	Increases welfare directly	Improved environment
Economic	Increases welfare by raising income	Increase in factors of production (physical capital, human capital, and natural capital)
		Accelerated innovation, through correcting market failures in knowledge
		Enhanced efficiency, through correcting nonenvironmental market failures and influencing behaviors
Social	Increases welfare through distributional effects, reduced volatility, and other social indicators	Increased resilience to natural disasters, commodity price volatility, and economic crises
		Job creation and poverty reduction

better measure of trade-offs than traditional national income accounting. As such, it is central to green growth strategies.

In sum, although many observers fear that green policies require incurring large costs now for benefits that will materialize only in the long term, the reality is that many of the benefits can occur in the short and medium term. Moreover, green policies can contribute to growth. Action therefore needs to be taken now—at least on issues that carry a risk of lock-in and irreversibility—to minimize regret and avoid costly policy reversals. In the next two chapters, we look at the cross-cutting issues of market and governance, beginning with the range of tools that can be marshaled to change behavior with respect to environmental and natural resources—tools that aim to improve social welfare through greener growth.

Notes

1. Kuznets argued that as a country develops and national income rises, inequality increases, but once a certain national income level is reached, inequality then declines. His now disproved theory was extended to the environment, where it has also been rejected (Andreoni and Levinson 2001; Barbier 1997; Brock and Taylor 2010).
2. Another common interpretation is that the environmental Kuznets curve reflects structural transformation of an economy. As economies become more industrial, environ-

mental quality deteriorates. But as economies shift from industry to services, environmental quality improves.
3. In some cases, even specialists debate the importance of these relationships.
4. Later efforts to explicitly model the environment into an endogenous growth framework include work by Smulders (1994) and Bovenberg and Smulders (1996); for a review, see Smulders (1999).
5. Few studies examine the potential for substituting other inputs for natural capital (Markandya and Pedroso-Galinato 2007).
6. It may be possible to compensate for the loss of natural capital with other types of capital in the short term but not the long term. An example would be increasing the use of fertilizer to compensate for soil degradation—a short-term solution that is not sustainable over the long term.
7. For an illustration of this point in the context of South Africa, see World Bank (2011).
8. This argument on the impact of green policies on productivity is the macro-scale equivalent of the Porter hypothesis (Porter and van der Linde 1995), which states that regulation can enhance innovation and business performance at the micro scale (for a review, see Ambec and others 2011).
9. A frequently asked question is whether public support of green innovation should target green innovation or general innovation. The opposite question—can green innovation policies accelerate innovation in general?—is posed here.
10. Hallegatte (2011) suggests that development can increase or decrease risk, depending

on its structure and pattern. Green growth strategies aim to make development risk decreasing, thereby increasing the resilience of the economic system.

11. For instance, the GDP losses associated with a carbon tax differ widely depending on how tax revenues are used (Goulder 1995).

References

Acemoglu, D., P. Aghion, L. Bursztyn, and D. Hemous. 2012. "The Environment and Directed Technical Change." *American Economic Review* 102 (1): 131–66.

Ambec, S., M. A. Cohen, S. Elgie, and P. Lanoie. 2011. *The Porter Hypothesis at 20: Can Environmental Regulation Enhance Innovation and Competitiveness?* Washington, DC: Resources for the Future.

Ambrosi P., J.-C. Hourcade, S. Hallegatte, F. Lecocq, P. Dumas, and M. Ha Duong. 2003. "Optimal Control Models and Elicitation of Attitudes towards Climate Damages." *Environmental Modeling and Assessment* 8 (3): 133–47.

Andreoni, J., and A. Levinson. 2001. "The Simple Analytics of the Environmental Kuznets Curve." *Journal of Public Economics* 80 (2): 269–86.

Aubertot J. N., J. M. Barbier, A. Carpentier, J. J. Gril, L. Guichard, P. Lucas, S. Savary, I. Savini, and M. Voltz., ed. 2005. *Pesticides, agriculture et environnement: réduire l'utilisation des pesticides et limiter leurs impacts environnementaux.* Expertise scientifique collective, synthèse du rapport, INRA et Cemagref (France).

Barbier, E. 1997. "Environmental Kuznets Curve Special Issue: Introduction." *Environment and Development Economics* 2: 369–81.

Blanchard, O. J., and J. Gali. 2010. "The Macroeconomic Effects of Oil Price Shocks: Why Are the 2000s So Different from the 1970s?" NBER Working Paper 13368, National Bureau of Economic Research, Cambridge, MA.

Bovenberg, A. L., and S. Smulders. 1996. "Transitional Impacts of Environmental Policy in an Endogenous Growth Model." *International Economic Review* 37 (4): 861–95.

Brock, W. A., and M. S. Taylor. 2010. "The Green Solow Model." *Journal of Economic Growth* 15 (2): 127–53.

Camerer, C., and H. Kunreuther. 1989. "Decision Processes for Low Probability Events: Policy Implications." *Journal of Policy Analysis and Management* 8 (4): 565–92.

Chapin, F. S., III, E. S. Zavaleta, V. T. Eviner, R. L. Naylor, P. M. Vitousek, H. L. Reynolds, D. U. Hooper, S. Lavorel, O. E. Sala, S. E. Hobbie, M. C. Mack, and S. Diaz. 2000. "Consequences of Changing Biodiversity." *Nature* 405: 234–42.

Costello, C., S. D. Gaines, and J. Lynham. 2008. "Can Catch Shares Prevent Fisheries Collapse?" *Science* 321 (5896): 1678–81.

Dasgupta, P., and G. Heal. 1974. "Optimal Depletion of Exhaustible Resources." *The Review of Economic Studies* 41 (1974): 3–28. http://www.jstor.org/stable/2296369.

Davis, K., S. J. Caldeira, and H. D. Matthews. 2010. "Future CO_2 Emissions and Climate Change from Existing Energy Infrastructure." *Science* 329 (5997): 1330–5.

Duhigg, C. 2009. "That Tap Water Is Legal but May Be Unhealthy." *New York Times*, December 16. http://www.nytimes.com/2009/12/17/us/17water.html.

Fischer, C., and R. G. Newell. 2008. "Environmental and Technology Policies for Climate Mitigation." *Journal of Environmental Economics and Management* 55 (2): 142–62.

Foa, R. 2009. "Social and Governance Dimensions of Climate Change Implications for Policy." Policy Research Working Paper 4939, World Bank, Washington, DC.

Gerlagh, R. 2006. "ITC in a Global Growth-Climate Model with CCS: The Value of Induced Technical Change for Climate Stabilization." *Energy Journal,* Special issue on Induced Technological Change and Climate Change: 55–72.

Gillingham, K., R. Newell, and K. Palmer. 2009. "Energy Efficiency Economics and Policy." *Annual Review of Resource Economics* 1: 597–619.

Goulder, L. 1995. "Environmental Taxation and the 'Double Dividend': A Reader's Guide." *International Tax and Public Finance* 2 (2): 157–83.

Goulder L. H., and K. Mathai. 2000. "Optimal CO_2 Abatement in the Presence of Induced Technological Change." *Journal of Environmental Economics and Management* 39 (1): 1–38.

Goulder, L. H., Parry, I. W. H. 2008. "Instrument Choice in Environmental Policy." *Review of Environmental Economics and Policy* 2: 152–74.

Graff Zivin, J. S., and M. J. Neidell. 2011. "The Impact of Pollution on Worker Productivity." NBER Working Paper 17004, National Bureau of Economic Research, Cambridge, MA.

Gregorio, J. D., O. Landerretche, and C. Neilson. 2007. "Another Pass-Through Bites the Dust? Oil Prices and Inflation." *Journal of LACEA Economia* 7 (2): 155–208.

Grubb, M., T. Chapuis, and M. H. Duong. 1995. "The Economics of Changing Course: Implications of Adaptability and Inertia for Optimal Climate Policy." *Energy Policy* 23 (4–5): 417–31.

Guivarch C., and S. Hallegatte. 2011. "Existing Infrastructure and the 2°C Target." *Climatic Change Letters* 109 (3–4): 791–825.

Gusdorf, F., and S. Hallegatte. 2007. "Compact or Spread-Out Cities: Urban Planning, Taxation, and the Vulnerability to Transportation Shocks." *Energy Policy* 35 (10): 4826–38.

Gusdorf, F., S. Hallegatte, and A. Lahellec. 2008. "Time and Space Matter: How Urban Transitions Create Inequality." *Global Environment Change* 18 (4): 708–19.

Ha-Duong, M., M. Grubb, and J.-C. Hourcade. 1997. "Influence of Socioeconomic Inertia and Uncertainty on Optimal CO_2–Emission Abatement." *Nature* 390 (6657): 270–3.

Hallegatte, S. 2011. "How Economic Growth and Rational Decisions Can Make Disaster Losses Grow Faster than Wealth." Policy Research Working Paper 5617, World Bank, Washington, DC.

Hallegatte, S., G. Heal, M. Fay, D. Treguer. 2011. "From Growth to Green Growth: A Framework." Background paper for the Flagship Report on Green Growth, Policy Research Working Paper 5872, World Bank, Washington, DC.

Hallegatte, S., J.-C. Hourcade, and P. Dumas. 2007. "Why Economic Dynamics Matter in Assessing Climate Change Damages: Illustration on Extreme Events." *Ecological Economics* 62 (2): 330–40.

Hanna, R. 2011. "The Effect of Pollution on Labor Supply: Evidence from a Natural Experiment in Mexico City." NBER Working Paper 17302, National Bureau of Economic Research, Cambridge, MA.

Heal, G., and W. Schlenker. 2008. "Economics: Sustainable Fisheries." *Nature* 455 (7216): 1044–5.

Jaccard, M., and N. Rivers. 2007. "Heterogeneous Capital Stocks and the Optimal Timing for CO_2 Abatement. *Resource and Energy Economics* 29 (1): 1–16.

Kenworthy, J. and F. Laube. 2001. *Millennium Cities Database for Sustainable Transport.* Brussels: International Union of Public Transport and Institute for Sustainability and Technology Policy.

Lecocq, F., J. Hourcade, and M. Ha Duong. 1998. "Decision Making under Uncertainty and Inertia Constraints: Sectoral Implications of the When Flexibility." *Energy Economics* 20 (4–5): 539–55.

Malthus, T. (1798) 1965. *First Essay on Population.* London: J. Johnson. Reprint, New York: A. M. Kelley.

Manne, A., and R. Richels. 2004. "The Impact of Learning-by-Doing on the Timing and Costs of CO_2 Abatement." *Energy Economics* 26 (4): 603–19.

Markandya, A., and S. Pedroso-Galinato. 2007. "How Substitutable Is Natural Capital?" *Environmental & Resource Economics (European Association of Environmental and Resource Economists)* 37 (1): 297–312.

Meinshausen, M., N. Meinshausen, W. Hare, S. Raper, K. Frieler, R. Knutti, D. Frame, and M. Allen. 2009. "Greenhouse Gas Emissions Targets for Limiting Global Warming to 2°C." *Nature* 458: 1158–62.

Multignier, L., J. R. Ndong, A. Giusti, M. Romana, H. Delacroix-Maillard, S. Cordier, B. Jégou, J. P. Thome, and P. Blanchet. 2010. "Chlordecone Exposure and Risk of Prostate Cancer." *Journal of Clinical Oncology* 28 (21): 3457–62.

Nordhaus, W. D. 1974. "Resources as a Constraint on Growth." *American Economic Review* 64 (May): 22–26.

———. 1992. "An Optimal Transition Path for Controlling Greenhouse Gases." *Science* 258 (5086): 1315–9.

———. 2007. "Who's Afraid of a Big Bad Oil Shock?" *Brookings Papers on Economic Activity* 2007 (2): 219–238. http://www.jstor.org/stable/27561607.

O'Neill, B. C., K. Riahi, and I. Keppo. 2009. "Mitigation Implications of Midcentury Targets That Preserve Long-Term Climate Policy Options." *Proceedings of the National Academy of Sciences of the United States* 107: 1011–6.

Otto, V. M., and J. Reilly. 2008. "Directed Technical Change and the Adoption of CO_2 Abatement Technology: The Case of CO_2 Capture and Storage." *Energy*

Economic 30: 2871–90. doi:10.1016/j.eneco.2007.07.001.

Popp, D., R. G. Newell, and A. B. Jaffe. 2009. "Energy, the Environment, and Technological Change." NBER Working Paper 14832, National Bureau of Economic Research, Cambridge, MA.

Porter, M., and C. van der Linde. 1995. "Toward a New Conception of the Environment-Competitiveness Relationship." *Journal of Economic Perspective* 9 (4): 97–118.

Rozenberg J., S. Hallegatte, A. Vogt-Schilb, O. Sassi, C. Guivarch, H. Waisman, and J.-C. Hourcade. 2010. "Climate Policies as a Hedge against the Uncertainty on Future Oil Supply."*Climatic Change Letters* 101 (3): 663–9.

Smulders, J. 1994. *Growth Market Structure and the Environment: Essays on the Theory of Endogenous Economic Growth.* Tilburg, the Netherlands: Tilburg University.

———. 1999. "Endogenous Growth Theory and the Environment." In *Handbook of Environmental and Resource Economics*, ed. J. C. J. M. van den Berg, 610–21. Cheltenham, United Kingdom: Edward Elgar.

Solow, R. M. 1956. "A Contribution to the Theory of Economic Growth." *Quarterly Journal of Economics* 70 (1): 65–94.

———. 1974. "The Economics of Resources or the Resources of Economics." *American Economic Review* 64: 1–14.

Sue Wing, I. 2006. "Representing Induced Technological Change in Models for Climate Policy Analysis." *Energy Economics* 28 (5–6): 539–62.

Tversky, A., and E. Shafir. 1992. "Choice under Conflict: The Dynamics of Deferred Decision." *Psychological Science* 3 (6): 358–61.

Wigley, T. M. L., R. Richels, and J. A. Edmonds. 1996. "Economic and Environmental Choices in the Stabilization of Atmospheric CO_2 Concentrations." *Nature* 379 (6562): 240–3.

World Bank. 2009. *World Development Report 2010: Development and Climate Change.* Washington, DC: World Bank.

———. 2011. *South Africa: Economic Update. Focus on Green Growth.* Washington, DC: World Bank.

World Bank and DRC (Development Research Center of the State Council, the People's Republic of China). 2012. *Seizing the Opportunity of Green Development in China.* Supporting Report 3 for *China 2030: Building a Modern, Harmonious, and Creative High-Income Society*, Conference Edition, World Bank, Washington DC.

Zenghelis, D. 2011. *A Macroeconomic Plan for a Green Recovery.* London: Grantham Research Institute on Climate Change and the Environment.

Influencing Firms, Consumers, and Policy Makers through Market and Nonmarket Mechanisms | 2

Key Messages

- Because economic incentives promote efficient solutions, "getting the prices right" is key to greening growth without slowing it. Complementary policies will be needed to mitigate negative distributional impacts.
- Economic incentives cannot induce all of the

changes needed to protect the environment, given market failures, behavioral biases, and political economy considerations.
- Other tools—such as information judiciously deployed to influence economic actors, and norms and regulations—are also needed.

The starting point in greening growth is an understanding of why so much of traditional economic growth has been "non-green"—that is, why the world is not using environmental assets efficiently, a reality that is harming economic growth and the environment.

For economists, achieving greener growth is fundamentally about changing the incentives that have led to environmental degradation and depletion—that is, "getting the prices right." The reasons markets are failing to appropriately price the environment and thus create incentives to encourage greener growth are many (Sterner 2003). They include institutional and policy failures; market failures, such as externalities,

the public-good nature of many environmental goods; and missing or incomplete property rights (box 2.1). With a common pool resource like a fishery or a shared aquifer, for example, the lack of property rights (such as individual quotas) can lead to overexploitation and ultimately a collapse of the resource.

For psychologists, achieving greener growth is about compensating for behavioral biases, tailoring information and messages to the way people learn, and improving the way in which environmentalists and economists communicate the costs and benefits of greener behaviors. Examples include social marketing campaigns that changed social norms around water usage in Australia or

---

BOX 2.1   Institutional and market failures that help explain why growth is often environmentally unsustainable

Growth may be environmentally unsustainable because of *institutional and policy failure*. Institutions and governments may themselves face bad incentives, driven by political economy. Or they may lack information on the overall impact of the policies they promote. Subsidizing energy "to benefit the poor" is a classic example—the subsidy encourages energy consumption, thereby increasing emissions of local air pollutants that often disproportionately affect the health of the poor. Moreover, it is generally the nonpoor who benefit most from energy subsidies, because they can afford an energy-intensive lifestyle.

Alternatively, *market failures* may be to blame. Under some technical assumptions, competitive markets are an efficient means of allocating goods. But real markets deviate from the ideal in a multitude of ways that can have severe consequences for the environment and social welfare. Examples include the following:

- *Externalities*. These are uncompensated damages imposed by one economic agent on another. For example, a factory owner can maximize profits from production by releasing untreated effluents into a river rather than incurring the costs of treatment. But the resulting water pollution can damage the health of people drinking the water downstream. This health damage is external to the profit-maximizing decisions of the factory owner, with the result that the social benefits from production are less than private profits.
- *Public goods*. Many environmental assets have a public-good nature—they provide services, such as amenities or the regulation of water flow, that

are nonrival (one person's enjoyment of the amenity does not decrease another person's enjoyment) and nonexcludable (there is no practical way to prevent people from enjoying an amenity such as a beautiful view). The result is that public goods are typically underprovided by private markets, because there is no way for private actors to appropriate all the benefits from providing the public good.
- *Information asymmetries and agency problems*. If different agents have different information, environmental impacts can result. Factory owners typically have much more information about pollutants, treatment measures, and treatment costs than environmental regulators, which can reduce the effectiveness of regulation. Landlord-tenant relationships lead to a type of agency problem with regard to energy efficiency: If the landlord pays the energy bills, the tenant has no incentive to conserve energy; if the landlord owns the furnace but the tenant pays the energy bills, the landlord has no incentive to invest in a more efficient furnace.
- *Missing or incomplete property rights*. For common pool resources (for example, a fishery or a shared aquifer), the lack of property rights (such as individual quotas) can lead to overexploitation and ultimately the collapse of the resource. From an economic perspective, overexploitation manifests itself as dissipation of resource rents: in the absence of quotas, exploitation efforts by users of the common pool drives up costs to the point at which economic profits drop to zero.

Source: Sterner 2003.

---

littering behavior in the United States. So for psychologists, incentives also matter but they must be tailored to how people process information and react to it.

Unfortunately, inappropriate incentives, or the lack of incentives, led to the current widespread inefficiency in the way natural resources are used. This chapter examines the range of tools that can be marshaled to increase efficiency by changing behavior with respect to the environment

and natural resources—tools that aim to increase social welfare through greener growth. The tools fall into the following areas:

- Incentivizing: providing effective market signals to spur green growth
- Informing and nudging: using information and framing to influence economic actors
- Imposing: using rules and regulations.

Incentivizing, informing and nudging, or imposing—some combination of the three is likely to be needed. Determining the best mix requires a solid understanding of how individual decisions are made and framed. Behavioral economics and social psychology thus provide indispensable insights into how to green growth. Economists will ignore them at their peril.

Incentivizing: Providing effective market signals to spur green growth

Economic incentives promote efficient solutions

Economic incentives—traditional price and quantity instruments—are critical to promoting green outcomes, because they change behavior in a manner that typically leads to least-cost solutions. The intuition behind this approach can be seen in markets for tradable pollution emission rights. Because polluting firms use different technologies for production, their pollution abatement costs differ, often markedly. Firms with high marginal abatement costs therefore tend to prefer to pollute more and purchase permits from firms that have low marginal abatement costs and find it profitable to invest in less polluting processes and sell their pollution rights. This trade allows the market to minimize the overall cost of achieving a given pollution target.

Economists recommend a variety of incentive-based instruments to reduce environmental damage and depletion—such as taxes, tradable permits, subsidies, deposit-refund schemes, and refunded emission payments—that focus on either price or quantity. In the case of carbon dioxide (CO_2), for example, the debate has centered on emission taxes, subsidies, and tradable emission permits.

Price instruments. These instruments aim to change behavior by ensuring that the prices paid for goods and services reflect their full social costs, including externalities. To the extent that environmental taxes replace other distortive taxes (say, on labor), there

can be a double dividend. Countries in the Organisation for Economic Co-operation and Development (OECD) have imposed some 375 environment-related taxes and about 250 environment-related fees and charges (OECD 2006). However, about 90 percent of revenues from these taxes comes from taxes on fuels and cars (OECD 2011). The majority of OECD countries also tax water usage in agriculture. Although they appear to have improved water efficiency, these price instruments still fall short of full cost recovery (OECD 2010, cited in OECD 2011).

In addition to reflecting social and environmental costs in prices through taxes, "full-cost pricing" implies the phasing out of harmful subsidies, such as subsidies on fossil fuels, fisheries, forestry, water use, land use, and agriculture. These subsidies not only encourage carbon emissions, resource depletion, and environmental degradation, they also distort trade and strain public finance. Reforming them should be a high priority, although it may not be easy.

Quantity instruments. Unlike pollution taxes and subsidy reforms, which affect existing markets, quantity instruments (such as tradable permit schemes) create new markets for pollution allowances by affecting the costs of production. Once these new markets reach equilibrium and the permit price is determined, the cost of acquiring pollution permits affects the costs of production in a manner equivalent to a pollution tax. Tradable permits or quotas have also shown good results in managing renewable environmental assets, notably fisheries.

"Cap and trade" schemes for pollution emissions have become the dominant market-based approach to controlling oxides of sulfur (SO_x) and nitrogen oxides (NO_x) in the United States, in the European Union's Emission Trading Scheme for CO_2, and in many other jurisdictions. The basic principle is that regulators determine the total allowable emissions per year (the cap) and allocate permits to polluters based on a variety of schemes (including "grandfathering" based on historical emissions or auctioning of all permits); firms are then free to trade permits. The evidence on the efficiency of the U.S. SO_x trading scheme is positive: markets have been liquid and permit prices (hence, total cost to firms) have been lower than originally estimated (Fullerton and others 1997). Moreover, international experience with CO_2 emission trading schemes suggests that they can be used to assign a price to polluting emissions from large sources, although implementation can be difficult (box 2.2).

Price versus quantity instruments. Although price schemes and cap and trade schemes are theoretically equivalent instruments, they have distinctive characteristics in practice (World Bank 2010). For example, permit systems create certainty regarding emission reductions but uncertainty about price; taxes provide certainty regarding price but uncertainly about emission reductions. They also differ regarding economic and administrative efficiency and their ability to

generate revenues (theoretically both do, but in practice countries have tended to allocate permits free of charge). As such, many jurisdictions, particularly in Europe, have opted for hybrid schemes to control carbon emissions: tradable permits for large emitting sectors and taxes for smaller sectors characterized by many actors, such as transport.

But imperfect markets and political economy complicate matters

Although in theory, economic incentive–based instruments are the most effective, in practice, market imperfections and political economy mean that additional measures may be needed to make these instruments more efficient. One well-known case concerns innovation and long-lived investments, for which prices are not always efficient (see chapter 3). But there are other circumstances

---

BOX 2.2   Lessons from CO_2 emission trading schemes

A review of existing and proposed carbon trading schemes in Alberta, Australia; the European Union (EU); New Zealand; Switzerland; Tokyo; and the United States (both national and state-level schemes) shows that these schemes are complex to implement but can be used to create a price of carbon for large emitters. To implement them effectively, policy makers should keep in mind the following dos and don'ts:

- *Targets.* Ambitious long-run targets are needed if firms are to invest in reducing their carbon footprints.
- *Allocation.* Free allocation of permits to producers in the electricity generation sector should be avoided, because it leads to windfall profits at the expense of consumers (electric utilities are typically free to pass costs along to consumers). Free allocation to new entrants should also be avoided, because it risks locking in high-carbon footprints (by, in effect, subsidizing a new source of emissions). The EU Emission Trading Scheme is reducing the free allocation of permits.
- *Start-up.* Trading schemes have tended to overallocate permits in the initial phase, leading to a price

collapse. Allowing permits to be banked—that is, allowing permits from one period to be used in subsequent periods—can overcome this problem, but this solution simply carries forward the surplus permits into the next phase. Other options include establishing a price floor, with cancellation of any unsold permits, or initially using a fixed price to aid the collection of data on emissions and abatement costs that can then be used to determine the subsequent allocation.
- *Offsets or links to other trading zones.* Trading outside the permit scheme can help reduce permit prices, but doing so runs counter to policy goals to reduce domestic emissions and provide incentives for innovation in achieving this reduction.
- *Support to carbon-intensive sectors.* Concerns about the competitive impacts on carbon-intensive sectors will lead to lobbying for financial support to these sectors. Any support should be time limited, and communicated as such, to reduce fiscal costs and provide incentives for firms to invest in less polluting technologies.

Source: IEA 2010.

in which narrow reliance on incentive-based instruments is misplaced. These include cases when:

Feasible alternatives are lacking. For pricing mechanisms to be successful in addressing environmental issues, feasible alternatives must be readily available or easily brought to market. One example is high fuel prices, which will be more effective at reducing individual car use if public transport is available or cities have been designed in such a way that walking or cycling are options. Another example is the emissions pricing scheme of the U.S. acid rain program, which successfully reduced SO_2 because the required technologies were available and well understood (Zysman and Huberty 2010). In this case, prices were a powerful incentive for adopting existing alternative technologies.

Market imperfections exist. Prices may be ineffective incentives because of market imperfections or imperfect contracts. For example, contracts may need to be designed in a particular way to address the principal-agent problem (the difficulty of motivating one party [the agent] to act on behalf of another [the principal]). An example is when building owners are responsible for insulation and heating systems but tenants pay energy bills; if owners cannot transfer the cost of higher energy efficiency through higher rents, they will under-invest in energy efficiency regardless of energy prices.

Another example is flood insurance if it is not "risk-based"—that is, if the premium is not calculated as a function of the risk level, which is itself based on the characteristics and location of the asset. Insurance that is not risk-based creates a moral hazard problem, as it reduces incentives to invest in prevention. Households or businesses investing in risk mitigation improvements (such as a reinforced roof or windows) are not rewarded fully for their investments. Moving toward a "risk-based" premium would encourage prudent behavior. However, this approach is difficult to implement with one-year insurance contracts, because investing in risk mitigation produces benefits over decades—meaning that a homeowner who sells his

or her house may not be able to recoup the benefits from the investment. In this case, attaching a long-term insurance contract to the property rather than the owner could help create the right incentives (Kunreuther and Michel-Kerjan 2012).

Prices are difficult to change. The fact that so much pricing is currently inefficient suggests complex political economy considerations. Whether it takes the form of preferential access to land and credit or access to cheap energy and resources, every subsidy creates its own lobby. Large enterprises (both state owned and private) have political power and lobbying capacity. Energy-intensive export industries, for example, will lobby for subsidies to maintain their competitiveness. In emerging economies, industries that are likely to be most affected by climate change policies are export-based industries, which are also the most influential and most able to oppose environmental policies (Mattoo and others 2011; Victor 2011). Thus, governments need to focus on the wider social benefits of reforms and need to be willing to stand up to lobby groups (box 2.3).

In considering pricing reforms or the introduction of new taxes, policy makers need to consider social impacts. Increasing energy prices, for example, has far-reaching impacts, because energy is used pervasively in production and in households. And although energy subsidies almost invariably benefit the rich much more than the poor, their removal can have devastating impacts on the purchasing power of the poor (Arze del Granado and others 2010).[1]

To prevent this from happening, policy makers need to adopt complementary policies, such as the use of existing safety nets (where available), alternative short-term mitigation measures and subsidies, and energy-pricing solutions. In middle- and high-income countries, social safety nets can be used for compensation. In low-income countries, where safety nets are often lacking, ad hoc measures are frequently necessary. Information to target support is often not available, especially in urban areas, where geographic targeting is very inefficient (Kanbur 2010).

BOX 2.3   The political economy of subsidy reform

What lessons have been learned about subsidy reform? An analysis of the political economy of subsidy reform—which looks at the few attempts that have been successful—suggests the need for careful analysis of the likely social impact of the reform and implementation of a program of appropriate support for those affected (Nikoloski 2012). Other elements of success include political will and institutional capacity, as well as an effective communications and outreach strategy that explains the justification for the reform and the benefits to be derived from it. As for the timing and pace of the reform, there is no clear lesson as to whether "big bang" or gradual approaches are more successful.

Another study, which focuses on petroleum product subsidies, confirms the importance of addressing the political logic that led to subsidy creation and either compensating the political interest that would otherwise oppose reform or finding a way to insulate the reform from its opposition—advice that applies to any subsidy reform (Victor 2009). In addition, it is critical to ensure the transparency of the costs and purpose of the subsidy. Reforming a subsidy may be easier if all members of society are fully aware of the costs they are paying and the extent to which they or others are benefiting.

Moreover, the political economy of reform will likely require compensatory transfers to the middle class. In the Islamic Republic of Iran, for example, where the law that reformed fuel and food subsidies stipulated that 50 percent of the revenues raised had to be redistributed to households, the initial thought was to target the bottom 30–50 percent of the income scale. In the end, 80 percent of households received significant transfers (Guillaume and others 2011)—no doubt contributing to the success of the reform.

In the end, the redistributive impacts of a carbon price scheme depend on how revenues from the scheme are used. Compensatory measures can offset unwanted distributional effects. However, such schemes require the institutional capacity to manage the classical challenges of redistributive policies: political acceptability, imperfect information and targeting, and behavioral issues.

To be effective, incentives must reflect behaviors

Designing effective environmental policies requires a good understanding of how behaviors are determined and how they can be influenced.[2] The hypothesis of rational behavior—under which price-based instruments are optimal—is only a rough approximation of how people actually make decisions. In practice, individuals make decisions in a variety of ways: "by the head" (based on calculation), "by the heart" (based on emotion), and "by the book" (based on rules) (Weber and Lindemann 2007). Alternative or complementary policies and measures are therefore needed to address behavioral biases or changes in values and preferences.

Four types of behavioral biases are particularly important. First, "cognitive myopia" prevents people from accurately balancing future benefits and immediate costs and from assessing the desirability of reductions in immediate benefits in exchange for future gains (Ainslie 1975; Benartzi and Thaler 2004).

Second, individuals are inconsistent in their treatment of time (Ainslie 1975): they apply high discount rates to costs and benefits that will occur at some point in the future, discounting much less when both time points are in the future and one occurs later than the other, in a kind of "hyperbolic discounting." These biases explain why it is difficult to implement policies that entail immediate costs but future benefits even if the result is a net (discounted) gain. A classic example is the failure of consumers to buy more energy-efficient appliances even when future energy savings would more than compensate for higher up-front purchase costs (Gillingham and others 2009).

Third, individuals suffer from "loss aversion"—that is, they weigh losses more than gains, evaluating both relative to a reference point (Tversky and Kahneman 1992). If individuals use the current situation as the reference point, they will consider the cost of environmental policy as a loss and weigh it more heavily than the gain (averted environmental damages). If the reference point is the future, when the loss is the environmental destruction, they will weigh it more heavily than the gain (the averted cost of environmental policies). Weber and Johnson (2012, 16–17) make the following observation about farmers:

Skillful insurance salespeople have long known that they need to move a farmer's reference point, away from its usual position at the status quo, down to the level of the possible large loss that could be incurred in case of drought. By focusing the insuree's attention on the severity of the possible loss and resulting consequences, all smaller losses (including the insurance premium) are to the right of this new reference point, making this a decision in the domain of (forgone) gains, where people are known to be risk averse and will choose the sure option of buying the insurance.

Fourth, individuals have an aversion to ambiguity, which causes them to delay making decisions (Tversky and Shafir 1992).[3] Aversion to ambiguity is particularly problematic for environmental issues, such as climate change, that involve huge uncertainties: while it disappears if decision makers regard themselves as expert in a domain (Heath and Tversky 1991), few people consider themselves experts in environmental policy.

Different behavioral changes can be triggered by different learning processes—such as learning by being hurt, being told, and observing and imitating (Weber and Johnson 2012).

Learning by being hurt. Learning by being hurt refers to learning from personal experience. Because recent events have a strong impact, which recedes over time (Hertwig and others 2004), reactions to

low-probability, high-severity events often appear erratic. In particular, people usually overreact when a rare event eventually occurs (Weber and others 2004). For instance, extremely ambitious flood defense projects were designed after each big flood in New Orleans, but none has been completed so far, as public interest in the issue faded a few years after each event. This tendency to overreact to recent events and then forget needs to be taken into account in developing green growth strategies, especially for disaster risk management (Hallegatte 2011).

Learning by being told. Learning by being told involves the absorption of objective information. For instance, hydrometeorological data can be collected and analyzed to generate quantified risk assessments that help individuals make informed choices. But providing information will not be enough to induce appropriate risk management or environment-friendly behavior, because people treat abstract information on distant events differently from concrete, emotionally charged information linked with real-world experience (Trope and Liberman 2003). So what is needed is a combination of communication tools that accounts for this bias and practical information on what needs to be done—for instance, rules to save energy or water or how to react in case of disasters.

Learning by observing and imitating. Learning by observing and imitating has the concreteness that "being told" does not have, making action more likely. One way of encouraging learning by observing and imitating is to help individuals compare their behaviors with more environment-friendly ones and to provide them with feedback on their consumption and with tips on how to change their behaviors. In one experiment, an Internet-based tool that combined feedback on past consumption, energy saving tips, and goal setting was used to encourage households to reduce their energy consumption. Households with access to the tool reduced their direct energy consumption by 5 percent; household without access to the tool increased their consumption by

0.7 percent (Abrahamse and others 2007). Indicators are thus critical—even when they are imperfect—because they allow individuals to monitor their effort.

All of these biases vary with culture and education (Weber and Hsee 1998). For instance, individuals with greater ability to reason with numbers are more likely to rely on calculation-based processes to make their decisions (Peters and others 2006). This diversity means that policy makers may need to align their approaches with the cognitive biases present in a given country or population.[4]

Informing and nudging: Using information and framing to influence economic actors

Many motives other than price signals drive individuals' behavior. It is therefore critical that information on the environmental consequences of their actions go beyond price. Information needs to be framed in a manner that accounts for behavioral biases and the ways in which people learn and make decisions. Governments have a role to play to ensure that the required information is produced and disseminated effectively. Fortunately, they can rely on the experience gained from decades of public health campaigns. However, a vibrant civil society will be essential to ensure that action follows information.

Informing to influence policy makers: The role of green accounting

Environmental assets are seldom traded through markets and thus do not have readily identifiable prices. In such cases, development decisions (such as building a road through a rainforest) are often made with incomplete information. As a result, they may not maximize social benefits. Given that the outputs of environmental projects generally do have a readily identified economic value—a road may increase the access of farmers to markets and thus increase food production—it is vital that economic values for environmental assets be comparable to other economic values.

Environmental valuation can help in a number of ways:

- It estimates people's willingness to pay for environmental goods and services or willingness to accept compensation for the loss of an environmental asset (Bolt and others 2005; Ley and Tran 2011).
- It assesses the value of the services provided by natural ecosystems. Because ecosystem services are typically provided as externalities—for example, an upland forest provides water regulation services to lowland farmers—the natural systems providing these services may be at risk when decisions are made that ignore the flow of services from natural areas and their benefits to people.
- It establishes the schedule of marginal benefits associated with the provision of different quantities of environmental goods and services—such as changes in the volume of pollution emitted. This information is useful when setting tax rates on environmental "bads" or when determining total quota sizes, such as the number of pollution emission permits that will be issued in a given time period.
- It facilitates "green accounting" (box 2.4), which focuses on a country's stock of assets (its wealth) rather than relying on a flow measure such as GDP. As such, it promotes good economic management, identifies situations in which economic growth is not wealth creating (because the growth degrades natural resources faster than it creates wealth), and assesses whether a country's economic trajectory is sustainable. However, green accounting and environmental valuation are not substitutes for price signals, because they do not affect incentives faced by individuals and firms.

Informing and nudging to influence individuals: Tackling behavioral biases

Good design and careful interventions can help align individual preferences with social goals and address behavioral biases.

BOX 2.4   What is "green accounting"?

All accounts serve two purposes: a scorekeeping purpose, providing indicators on how well you are doing, and a management purpose, providing detailed statistics so that anybody who does not like the "score" has the information to understand and do something about it.

In standard national accounting, GDP is measured as the market value of all goods and services produced by a country within a specified time period. Changes in GDP indicate whether the economy is growing, but not whether this growth is sustainable. In particular, the use or misuse of natural capital is not taken into account.

Green accounting extends national accounts to include the value of the damage and depletion of the natural assets that underpin production and human well-being. In particular, net saving, adjusted for the depreciation of produced assets and the depletion and degradation of the environment, indicates whether well-being can be sustained into the future. Negative net saving indicates that it cannot, because the assets that support well-being are being depleted

(Asheim and Weitzman 2001; Dasgupta and Mäler 2000; Hamilton and Clemens 1999).

At the regional level, East Asia and South Asia have exhibited strong wealth creation over more than a decade. In contrast, Sub-Saharan Africa, where the depletion of oil and minerals has been offsetting savings by the public and private sectors, displays a worrisome trend (figure B2.4.1). At the country level, China's near 10 percent annual GDP growth is being partly offset by environmental depletion and degradation, reducing its adjusted net national income growth to an estimated 5.5 percent (World Bank and DRC 2012).

With green accounting, the scorekeeping indicators (such as wealth accounts) can be used alongside GDP to better assess how well a country is doing for the long term. It also provides detailed accounts for management of natural capital, which many countries have adopted over the past 20 years—especially for water, energy, and pollution. However, few countries have adopted the revised macroeconomic indicators.

FIGURE B2.4.1   Some regions are doing better than others in wealth creation
(net saving by region, 1975–2008)

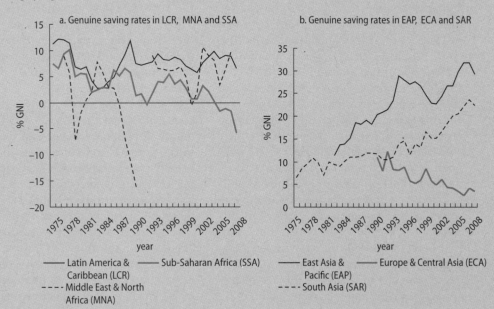

a. Genuine saving rates in LCR, MNA and SSA

b. Genuine saving rates in EAP, ECA and SAR

——— Latin America & Caribbean (LCR)
——— Sub-Saharan Africa (SSA)
- - - - Middle East & North Africa (MNA)

——— East Asia & Pacific (EAP)
——— Europe & Central Asia (ECA)
- - - - South Asia (SAR)

Source: World Bank 2011.
Note: GNI = gross national income.

(continued next page)

BOX 2.4   (continued)

A new partnership—Wealth Accounting and Valuing Ecosystem Services (WAVES)—is expanding efforts to account for ecological services. Botswana, a WAVES partner country, has defined one of its overarching objectives as to continue to grow while diversifying away from diamonds (which currently account for about 35 percent of national income) and eradicating poverty. Several natural resource–based sectors are being tapped to play a lead role in this development strategy, including nature-based tourism, mining (especially coal for export), and irrigated agriculture.

Water plays a critical role in Botswana's development, given its scarcity; the increasing reliance on shared, international water resources; and the water-intensive nature of sectors identified for economic growth and diversification. A key component of WAVES in Botswana will be the establishment of water accounts—physical supply and use accounts as well as monetary accounts (for supply costs, tariffs paid, and the value of water in different uses). Water accounts will enable Botswana to answer the following questions: Is there enough water in the right places to support the diversification strategy? What are the economic trade-offs among competing users? How can incentives for water efficiency be created? In the wake of the recent privatization of water under full cost recovery management, what will happen to poor households' access to water resources? The answers to these questions are critical for helping policy makers chart the best path forward.

Avoiding fear mongering. Given cognitive myopia and people's tendency to weigh emotion-filled consequences more heavily than abstract consequences, policy makers may be tempted to scare people into adopting environment-friendly behavior. Using "catastrophism" to make people change their behavior is ineffective, however, for two reasons. First, fear is only briefly effective. Once people get used to the problem, they revert back to their initial behavior (Weber 1997). For example, farmers informed about weather risks have a tendency to implement one mitigating measure (such as buying insurance), after which they consider their vulnerability problem solved, without considering how additional action may help.

Second, people have only a limited ability to worry; an increase in worry about one hazard decreases worry about other hazards (Weber 1997, 2006). This means that a policy based on fear leads to competition among hazards, and success in one area (for example, climate change) comes at the cost of failure in others (for example, water pollution).

Greening default options. An important behavioral bias that environmental policy makers can use to their advantage is the tendency of people to stick with the default option (box 2.5). In European countries, where organ donation is the default option, more than 85 percent of people are organ donors. In contrast, in neighboring countries where people must designate themselves as organ donors, less than 30 percent of people do so (Johnson and Goldstein 2003). In the United States, automatically enrolling employees in saving programs and requiring them to opt out if they preferred not to participate increased participation from 37 percent (under the opt-in design) to 86 percent (Madrian and Shea 2001).

Using nudging. In recent years, behavioral economists and the behavior change community overall have stepped up their interest in the potential role of nudges to influence behaviors. This approach advocates tweaking "choice architectures" to nudge people to make better decisions about their health, the environment, or other desirable outcomes without restricting their freedom of choice (Thaler and Sunstein 2009). To count as a nudge, the intervention must be easy, inexpensive, and voluntary. Nudges are increasingly being used to stimulate green behaviors; studies show promising results. For example, an electrical outlet (designed by Muhyeon Kim) that displays how much power it is using makes people more conscious of their energy use (figure 2.1). The Danish Nudging

---

BOX 2.5   Changing the default option to spur the use of renewable energy

To spur, rather than coerce, the purchase of renewable energy, policy makers could rewrite the default electricity purchase contract to include a minimum share of electricity produced from renewable sources. Consumers would have to opt out to purchase their electricity without this constraint, at a lower cost.

A study of the impact of such "green default" in electricity provision provides support for this

approach (Picherta and Katsikopoulos 2008). It looked at two cases in which electricity providers offered green options with more renewable energy and a higher price as the default option. In both cases, fewer than 5 percent of customers decided to shift to less expensive, less green options.

FIGURE 2.1   Energy-reporting electrical outlet

Source: Webster 2012.
Note: Designer Muhyeon Kim has designed a switch that displays how much power it is using. Research has found that people are more conscious of their energy use when they can see it in action.

Network even hosts a Web site, iNudgeYou.com, dedicated to sharing applications and study findings.

Framing decisions judiciously. The way economic actors react to policies depends on many factors, including how the policy is presented, or framed. Firms know this well, which is why they rely on marketing tools and branding in addition to price signals. By priming or framing personal behavior as part of a larger social goal, the public and private sectors can induce people to behave in more environment-friendly ways, particularly when they act as groups, as group decisions have been found to be made with less selfishness

than individual decisions (Milch and others 2007). By framing environmental protection as a "social project," policy makers can make individuals think in terms of social and collective goals. For example, surveys show that many passengers are willing to pay more for flights to account for the environmental damage that flying causes. However, their willingness to do so depends partly on what the surcharge is called: simply relabeling a carbon "tax" as a carbon "offset" increases its acceptability (Hardisty and others 2010).

In addition, people are more likely to accept increases in energy prices if they perceive them as needed to reach an ambitious and positive social goal than if they perceive them as top-down government decisions to reduce oil imports or protect the climate. Germany presented its decision to gradually replace its nuclear plants with renewable energy sources as a collective national project that positions it as a leader in the transition toward a greener economy. This framing makes it more likely that the public will accept the resulting increases in the price of electricity. It also reduces the risk that the decision will be reversed by the next government. The certainty afforded by the decrease in the chance of policy reversal increases incentives for long-term investments in research and development and new technology.

It may be more efficient to change the values related to the emotional part of decisions than to count on prices and other policies to counteract emotion-based decisions. For instance, many consumers prefer big and inefficient cars for status-related reasons. As long as such cars provide status, raising their price may not reduce consumers' desire to own them. For this reason, price mechanisms may be less effective than efforts to make green and efficient cars a status symbol (Griskevicius and Tybur 2010). Ideally, price mechanisms and behavioral changes can reinforce each other, as recent trends in French car purchases show (box 2.6).

It may also be more efficient to influence consumer behavior through advertising than through price—witness the hundreds of billions of dollars firms spend every year to advertise consumer products (Bertrand and others 2009). What is true for commercial consumption choices is likely to be true for environmental behaviors.

Informing and nudging to influence firms: Enabling public pressure and focusing managers' attention

Information allows citizens or governments to put pressure on businesses—the goal of programs that collect and disseminate information about firms' environmental performance. This approach has been deemed the "third wave" in environmental regulation, after command-and-control and market-based approaches (Tietenberg 1998). Studies show that it is making significant inroads in terms of environmental benefits.

One type of disclosure program relies on emissions data without using them to rate or otherwise characterize environmental performance. Regulations requiring U.S. electric utilities to mail bill inserts to consumers reporting the extent of their reliance on fossil fuels led to a significant decrease in fossil fuel use (Delmas and others 2007). Another type of scheme involves reporting regulatory violations. A policy of publicly disclosing the identity of plants that are noncompliant or "of concern" spurred emissions reductions in a sample of pulp and paper plants in British Columbia (Foulon and others 2002).

Performance evaluation and ratings programs (PERPs) report emissions data and use them to rate plants' environmental performance. Examples include China's GreenWatch program; India's Green Rating Project (GRP); Indonesia's Program for Pollution Control, Evaluation, and Rating (PROPER); the Philippines' EcoWatch program; and Vietnam's Black and Green Books initiative (box 2.7). These programs—which require no enforcement capacity or even a well-defined set of environmental regulations but do require an active civil society, local activism, or both—are particularly helpful in developing countries, where weak formal institutions make traditional enforcement of environmental regulations difficult. Thanks to advances in information technology, the administrative cost of such programs (mainly data collection and dissemination) is falling (Dasgupta and others 2007).

Public disclosure can improve environmental performance through a variety of channels. It can have the following effects (Powers and others 2011):

- Affect demand for firms' products (output market pressure).
- Affect demand for publicly traded companies' shares and the ability of such companies to hire and retain employees (input market pressure).
- Encourage private citizens to sue polluters (judicial pressure).

BOX 2.6   Modifying car buyer behavior in France

From 2003 to 2009, the average emissions of new cars in France decreased, dropping precipitously in 2008 when the government introduced a "feebate" that increased the price of high-energy and reduced the price of low-energy-consuming cars (figure B2.6.1). The average willingness to pay for a reduction of 10 grams of CO_2 per kilometer increased by €536 during the period. This shift in preferences accounts for 20 percent of the overall decrease in average CO_2 emissions of new cars—of which 34 percent is related to the type of cars on the market and 46 percent to price effects (gasoline prices and the feebate). The biggest preference changes occurred among young people and rich people.

FIGURE B2.6.1   A sudden shift to greener cars
(average CO$_2$ emission of new cars in France, 2003–09)

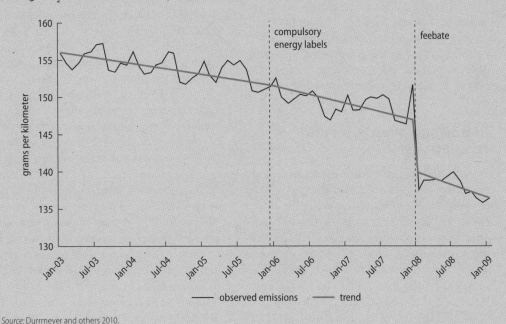

Source: Durrmeyer and others 2010.

BOX 2.7   How are PERPs faring in developing countries?

Performance evaluation and ratings programs (PERPs)—which are increasingly being used throughout the world—appear to generate environmental benefits. Indonesia's Program for Pollution Control, Evaluation, and Rating (PROPER) spurred significant emissions reductions in wastewater discharges (García and others 2007, 2009). A qualitative evaluation of PERPs in China, Indonesia, the Philippines, and Vietnam found that in all programs examined a large number of plants initially rated "noncompliant" rose to "compliant" over time (in contrast, plants rated "flagrant violators" and "compliant" tended to remain in these categories) (Dasgupta and others 2007). This evidence is consistent with the findings of other studies that concluded that performance ratings led to improvements among plants with moderately poor performance records but not among plants with either very bad or good records (García and others 2007; Powers and others 2011).

- Build support for new pollution control legislation or more stringent enforcement of existing legislation (regulatory pressure).
- Enhance pressure from community groups and nongovernmental organizations (community pressure).
- Provide new information to managers about their plants' discharges and options for reducing them (managerial information) (Blackman and others 2004; Tietenberg 1998).

The impact of information disclosure goes beyond its effect on environmentally conscious consumers. Even when environmental concerns are low and consumers are unlikely or unable to change their consumption patterns, disclosure can create an incentive for businesses to reduce their environmental impacts.

Imposing: Using rules and regulations

Price-based instruments such as taxes and polluting permits are generally considered preferable to norms and standards, under the simplifying assumptions of economic modeling (competitive industry, no enforcement cost, and so forth) (Baumol and Oates 1988; Morgenstern and others 1999). This may not be the case when additional complexities are considered (Helfland 1999).

When enforcement costs and political economy constraints (such as reaction against increases in fuel prices) are factored in, standards-based solutions may be more efficient than incentive-based solutions in some contexts. Moreover, introducing a new standard may prove easier, especially in sectors that are already regulated, than increasing (or introducing) prices. In such cases, existing institutions can be relied upon to enforce new norms, and complex policy making may not be necessary.

That said, the enforcement costs of norms and standards should not be underestimated. Enforcement of a norm on emissions or a trading scheme requires the establishment of emission measurement and reporting systems, which are costly to create and operate.

Norms and regulations can also have negative side effects, by favoring incumbent firms at the expense of new entrants, thereby reducing the ability of the economy to innovate and grow (Copeland 2012). To avoid such a risk, policy makers must design environmental regulation in a way that does not create additional barriers to entry into markets, especially for small firms, which are often innovative and create the most jobs.

Policy makers must also avoid the risk of a rebound effect. Promoting water conservation technologies may increase the acreage of crops requiring irrigation, resulting in an increase in total water consumption (Pfeiffer and Lin 2010). Improving the fuel efficiency of automobiles, by making it cheaper to drive, leads to an increase in car use, reducing by 30 percent any energy gain reaped by improved technology (Sorrel and others 2009) (box 2.8).

BOX 2.8   What is the best way to promote vehicle fuel economy?

Are incentive-based measures or norms and regulations more effective in increasing individual car fuel economy? Proponents of incentives argue that higher fuel prices are more efficient than stricter fuel efficiency standards. The latter, they contend, increase the costs of new vehicles, causing car owners (including organizations with fleets) to wait longer to replace their cars. The result is that fuel consumption remains the same rather than decreasing as owners continue to drive aging, and therefore less fuel-efficient, cars. In addition, when car owners do purchase more fuel-efficient cars with unchanged fuel price, their ability to drive more for the same price can result in rebound effects, thus reducing energy savings and leading to increased traffic congestion. In contrast, fuel taxes cause car owners to drive less, thereby not only decreasing local pollution but also reducing traffic congestion and accidents. In addition, by increasing

(continued next page)

BOX 2.8   (continued)

tax revenues, fuel taxes can potentially allow other, more distorting taxes to be reduced without affecting the budget.

Proponents of fuel efficiency standards argue that consumers may not appropriately value fuel economy when buying a car (Greene 2010). If consumers under-value fuel economy, fuel efficiency standards will improve welfare. They also argue that opposition to fuel taxes makes their imposition difficult politically.

The debate over which approach is better ulti-mately depends on the mitigation burden that should be borne by the automobile sector—that is, pick-ing an appropriate carbon price as the basis for fuel taxes. The problem is that there is no consensus as to what could constitute an "appropriate" carbon

price. Moreover, the carbon prices that have been implemented in the industrial sector (for example, the European Union's Emission Trading System) are not high enough to trigger manufacturer's invest-ments in the technologies needed to dramatically reduce emissions (Vogt-Schilb and Hallegatte 2011).

In such a situation, fuel efficiency standards, like the ones implemented in Australia, Canada, China, the European Union, Japan, the Republic of Korea, and the United States (An and others 2007), are a reason-able second-best solution, particularly when they are announced early enough to let manufacturers adapt their investments plans accordingly (figure B2.8.1). Standards are best applied in combination with price increases to minimize the risk of rebound.

Figure B2.8.1   Fuel efficiency standards are key to reducing emissions from the transport sector
(historical fleet CO$_2$ emissions and current or proposed standards, 2000–25)

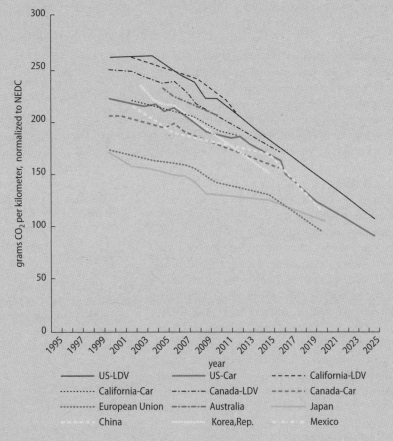

Sources: International Council on Clean Transportation; An and others (2007).
Note: The NEDC is a driving cycle used in Europe to assess car emissions. LDV = light duty vehicle.

The efficiency of market-based instruments is compromised by the existence of market failures that cannot be fixed. Emission intensity standards, for example—which are widely considered to be less effective than emission taxes—can be preferable in sectors where production has positive external consequences (for example, knowledge creation, transportation), because they generally have less of an impact on output. Emission intensity standards can also improve social welfare relative to emission taxes in the presence of market power (Holland 2009). The idea that a unique carbon price in the economy is the optimal policy has been challenged in situations in which future carbon prices are unpredictable (Vogt-Schilb and Hallegatte 2011); technologies exhibit lock-ins, making it difficult to disseminate new technological options (Kalkuhl and others 2011); or labor markets or revenue-raising taxes are distortionary (Richter and Schneider 2003).

Norms and standards are usually costly in economic terms. They should not be implemented without a detailed analysis of their costs and benefits—but predicting and measuring the economic cost of regulations and norms is difficult. For instance, a pollution regulation can increase production costs for industries and lead to reduced output and employment, but it can also favor more labor-intensive technologies and create jobs. A study of pulp and paper mills, plastic manufacturers, petroleum refiners, and iron and steel mills in the United States finds that the impact of regulation on employment is industry specific and the overall impact insignificant (Morgenstern and others 2002). When they target local public goods, regulations can even lead to net economic gains—by reducing health impacts from pollution, decreasing health costs, and increasing labor productivity, for instance.

In an analysis of U.S. environmental regulations, Morgenstern and others (1999) find that ex ante estimates of total (direct) costs tend to exceed actual costs, suggesting that environmental regulations may be less costly than usually predicted. The overestimation of total costs arises not from an overestimation of per unit abatement costs (how much it costs to reduce pollution by one unit) but from errors in the quantity of emission reductions achieved (how much pollution is reduced by a given regulation). This finding suggests that if regulation costs are often overestimated, so may their benefits.

In sum, rules and regulations are generally considered second-best solutions in situations with perfect markets (markets with perfect information and competitive industries). In the real world, where settings are imperfect, they can be a useful complement to price-based incentives. In the next chapter we look at the need to navigate between market and governance failures through the careful use of innovation and industrial policies.

Notes

1. In a review of energy subsidies across more than 30 countries, Arze del Granado and others (2010) estimate that it costs $33 to transfer $1 to poor households through a gasoline subsidy. The figure is high because the vast majority of gasoline is consumed by higher-income households.
2. Weber and Johnson (2012) provide a comprehensive review of this issue in a background paper for this report.
3. The Ellsberg paradox (Ellsberg 1961) shows that when faced with a choice between risk (which is represented by known probabilities) and uncertainty (in which probabilities are not available) decision makers display a preference for risk. This tendency is known as *ambiguity aversion*.
4. This is a different issue from cultural differences, which may make certain policies unacceptable (rather than ineffective) in particular countries. For example, London successfully adopted congestion charges, whereas such schemes are considered exclusionary in France, which explains why they have not been applied in Paris to date.

References

Abrahamse, W., L. Steg, C. Vlek, and T. Rothengatter. 2007. "The Effect of Tailored Information, Goal Setting, and Tailored Feedback on Household Energy Use,

Energy-Related Behaviors, and Behavioral Antecedents." *Journal of Environmental Psychology* 27 (4): 265–76.

Ainslie, G. 1975. "Specious Reward: A Behavioral Theory of Impulsiveness and Impulse Control." *Psychological Bulletin* 82 (July): 463–96.

An, F., D. Gordon, H. He, D. Kodjak, and D. Rutherford. 2007. *Passenger Vehicle Greenhouse Gas and Fuel Economy, Standards: A Global Update.* Washington, DC: International Council on Clean Transportation.

Arze del Granado, J., D. Coady, and R. Gillingham. 2010. "The Unequal Benefits of Fuel Subsidies: A Review of Evidence for Developing Countries." IMF WP/10/02, International Monetary Fund, Washington, DC.

Asheim, G. B., and M. L. Weitzman. 2001. "Does NNP Growth Indicate Welfare Improvement?" *Economics Letters* 73 (2): 233–9.

Baumol, W. and W. Oates. 1988. *The Theory of Environmental Policy.* 2nd ed. Cambridge: Cambridge University Press.

Benartzi, S., and R. H. Thaler. 2004. "Save More Tomorrow: Using Behavioral Economics to Increase Employee Saving."*Journal of Political Economy* 112 (S1): 164–87.

Bertrand, M., D. Karlan, S. Mullainathan, E. Shafir, J. Zinman. 2009. "What's Advertising Content Worth? Evidence from a Consumer Credit Marketing Field Experiment," Center Discussion Paper 968, Yale University, Economic Growth Center, New Haven, CT.

Blackman, A., S. Afsah, and D. Ratunanda. 2004. "How Does Public Disclosure Work? Evidence from Indonesia's PROPER Program." *Human Ecology Review* 11 (3): 235–46.

Bolt, K., G. Ruta, and M. Sarraf. 2005. *Estimating the Cost of Environmental Degradation.* Washington, DC: World Bank Environment Department.

Copeland, B. R. 2012. "International Trade and Green Growth." Paper presented at the Green Growth Knowledge Platform inaugural conference, Mexico City, January 12–13.

Dasgupta, P., and K.-G. Mäler. 2000. "Net National Product, Wealth, and Social Well-Being." *Environment and Development Economics* 5: 69–93.

Dasgupta, S., D. Wheeler, and H. Wang. 2007. "Disclosure Strategies for Pollution Control." In *International Yearbook of Environmental and Resource Economics 2006/2007: A Survey of Current Issues,* ed. T. Teitenberg and H. Folmer. Northampton: Edward Elgar.

Delmas, M., M. Montes-Sancho, J. Shimshack 2007. "Information Disclosure Policies: Evidence from the Electricity Industry." Working Paper, Department of Economics, Tufts University.

Durrmeyer, I., X. D'Haultfoeuille, and P. Février. 2010. "The Willingness to Pay for Global Warming Reduction: Lessons from the French Automobile Market." Congrès de l'Association Française de Science Economique.

Ellsberg, D. 1961. "Risk, Ambiguity and the Savage Axioms." *Quarterly Journal of Economics* 75: 643–79.

Foulon J., P. Lanoie, and B. Laplante. 2002. "Incentives for Pollution Control: Regulation or Information?" *Journal of Environmental Economics and Management* 44 (1): 169–87.

Fullerton, D., S. P. McDermott, and J. P. Caulkins. 1997. "Sulfur Dioxide Compliance of a Regulated Utility." *Journal of Environmental Economics and Management* 34 (1): 32–53.

García, J. H.,Afsah S, Sterner T 2009. "Which Firms Are More Sensitive to Public Disclosure Schemes for Pollution Control? Evidence from Indonesia's PROPER Program." *Environmental and Resource Economics* 42 (2): 151–68.

García, J. H., T. Sterner, S. Afsah 2007. "Public Disclosure of Industrial Pollution: The PROPER Approach for Indonesia?" *Environment and Development Economics* 12: 739–56.

Gillingham, K., R. Newell, and K. Palmer. 2009. "Energy Efficiency Economics and Policy." *Annual Review of Resource Economics* 1: 597–619.

Greene, D. L. 2010. "How Consumers Value Fuel Economy: A Literature Review." EPA–420–R–10–008, U.S. Environmental Protection Agency, Washington, DC.

Griskevicius, V., and J. M. Tybur. 2010. "Going Green to Be Seen: Status, Reputation, and Conspicuous Conservation." *Journal of Personality and Social Psychology* 98 (3): 392–404.

Guillaume, D., R. Zytek, and M. R. Farzin. 2011. "Iran: The Chronicles of the Subsidy Reform." IMF Working Paper WP 11/167, International Monetary Fund, Washington, DC.

Hallegatte, S. 2011."How Economic Growth and Rational Decisions Can Make Disaster

Losses Grow Faster Than Wealth." Policy Research Working Paper 5617, World Bank, Washington, DC.

Hamilton, K., and M. Clemens. 1999. "Genuine Savings Rates in Developing Countries." *World Bank Economic Review* 13 (2): 333–56.

Hardisty, D. H., E. J. Johnson, and E. U. Weber. 2010. "A Dirty Word or a Dirty World? Attribute Framing, Political Affiliation, and Query Theory." *Psychological Science* 21 (1): 86–92.

Heath, C., and A. Tversky. 1991. "Preference and Belief: Ambiguity and Competence." *Journal of Risk and Uncertainty* 4: 5–28.

Helfland, G. E. 1999. "Standards versus Taxes in Pollution Control." In *Handbook of Environmental and Resource Economics*, ed. J. C. J. M. van den Bergh, 223–34. Cheltenham: Edward Elgar.

Hertwig, R., G. Barron, E. U. Weber, and I. Erev. 2004. "Decisions from Experience and the Effect of Rare Events." *Psychological Science* 15: 534–9.

Holland, S. P. 2009. "Taxes and Trading versus Intensity Standards: Second-Best Environmental Policies with Incomplete Regulation. Leakage or Market Power?" NBER Working Paper 15262, National Bureau of Economic Research, Cambridge, MA.

IEA (International Energy Agency). 2010. *Reviewing Existing and Proposed Emission Trading Systems*. Paris: IEA.

Johnson, E. J., and D. Goldstein. 2003. "Do Defaults Save Lives?" *Science* 302 (5649): 1338–9.

Kalkuhl, M., O. Edenhofer, and K. Lessmann. 2011. *Learning or Lock-In: Optimal Technology Policies to Support Mitigation*. Munich: CESifo Group.

Kanbur, R. 2010. "Macro Crisis and Targeting Transfers to the Poor." In *Globalization and Growth: Implications for a Post-Crisis World*, ed. M. Spence and D. Leipziger. Washington, DC: World Bank and the Commission on Growth and Development.

Kunreuther, H., and E. Michel-Kerjan. 2012. "Impact of Behavioral Issues on Green Growth Policies and Weather-Related Disaster Reduction in Developing Countries." Paper presented at the Green Growth Knowledge Platform inaugural conference, Mexico City, January 12–13.

Ley, E., and N. B. Tran. 2011. "The Role of Prices." Background Paper for the Green Growth Report. World Bank, Washington, DC.

Madrian, B., and D. Shea. 2001. "Behavior." *Quarterly Journal of Economics* 116: 1149–87.

Mattoo, A., A. Subramanian, D. van der Mensbrugghe, and J. He. 2011. "Can Global De-Carbonization Inhibit Developing Country Industrialization?" *World Bank Economic Review* doi:10.1093/wber/lhr04.

Milch, K. F., E. U. Weber, K. C. Appelt, M. J. J. Handgraaf, and D. H. Krantz. 2007. "From Individual Preference Construction to Group Decisions: Framing Effects and Group Processes." Mimeo.

Morgenstern, R., W. Harrington, and P.-K. Nelson. 1999. "On the Accuracy of Regulatory Cost Estimates," Discussion Paper 99-18, Resources for the Future, Washington, DC.

Morgenstern, R. D., W. A. Pizer, J.-S. Shih. 2002. "Jobs Versus the Environment: An Industry-Level Perspective." *Journal of Environmental Economics and Management* 43: 412–436.

Nikoloski, Zlatko. 2012. "The Political Economy of Energy Subsidies: Country Narratives." MNA Urban and Social Development Unit, World Bank Washington, DC.

OECD (Organisation for Economic Co-operation and Development). 2006. *The Political Economy of Environmentally Related Taxes*. Paris: OECD.

———. 2010. *Pricing Water Resources and Water and Sanitation Services*. Paris: OECD.

———. 2011. *Towards Green Growth*. Paris: OECD.

Peters, E., D. Västfjäll, P. Slovic, C. K. Mertz, K. Mazzocco, and S. Dickert. 2006. "Numeracy and Decision Making." *Psychological Science* 17: 407–13.

Pfeiffer, L., and C.-Y. C. Lin. 2010. "The Effect of Irrigation Technology on Groundwater Use." *Choices* 25 (3).

Picherta, D., and K. V. Katsikopoulos. 2008. "Green Defaults: Information Presentation and Pro-Environmental Behaviour." *Journal of Environmental Psychology* 28: 63–73.

Powers, N., A. Blackman, T. Lyon, and U. Narain, 2011. "Does Disclosure Reduce Pollution? Evidence from India's Green Rating Project." *Environmental & Resource Economic*, 50 (1): 131–55.

Richter, W. F., and K. Schneider. 2003. "Energy Taxation: Reasons for Discriminating in Favor of the Production Sector." *European Economic Review* 47 (3): 461–76.

Sorrell, S., J. Dimitropoulos, and M. Sommerville. 2009. "Empirical Estimates of the Direct

Rebound Effect: A Review." *Energy Policy* 37: 1356–71.

Sterner, T. 2003. *Policy Instruments for Environmental and Natural Resource Management*. Washington, DC: Resources for the Future Press.

Thaler, Richard H., and Cass R. Sunstein. 2009. *Nudge: Improving Decisions About Health, Wealth and Happiness*. New York: Penguin.

Tietenberg, T. H. 1998. *Environmental Economics and Policy*. Boston: Addison-Wesley.

Trope, Y., and N. Liberman. 2003. "Temporal Construal." *Psychological Review* 110: 403–21.

Tversky, A., and D. Kahneman. 1992. "Advances in Prospect Theory: Cumulative Representation of Uncertainty." *Journal of Risk and Uncertainty* 5 (4): 297–323.

Tversky, A., and E. Shafir. 1992. "The Disjunction Effect in Choice under Uncertainty." *Psychological Science* 3 (5): 305–9.

Victor, D. 2009. *Untold Billions: Fossil-Fuel Subsidies, Their Impacts and the Path to Reform*. International Institute for Sustainable Development, Global Subsidies Initiative, Geneva. http://www.globalsubsidies.org/en/research/political–economy.

———.2011. "National Effects of Global Policy." *Nature Climate Change* 2: 24–5.

Vogt-Schilb, A., and S. Hallegatte. 2011. "When Starting with the Most Expensive Option Makes Sense: Use and Misuse of Marginal Abatement Cost Curves." Policy Research Working Paper 5803, World Bank, Washington, DC.

Weber, E. U. 1997. "Perception and Expectation of Climate Change: Precondition for Economic and Technological Adaptation." In *Psychological Perspectives to Environmental and Ethical Issues in Management*, ed. M. Bazerman, D. Messick, A. Tenbrunsel, and K. Wade-Benzon, 314–41. San Francisco, CA: Jossey-Bass.

———. 2006. "Experience-Based and Description-Based Perceptions of Long-Term Risk: Why Global Warming Does Not Scare Us (Yet)." *Climatic Change* 70: 103–20.

Weber, E. U., and C. Hsee. 1998. "Cross-Cultural Differences in Risk Perception, but Cross-Cultural Similarities in Attitudes towards Perceived Risk." *Management Science* 44 (9): 1205–17.

Weber, E. U., and E. J. Johnson. 2012. "Psychology and Behavioral Economics Lessons for the Design of a Green Growth Strategy." Paper presented at the Green Growth Knowledge Platform inaugural conference, Mexico City, January 12–13.

Weber, E. U., and P. G. Lindemann. 2007. "From Intuition to Analysis: Making Decisions with Our Head, Our Heart, or by the Book." In *Intuition in Judgment and Decision Making*, ed. H. Plessner, C. Betsch, and T. Betsch, 191–208. Mahwah, NJ: Lawrence Erlbaum.

Weber, E. U., S. Shafir, and A.-R. Blais. 2004. "Predicting Risk-Sensitivity in Humans and Lower Animals: Risk as Variance or Coefficient of Variation." *Psychological Review* 111 (2): 430–45.

Webster, George. 2012. "Is a 'Nudge' in the Right Direction All We Need to Be Greener?" CNN, updated Friday February 12. http://www.cnn.com/2012/02/08/tech/innovation/green-nudge-environment-persuasion/index.html

World Bank. 2010. *World Development Report 2010: Development and Climate Change*. Washington, DC: World Bank.

———. 2011. *The Changing Wealth of Nations: Measuring Sustainable Development in the New Millennium*. Washington, DC: World Bank.

World Bank and DRC (Development Research Center of the State Council, China). 2012. "Seizing the Opportunity of Green Development in China." Supporting Report 3 for *China 2030: Building a Modern Harmonious, and Creative High-Income Society*. Washington, DC: World Bank.

Zysman J., and M. Huberty. 2010. "An Energy Systems Transformation: Framing Research Choices for the Climate Challenge." *Research Policy* 38 (9): 1027–29.

Green Innovation and Industrial Policies | 3

Key Messages

- Innovation and industrial policies are potentially useful tools to spur green growth, as they can correct market (environmental and nonenvironmental) failures, but they should be designed to minimize risks from capture and rent-seeking behaviors.
- More advanced countries need to invest in frontier innovation through research and development; lower-income countries (with more limited technological capacity) should focus on adapting and disseminating technologies already developed and demonstrated.
- Although green growth and trade interact, it is not through the much publicized but seldom observed "pollution haven" effects. Green policies create opportunities for developing exports of green products; meanwhile, imports facilitate the adoption of greener, more efficient technologies.

Brazil has supported the development of a biofuel industrial sector for decades. China is subsidizing research and development (R&D) and industrial production of photovoltaic (PV) panels, most of which it exports. Morocco is investing public resources in producing electricity from concentrated solar power and plans to sell renewable energy to Europe. In all three cases, the policy objective is both to produce environmental benefits and to create growth and jobs.

These countries are not alone in pursuing such approaches. Indeed, most countries tap these types of environmental policies—which really amount to green innovation policies and green industrial policies. Some commonly used policies include R&D subsidies for drought-resistant crops, national strategies for electric cars, and efforts to create new green industries such as China's promotion of solar PV production.

Why are these policies even needed? Getting prices right is critical to addressing environmental externalities and providing the right signal for economic agents to modify their consumption, production, and investment patterns. But as chapter 2 showed, doing so is difficult because of behavioral quirks, political reasons, market or contract imperfections, and low price elasticities (how responsive quantities demanded or provided are to a certain price change).

And prices are notoriously limited instruments for transforming economies or triggering investments with long-term or uncertain payoffs. Indeed, they are ill-suited to address the "classic" market failures usually invoked to justify innovation and industrial policies:

knowledge externalities, latent comparative advantage and increasing returns, information asymmetries, capital market imperfections, and the coordination needed across industries to permit a technological transition (box 3.1).

Further, for green growth, getting the price right requires pricing externalities, which requires government intervention. Future government policies (on carbon prices or pollution limits) determine the size and

---

BOX 3.1   Market failures that can justify innovation and industrial policies

Many market failures may justify the broad innovation policies and more targeted innovation and industrial policies that aim to support a specific green industry, firm, or technology:

- *Knowledge externalities and capital market imperfections.* Absent government intervention, knowledge spillovers create a gap between the private and social returns to producing knowledge that typically leads to under-provision of knowledge. And this is amplified by information asymmetry in capital markets. Competitive innovation projects may struggle to find financing, making it difficult for new businesses and activities to start. This is especially true because young businesses have more difficulty securing financing than large established companies, even though they may be very innovative.
- *Latent comparative advantages and increasing returns.* Latent comparative advantages—that is, future as opposed to current comparative advantages—are sometimes cited as a justification for industrial policies (Harrison and Rodríguez-Clare 2009; Khan 2009; Rodrik 2004). Industrial policies may be warranted if the advantage includes learning or increasing returns to scale, which require support at an early stage. When two or more technologies (some not even invented) are substitutes, profit-maximizing innovators may focus on improving the productivity of existing technologies ("building on the shoulders of giants") because the market for these technologies is large and the returns are higher. Support—through production

subsidies or trade protection—can be provided to foster new technologies.
- *Coordination failures.* Industrial policies may be warranted to address coordination failures within and across industries (Murphy and others 1989; Okuno-Fujiwara 1988; Pack and Westphal 1986; Rodenstein-Rodan 1943; Trindade 2005). The idea is that developing a comparative advantage in an activity can depend on another activity in the region or country. (Morocco is hoping to develop a concentrated solar industry, which requires creating the demand, the needed transmission lines, and the domestic supply chain for those parts in which Morocco can develop a competitive advantage—such as mirrors.) An industrial policy through which the government acts as the precommitment mechanism can solve this problem (Rodrik 2004). The same argument holds for "soft" industrial policies—policies that support particular clusters by increasing the supply of skilled workers, encouraging technology adoption, and improving regulation and infrastructure (Harrison and Rodríguez-Clare 2009).
- *International rent shifting.* Some industries are characterized by fixed costs or indivisibilities limiting the number of entrants and creating oligopolies, with significant rents for installed businesses. A classic example is the competition between Airbus and Boeing (Baldwin and Krugman 1988; Helpman and Krugman 1989). Depending on the case, it can be welfare enhancing to either introduce specific taxes to capture and redistribute the rent or support new entrants to increase competition and reduce rents.

(continued next page)

BOX 3.1   (continued)

- *Spatial, redistributive, and political economy motivations.* Industrial policies are frequently used to promote regional balance and stimulate job growth and other economic activity where unemployment is worse, the population poorer, or a geopolitical reason exists to promote production in an area (such as Manaus in Brazil). Industrial policies are also used to smooth economic transitions—when,

for example, structural change or trade liberalization leads to unemployment and workers find it difficult to shift from sunset to sunrise industries. In this case, an industrial policy can support a declining industry to mitigate transitional costs and allow time for retraining and shifting workers toward growing industries.

---

profitability of the future green market. But because they cannot credibly commit to future policies, governments create policy risks for green firms. It thus makes sense for governments to share risks through investment subsidies. To the extent that such subsidies reduce the future cost of green policies, they enable today's governments to influence future policies: it is more likely that carbon prices will be implemented in the future if inexpensive low-carbon alternatives are available (Karp and Stevenson 2012).

For these reasons most countries resort to some form of innovation and industrial policies in their growth strategies. But given the mixed record of these policies—rife with both successes and failures—green growth strategies must heed the lessons from innovation and industrial policies over the past decades.

This chapter explores the concepts of green innovation and industrial policies and identifies their main benefits and potential pitfalls. It finds that they represent potentially useful tools for facilitating green growth, provided that they are tailored to country contexts and that care is taken to navigate between the risks of market and governance failures.

Innovation policies: Tailoring mixes of instruments to a country's innovation potential

Green innovation, which includes both the creation and commercialization of new

frontier technologies and the diffusion and adoption of green technologies new to the firm, is critical to greening growth processes.[1] Achieving greener growth requires both green innovation policies, supported sometimes by more targeted industrial policies, and environmental policies to create demand where the traditional environmental externalities are not fully reflected in market prices (box 3.2).

Green frontier innovation is growing fairly rapidly, albeit from a small base. But the lion's share of this growth is in high-income countries, raising concerns about the ability of developing countries to access and adapt new technologies tailored to their needs. A few large middle-income economies—Brazil, China, India—can become significant frontier green innovators; they are already leading in incremental process innovation in the wind, solar, and biofuel markets. Other countries need to rely on global frontier innovation efforts while developing the capacity to identify, adapt, and absorb relevant technologies that are new to their firms.

The challenge is to combine innovation and environmental policies to make them effective and ensure that they are suitably balanced among policies that support frontier innovation (relevant mostly for more technologically advanced countries); policies that promote catch-up innovation and the adoption and spread of suitably adapted technologies; and policies that improve domestic absorptive capacity, including strengthening local skills.

BOX 3.2   Shedding light on green innovation, technologies, and industrial policies

Green innovation is the development and commercialization of new ways to solve environmental problems through improvements in technology, with a wide interpretation of technology as encompassing product, process, organizational, and marketing improvements. In addition to frontier (new-to-the-world) innovations, this definition includes catch-up (new-to-the-firm) innovations—also known as *absorption*—which covers the diffusion (both across and within countries), adoption, adaptation (to local contexts), and use of green technologies.

Green technologies comprise many fundamentally different technologies to achieve more resource-efficient, clean, and resilient growth. They include technologies needed to achieve the following goals:

- Reduce pollution and achieve greater resource efficiency in buildings (thermal insulation and new materials, heating, energy-efficient lighting); production processes (new uses of waste and other by-products from firms); agriculture (from improved and resilient crop and livestock breeds, water management, and farming systems to mechanical irrigation and farming techniques); and infrastructure and urban design (such as land use zoning).
- Mitigate climate change through a cleaner energy supply (wind, solar, geothermal, marine energy, biomass, hydropower, waste-to-energy, hydrogen fuels); low-carbon end use (electric and hybrid vehicles, climate-friendly cement); and carbon capture and storage.
- Reduce vulnerability and adapt to climate change with tools for understanding climate risks, better

early-warning systems, and climate-resistant technologies (sea-walls; drainage capacity; reductions in the environmental burden of disease; water, forest, and biodiversity management).
- Support wealth creation from the more productive and sustainable uses of biodiversity, including natural cosmetics, pharmaceutical products, other sustainable bioprospecting, nature-based tourism, more sustainable production of plants and livestock, and ecosystem protection.

Green innovation policies are policies seeking to trigger green innovation by encouraging innovation broadly (horizontal policies) or supporting a specific technology (vertical policies).

Green industrial policies are policies aiming to green the productive structure of the economy by targeting specific industries or firms. They include industry-specific research and development subsidies, capital subsidies, and tax-breaks; feed-in tariffs; and import protection. They do not include policies targeting demand (such as consumer mandates), which can be met by imports without changing local production.

In practice, green innovation and industrial policies can be difficult to separate. Brazil's support for biofuels relies on a range of policy tools from broad innovation to targeted industrial policies, with the ultimate goal of triggering innovation. Germany's support for solar photovoltaic power amounts to innovation policy using industrial policy tools. Both countries would likely consider these efforts as part of their environmental policies.

Source: Dutz and Sharma 2012 and World Bank.

Frontier innovation and catch-up innovation

Since the mid-1990s green frontier innovation has increased substantially worldwide, mostly in high-income countries (figure 3.1a). In recent years the gap between developed and developing countries for green patents—those based on key greenhouse gas–mitigation technologies—continued to widen, with the richer countries granted some 1,500 patents in the United States compared with

only 100 patents granted to poorer countries. Within the developing world the East Asia and Pacific region has by far the largest number of patents; the Middle East and North Africa has the smallest number of patents (figure 3.1b). China, in 10th place globally in number of patents filed in more than one country, is the only emerging economy represented among the top 10 "high-quality" innovating countries (Dechezleprêtre and others 2011). The number and share of green patenting remains very small—less than 1 percent—in both developed and developing regions (figure 3.1c).

In the developing world a few technologically sophisticated countries are surfacing as significant innovators; appropriate green innovation policy in these countries is likely to differ from appropriate policy in other developing countries. A group of nine emerging economies (Argentina, Brazil, China, Hungary, India, Malaysia, Mexico, the Russian Federation, and South Africa) accounted for nearly 80 percent of all U.S. green patent grants to developing countries, over 2006–10.[2] And unlike the less technologically sophisticated countries, these "high flyer" economies display a sharp upward trend in green patenting, with their green patent grants more than doubling between 2000–05 (30 grants) and 2006–10 (more than 70 grants).

But even if there is little capacity for *frontier* green innovation in most developing countries, substantial capacity may exist for *catch-up* green innovation through the adoption and adaptation of green technologies as well as indigenous base-of-pyramid innovations, aimed at meeting the needs of poor consumers (box 3.3).

Trade data suggest that there is substantial potential for catch-up innovation. Environmental goods constitute a nontrivial and rising share of exports (3.4 percent in developing countries in 2010, 6 percent in high-income regions; figure 3.2). But, except for the East Asia and Pacific region, the share of green exports has not been rising, suggesting a need for greater diffusion of green technologies. The policy implication of this trend depends on the extent to which it reflects some underexploited comparative advantages in developing countries that account for lower levels of home production and export of green goods and services, whether driven by specific market or policy failures. Information on the extent to which weaker environmental regulations in many developing countries account for these differences could suggest appropriate policies.

FIGURE 3.1A   Green frontier innovation occurs mostly in high-income countries...

(number of green patents granted in the United States, developing versus high-income countries)

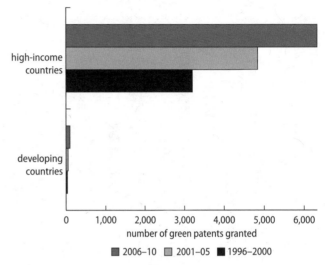

Source: Dutz and Sharma 2012, based on data from PATSTAT (the European Patent Office's Worldwide Patent Statistical Database).

FIGURE 3.1B   ... with East Asia leading the way in developing regions ...

(number of green patents granted in the United States, by developing region)

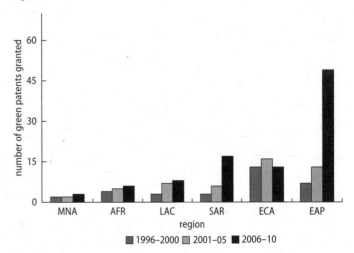

Source: Dutz and Sharma 2012, based on data from PATSTAT (the European Patent Office's Worldwide Patent Statistical Database).
Notes: Total U.S. Patent Office grants in OECD green technology areas. Developing regions are AFR (Africa), EAP (East Asia and Pacific), ECA (Europe and Central Asia), LAC (Latin America and the Caribbean), MNA (Middle East and North Africa), and SAR (South Asia).

FIGURE 3.1C ... but worldwide green patents remain low

(green patents granted as a percentage of all patent grants in the United States, by region)

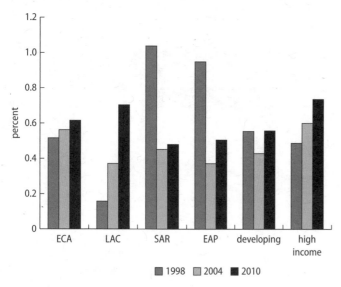

1998 2004 2010

Source: Dutz and Sharma 2012, based on data from PATSTAT (the European Patent Office's World-wide Patent Statistical Database).
Note: Ratio of three-year moving averages of U.S. Patent Office grants in OECD green technology areas to all U.S. Patent Office grants.

Even if developing countries are not increasing their exports of green products, they could have substantial potential for moving into green industries to the extent that they are producing nongreen goods that use inputs or technologies similar to those used to produce green goods. The concept of "proximity" between products is useful for examining this broader capability for green exports.[3] For example, a country with the ability to export apples will probably have most of the conditions suitable for exporting pears but not necessarily the conditions for producing electronics. Indeed, trade in green and close-to-green goods is about three to five times that of green goods alone, with East Asia and Pacific and Latin America and the Caribbean countries on par with high-income countries (figure 3.3). This difference suggests a potential for developing exports in green products.

As for green imports, studies show that, as a share of all imports, they are as important

---

BOX 3.3   What are green base-of-pyramid innovations?

Base-of-pyramid innovations are defined as innovations that meet poor consumers' needs. They include formal innovations for the poor—namely, innovations by global and local formal private companies and public institutions, whether fully privately provided, supported by public subsidies, or produced through public-private partnerships (such as medicines for neglected diseases and seeds for "neglected" soil types and climates). They also include informal innovations by local grassroots inventors, largely through improvisation and experimentation. Often facilitated by co-creation with poor consumers themselves, the innovations typically seek to better meet the needs of poor households at dramatically lower costs per unit, aided by significant scale-up in volumes. They thus seek "to do more (products) with less (resources) for more (people)" (Prahalad and Mashelkar 2010). Three examples are described below.

Aakash Ganga ("river from sky"). In Rajasthan, India, ancient rainwater harvesting systems have been modernized to collect safe drinking water. This low-cost adaptation in arid regions has spurred additional innovations, generating many co-benefits for efficiency and inclusiveness:

- Automation of the traditional surveying system with satellite imaging, which shortens design time, minimizes earthwork, and reduces material costs.
- Creation of a numbering plan for reservoirs, which facilitates co-investments.
- Inducement of demand for stretchable roofs, which has spurred more innovation.
- Introduction of accounting transparency, which has spurred policy debate on broader inequities in water affordability.

Novel uses of rice husks. Rice husks are one of India's most common waste products. Husk Power

(continued next page)

BOX 3.3 (continued)

Systems (HPS), winner of the 2011 Ashden Awards for sustainable energy, has adapted and converted a biomass gasification using diesel technology into a single-fuel rice husk gasifier for rural electrification. Households stop using dim kerosene lamps when they get HPS electricity, thereby saving on kerosene (and reducing CO_2 emissions) and facilitating evening studying and other productive activities. Tata Consulting Services sells a $24 Swach ("clean" in Hindi) water filter that uses ash from rice milling to filter out bacteria. It is intended for rural households that lack electricity and running water.

Affordable green housing. In Mexico, Vinte specializes in building affordable, sustainable housing for low- and middle-income families. Its research and development in new technologies helped it introduce innovations such as home designs that reduce energy costs by 75 percent.

Source: Dutz and Sharma 2012.

in developing countries as they are in high-income countries, indicating the international transfer of green technology as embodied in green consumer products (figure 3.4). Inasmuch as some of these products are used as inputs, this also indicates the greening of the input mix, which may reflect adoption and adaptation of technologies by local firms. For instance, the purchase of manufacturing equipment in international markets is the main channel through which Chinese producers acquired the technologies and skills necessary to produce PV panels (de la Tour and others 2011). And the importing of green products may be a response to domestic demand-side green policies in developing countries. However, there has not been any significant upward trend in any region.

The dissemination of green technologies can be accelerated through policies that increase adaptation and adoption capacity (such as education in relevant disciplines, especially sciences and engineering) and through trade and industrial policies (such as local content requirements and technology transfers). A good example is the success of the high-speed train program initiated in the Republic of Korea in 1993 by the purchase of the French Alstom TGV (*train à grande vitesse*). The contract included technology transfers (partly through training Korean workers in France) and the localization of 50 percent of manufacturing in Korea (Lee and Moon 2005). Today, Korea

FIGURE 3.2 Green exports are growing, especially in the East Asia and Pacific region

(export of green goods and services as a percentage of all exports, 2000, 2005, 2010)

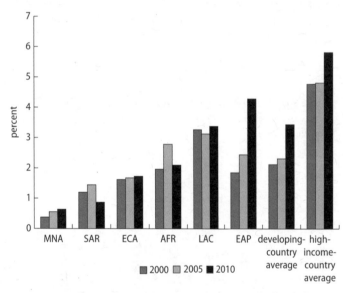

Source: Dutz and Sharma 2012, based on data from COMTRADE + OECD list of environmental six-digit harmonized system categories.
Note: Developing regions are AFR (Africa), EAP (East Asia and Pacific), ECA (Europe and Central Asia), LAC (Latin America and the Caribbean), MNA (Middle East and North Africa), and SAR (South Asia).

is among the five top world competitors in exports of high-speed trains. In Morocco the contract for high-speed trains and the Casablanca tramway included a local factory (created by Alstom and Nexans) specializing in railway beam and wire production, which will produce for the local and international markets.

FIGURE 3.3   Developing countries may have a substantial unrealized potential for producing green exports

(export of green versus green plus close-to-green goods and services from developing regions, as a percentage of all exports from developing regions, 2000–10)

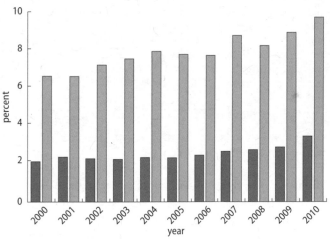

Source: Dutz and Sharma 2012, based on data from COMTRADE.

FIGURE 3.4   Green imports are vital worldwide

(imports of green goods and services, as a percentage of all imports, 2000, 2005, 2010)

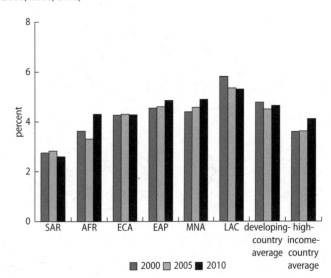

Source: Dutz and Sharma 2012, based on data from COMTRADE and OECD List of environmental six-digit harmonized system categories.
Note: Developing regions are AFR (Africa), EAP (East Asia and Pacific), ECA (Europe and Central Asia), LAC (Latin America and the Caribbean), MNA (Middle East and North Africa), and SAR (South Asia).

Green imports from higher-income countries may not, however, meet the needs of poorer consumers in low-income countries. In principle, home-grown base-of-pyramid innovations can offer a complementary supply of relevant green technologies (box 3.3). But few green base-of-pyramid innovations have been sufficiently scaled up to date, suggesting the need for more focused policy efforts in this area.

The adaptation of green technologies to local conditions is also critical for developing countries. Using green technologies efficiently requires them to be more varied than nongreen technologies, given the significant variance of the underlying environment by locality. For instance, turbine designs need to be adapted to work efficiently in India, where wind speeds are lower than in Europe. Such adaptations can yield important co-benefits, including more sustainable corporate cultures (box 3.4).

Fostering innovation

The policy instruments relevant to promoting the development, dissemination, and adaptation of green technologies will differ depending on the maturity of the technologies and the market failures the policies seek to address. No single green bullet exists, so countries will need to employ a mix of instruments (figure 3.5).

Policies to foster innovation should aim to strengthen entrepreneurship and local firm absorptive capacity, support new knowledge creation and commercialization, and support diffusion and adaptation of existing knowledge to new local contexts. The importance of each and the modalities used depend on a country's level of technological sophistication and implementation capacity.

Strengthening entrepreneurship and absorptive capacity: The importance of skills and the broader business environment
For firms to understand and assimilate the discoveries of others as well as create new technologies, they need strong absorptive

---

BOX 3.4   Rapidly growing champions of "new sustainability"

In principle, the home-grown green ideas of companies to reduce costs, motivate workers, and shape their business environments by forging new relationships should make it easier for their peers in developing countries to emulate such approaches. Several examples are described below.

Century Energy (Colombia) develops small-scale hydroelectric power plants in Colombian river basins, diverting fast-rushing stream water without the need for reservoirs and thus avoiding displacement. In the next 5 years it plans to develop up to 10 facilities, adding 250 megawatts of capacity to Colombia.

Energy Development Corporation (the Philippines) pioneered the use of watershed management and recharge reinjection in its geothermal power plants as a way to extend the economic life of its facilities and reduce maintenance costs. These practices have since been mainstreamed across the industry and are now a regular part of industry regulation.

Equity Bank agricultural financial products (Nairobi, Kenya) worked with mobile telecom provider Safaricom to create a mobile banking system on its existing platform. The system offers credit for inputs and supports farmers throughout the value chain of production, transport, processing, and marketing. It has partnered with groups such as the International Fund for Agricultural Development to reduce its risks when lending to smallholders.

Jain Irrigation Systems (Jalgaon, India) adapted drip irrigation systems to meet the needs of smallholder farmers. The company works closely with customers to teach "precision farming" (optimizing the balance among fertilizers, pesticides, water, and energy to increase output) and uses dance and song to explain the benefits of drip irrigation to illiterate farmers.

Natura Organic Cosmetics (São Paulo, Brazil) worked transparently with rural communities and local governments to adapt its formal business practices to the local context. It tapped traditional knowledge about how to extract raw materials sustainably (receiving the Forest Stewardship Council certificate for these raw materials), and then educated suppliers in sustainable sourcing and production practices (such as reusing, refilling, and recycling packaging and adopting a new green plastic derived from sugar cane, which is eventually expected to reduce greenhouse gas emissions by more than 70 percent). The company also gives bonuses to workers who find ways to reduce the firm's impact on the environment.

Source: IFC 2010; World Economic Forum 2011, cited in Dutz and Sharma 2012; and Russell Sturm (personal communication).

---

capacity. Absorption is a subset of innovation that focuses on the use of new-to-the-firm technologies rather than the creation and commercialization of new-to-the-world technologies. Absorption of existing technologies can be improved by tackling the cross-cutting business environment constraints that impede experimentation, global learning, and attracting and retaining talent, as well as enhancing human capital in the public and private sectors.

An important starting point is to ensure that the business environment does not constrain entrepreneurship and innovative behavior, whether green or complementary to green. Many cross-cutting policy measures are vital for creating a business environment that spurs and enables entrepreneurs and firms to create,

commercialize, absorb, and adapt knowledge. They include the following:

- *Policies to overcome the stigma of failure and encourage opportunities for reentry and renewed experimentation.* Making it easier to wind up businesses is one of the best ways to get more people to try new ideas, even though doing so involves difficult legal reforms and changes in attitude toward debt. Closing a terminally ill business takes fewer than 10 months and allows more than 90 cents on the dollar to be recovered in Singapore, Tokyo, or Toronto. By contrast, in Mumbai it still takes on average 7 years to recover roughly 20 cents on the dollar (World Bank 2012). Other policies include publicizing

FIGURE 3.5   Snapshot of technology creation and diffusion

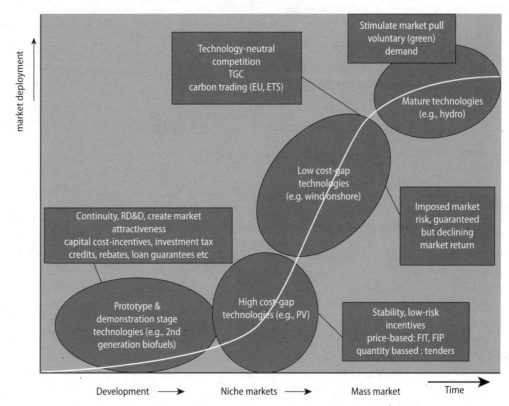

Source: IEA 2008 (*Deploying Renewables: Principles for Effective Policies* © OECD/International Energy Agency 2008, figure 1, page 25).
Note: FIT= feed-in tariffs; FIP = feed-in premiums; PV = photovoltaic; RD&D = research, development, and demonstration; TGC = tradable green certificate.

innovative role models (such as India's Tata Group's awarding of an annual prize for the best failed idea) and reducing the sunk costs of trying to commercialize an idea, such as removing impediments to deeper rental and resale markets.

- *Policies to facilitate global connectivity and learning.* Here the emphasis should be on linking up with international consortia and helping firms insert into global value chains. International mobility of workers was critical to the rapid development of wind energy capabilities in China and India. Suzlon, the leading Indian wind turbine manufacturer, established R&D facilities in Germany and the Netherlands to have its workers learn from European expertise. Goldwind, the leading Chinese manufacturer, sent employees abroad for training.[4]

Learning networks were also critical in the development of China's PV panel industry.[5] Mexico's Green Supply Chains Program—a public-private partnership program—highlights a way to diffuse eco-efficiency techniques to small- and medium-size enterprises.[6]

- *Policies to increase the livability and "stickiness" of cities to attract and retain talent.* Dense urban-industrial agglomerations spur technological upgrading and productivity growth by opening up opportunities and stimulating supplies of capital and skills. China's establishment of special economic zones, followed by a range of support by national and local governments for further industrial deepening in its three major urban/industrial agglomerations and in a number of inland cities, highlights how a mix of instruments can be used (Yusuf and others 2008).

In addition, green innovation, like innovation in general, depends on people who are able to generate and apply knowledge in the workplace and society at large. Required innovation skills include basic skills (reading, writing), technical skills (science, engineering), generic skills (problem solving, multicultural openness, leadership), managerial and entrepreneurial skills, and creativity and design skills.[7] The green economy requires greater emphasis on design and multidisciplinary teamwork, strategic leadership and adaptability, and knowledge of the sciences (CEDEFOP 2009; OECD 2011).

Even advanced developing countries are far behind high-income countries in the share of professionals engaged in creating knowledge and managing research projects. High-income countries like Denmark and Finland have about 15 researchers per 1,000 employees. By contrast, China, Mexico, and South Africa each has fewer than 2 researchers per 1,000 employees. And in developing countries the business sector plays a much smaller role

in the national R&D system than the higher education and government sectors. In the United States, four of five researchers work in businesses. By contrast, in Chile, China, Mexico, Poland, the Slovak Republic, South Africa, and Turkey the number of researchers per 1,000 employees in industry is less than 1. Developing country firms need more individuals with research and related creativity skills in the workforce if they are to play a greater role in accessing green technologies and adapting them for local use.

Thus, policies are needed to strengthen market signals so that tertiary education institutions and technical and vocational education and training systems are better attuned to firm demands. These institutions should ensure that the costs of skills upgrading are shared by students, employers, and the government in line with benefits, and that periodic independent and transparent national assessments are adopted to ensure quality and consistency (OECD 2009). In West Africa an effort to better monitor monsoon variability and impacts illustrates solutions to build relevant skills in a developing-country setting (box 3.5). This case highlights the need to attract West African scientists trained in

---

BOX 3.5   African monsoon multidisciplinary analyses

West Africa is extremely vulnerable to weather and climate variability because of its dependence on rain-fed agriculture, on which 80 percent of the Sahel's population relies. The African Monsoon Multidisciplinary Analyses (AMMA) is a research project funded by agencies from Africa, the European Union, France, the United Kingdom, and the United States to better monitor West African monsoon variability and the impacts on society and the environment, including on climate. To do so, the AMMA community was created in 2002. It now comprises more than 600 people from 30 countries, including 250 in Africa, among them 80 African PhD students. The AMMA community has established local university research programs in climatology, agronomy, and related social science fields, and has

convened functional research teams to build new capacity for improved early-warning systems. These teams and programs will continue to train cohorts of African specialists, thus cultivating a community whose mutual interest in AMMA–related issues will help ensure sustainability.

AMMA has done fairly well in building a partnership between the international community and Africans in phase one (2002–10). The main challenge for phase two (2010–20) is clarifying the needs of users (farmers, hydropower and flood managers, and health care professionals) and identifying what science can offer. Stronger user demand should increase political support for scientific resources.

Source: Thorncroft 2011.

better-equipped universities in high-income countries and the need to ensure enough local demand for established scientific and research facilities.

Promoting frontier innovation: Approaches depend on extent of local technological sophistication

Policies for frontier innovation include both supply-side "technology-push" elements (which reduce the costs of knowledge creation in advance of commercialization) and demand-side "market-pull" elements (which increase revenues from sales after commercialization). Key recommendations to guide the design of such policies include the following:

Limit local technology-push support to countries with enough technological capabilities. Government funding for early-stage and pre-commercialization technology is a vital element of many innovation systems, including direct funding of public labs and universities; grants, matching grants, and soft loans (which give the government control over what research is conducted); and indirect R&D tax subsidies (which allow firms to choose the most profitable research opportunities, switching some marginal projects from unprofitable to profitable). All these tools have their drawbacks. Grants allow coordination of research efforts with little or no duplication but may fail to integrate information from markets about what consumers want and are willing to pay for. They also run the risk of crowding out private R&D funding and need to be transparently allocated. Tax incentives may promote distorting tax avoidance rather than productive investment in countries with a weak tax enforcement system.

Despite these drawbacks, supply-push R&D support, through direct or indirect government funding, may generate new frontier innovations more effectively than demand-pull policies such as feed-in tariffs and regulations—at least where local technological capabilities and good governance mechanisms exist. For wind power, the marginal million dollars spent on public support to R&D in wind power technology generated 0.82 new inventions, whereas the same amount spent on demand-pull policies induced, at best, 0.06 new inventions (Dechezleprêtre and Glachant 2011).

Consider carefully structured public-private partnerships as only one of many measures to foster early-stage financing. Much of the investment needed for green growth will come from private business. Many of these investments face uncertain cash flows and require significant risk taking because they involve new technologies, including new business models. Once new ideas with commercial potential have progressed to the proof-of-concept stage, further financing and mentoring support for early-stage technology development (ESTD) are required.

The range of ESTD finance options includes both public and private resources. At this early stage, private sources are typically restricted to internal financing (personal savings and retained earnings), friends and family, angel investors (successful wealthy entrepreneurs), venture capital (VC), private equity, and private corporations (which fund ideas developed in-house, operate their own VC units, and acquire young start-up companies; see box 3.6). Among these sources, private equity and VC are uniquely suited to finance climate-friendly investments that are risky and fairly small. Although they will not provide more than a fraction of the resources needed, they can fill a key niche for driving green innovation.

However, developing the private equity and venture capital market for climate- and environment-friendly investments in emerging markets is hindered by capital market and carbon market barriers. These barriers include high management expenses, a shortage of good fund managers, long time horizons for investment returns and regulatory uncertainties, and the uncertainty of raising capital and having profitable exit opportunities for new technologies with no track record of historical returns. The public sector and international financial institutions can assist in capitalizing such

---

BOX 3.6   "Pinstripe greens": Private financiers making millions from clean-tech ventures

Although global venture capital investment in green energy declined with the 2008/09 recession and shares in clean-tech businesses have recently underperformed the wider market by a large margin, a world of U.S. solar titans, German wind moguls, Brazilian biofuel magnates, and Chinese battery tycoons has emerged over the past decade. One often hears that green energy could be the biggest economic opportunity of the 21st century. In 2010 the global clean energy sector (wind farms, solar parks, and related technologies) attracted a record $243 billion in new investment, nearly 5 times the volumes of 6 years earlier. Between 2000 and 2010 the global market for solar and wind power rose from $6.5 billion to $132 billion, the number of hybrid electric car models jumped from 2 to 30, and the number of certified green buildings grew from 3 to 8,138. Examples of private green financing include the following:

- *Khosla Ventures* is a venture capital firm founded by Vinod Khosla in 2004. Its clean-tech portfolio spans utility-scale and distributed generation,

electrical and mechanical efficiency, batteries, building materials, plastics and chemicals, agriculture, cellulosic alcohol, and advanced hydrocarbons. The portfolio also includes investments in a low-emission engine (with Bill Gates) and two-bladed wind turbines (with Goldman Sachs).

- *Bloomberg New Energy Finance* is a provider of analysis, data, and news about clean-tech, including renewable energy, energy-smart technologies, carbon, carbon capture and storage, renewable energy certificates, nuclear, power markets, and water. The company, founded by Michael Liebreich in 2004, has generated more than $1 billion in profits in 2011.

- *Suntech* is a Chinese company founded in 2001 by Dr. Zhengrong Shi and floated on the New York Stock Exchange in 2005. It is the world's largest producer of solar panels, with solar modules installed in more than 80 countries (and a low-carbon museum in Wuxi, west of Shanghai, opened by Al Gore).

Source: Dutz and Sharma 2012.

---

funds by anchoring new funds, financing new fund development, supporting pioneer investments, and supporting improved carbon payments. Even more important will be helping with the structure, management, and exit routes for venture capital investments—for example, by providing equity contributions to increase potential returns or reduce potential risks, which would play a helpful demonstration role if there is enough deal flow.[8] But experience suggests that the government role should be restricted to that of financial backer, and not manager, with funds administered professionally, free of bureaucratic burdens, and independent of political interference (Lerner 2009).

But capital market–based, arms-length forms of finance that structure and price each transaction on its merits require deep financial markets, which most developing countries still lack. Moreover, a number of other

factors—such as government R&D expenditures, the extent of patenting by entrepreneurial firms, and national environmental deployment policies designed with the long-term perspective of creating a market for environmental technologies—appear to be more important in affecting the amount of private financing of frontier innovation in the clean-tech sector.[9]

Provide global support for bottom-of-pyramid and neglected technologies. It is not advisable for countries with weak technological capabilities and no comparative advantage in creating frontier technologies to dedicate significant public resources to this objective. But given the global nature of benefits from many green innovations, stable, long-term global public spending on R&D should be increased and channeled into programs that facilitate the development and adoption of technologies applicable to developing countries.

Prize funds and advance market commitments—also called purchase guarantees—can be useful market-pull mechanisms for promoting R&D in neglected technologies.

- Prize funds are most appropriate when objectives can be well defined but the technologies are unknown. They may be particularly relevant for promoting more radical green innovations likely to be fostered not through the traditional linear R&D approach but rather through out-of-the-box new knowledge, involving co-creation and codesign by scientists, engineers, entrepreneurs, producers, and users from different disciplines.
- Advance market commitments work best when key characteristics of the desired technology are known and can be specified in a contract, typically for fairly homogeneous technologies rather than the more differentiated ones required for green growth. Although to date they have been used to provide affordable access to health care in low-income countries, they may help stimulate innovations and access to a few affordable green solutions—such as a nutrient-fortified staple food crop or improved storage technologies in contexts of land and water scarcity, climate change, and declining crop yields.

Promoting catch-up innovation: Facilitating technology access and stimulating technology adoption

Promoting green growth in developing countries is typically more about catch-up innovation and the diffusion and adaptation of already-existing technologies than about frontier innovation. Relevant policies need to facilitate access to existing technologies, as well as stimulate their uptake.

Policies to facilitate access to green technologies. The best way to facilitate access to green technologies is through openness to international trade, foreign direct investment, technology licensing, worker migration, and other forms of global connectedness. Many green technologies are embodied in technology licensing agreements and in equipment, machinery, and imported capital goods. Some are knowledge-based processes or business models that diffuse through movements of people attached to multinational corporations or from the diaspora. Some can be recreated by emulating imported final goods, copying lapsed patents, or studying and inventing around patents that are still in effect. Technology and skill transfer also occur through the purchase of manufacturing equipment on global markets, because suppliers usually provide worker training with their equipment. This channel was critical in the ability of Chinese producers to become world leaders in PV panel production (de la Tour and others 2011).

Other underused policies to boost access to existing technologies include patent buy-outs, compulsory licenses, patent pools, and open source approaches. A patent buy-out increases access to existing or future products that already benefit from adequate innovation incentives. Making it easier for countries to issue compulsory licenses under appropriate circumstances can help ensure more affordable access to patented green innovations by poorer households in low-income countries.[10]

Patent pools provide a one-stop voluntary licensing service that combines multiple patents and licenses them, with patent holders getting royalties on the sales of adapted, more affordable products, and generic manufacturers getting access to broader markets. An example is the Medicines Patent Pool, funded by the international drug-purchasing facility UNITAID, which increases access to HIV medicines in developing countries. In open source development, a body of original information is made available for anyone to use. Usually, any party using the original material must agree to make its enhancements publicly available. Open source projects are inherently royalty free. Both of these approaches could be used for neglected seeds for drought-prone, saline environments, or other green solutions for lower-income countries.

However, and perhaps most important, countries should avoid imposing tariffs on renewable energy technologies and subsidizing fossil fuels, given that most studies show that these tools do more than patent protection to limit the transfer of clean technologies (Barton 2007 and Copenhagen Economics 2009, as cited in Hall and Helmers 2010). A World Bank (2008) study finds that eliminating tariff and nontariff barriers in the top 18 developing countries ranked by greenhouse gas emissions would increase imports by 63 percent for energy-efficient lighting, 23 percent for wind power generation, 14 percent for solar power generation, and 4.6 percent for clean coal technologies.[11]

Policies to stimulate adoption of green technologies. Green technologies are often more costly for firms to adopt and are not always immediately more attractive to end-use customers. When feasible, ensuring that prices reflect the environmental externality and removing subsidies that favor brown technologies are the best tools with which to encourage the adoption and spread of green innovation.

When prices cannot be adjusted, demand-pull technology-deployment innovation policies (standards, regulations, public procurement) are needed. Demand-side policies include guaranteed feed-in tariffs for renewables, taxes and tradable permits for emissions pollution, tax credits and rebates for consumers of new technologies (compact fluorescent light bulbs), comparison labeling (to inform consumers about the relative efficiency of products), endorsement labeling ("CFC–free"), government regulations (limits to polluting emissions from industrial plants), and industry-driven standards (home and office building insulation). In contrast with radical innovation, demand-side policies appear to be effective in spurring firms to introduce incremental environmental innovations and adopt existing technologies.

Indeed, European Union surveys show that firms in most countries identify existing or future environmental regulations, followed by market demand from customers, as the main driver behind adopting incremental processes (Dutz and Sharma 2012). In high-income countries as a whole, most studies report that well-designed environmental regulations stimulate innovation by firms, as measured by R&D spending or patents. That said, the induced innovation may not be enough to fully overcome the added costs of regulation (Ambec and others 2011). As for designing environmental regulations, studies emphasize the need for stability, predictability, and a focus on end results rather than means—allowing firms to choose the most cost-effective approach to meet the end result.

Voluntary sustainability standards for products and processes can help local firms upgrade environmental practices, a form of catch-up innovation for business practices. Roundtables and other multi-stakeholder initiatives provide new ways to manage natural resources more sustainably and efficiently. The best-known are international initiatives that group together producers, processors, traders, and other actors in a commodity's supply chain with banks and civil society groups concerned about the harmful impacts of agriculture and aquaculture expansion. They aim at building consensus and setting voluntary standards on what constitutes responsible production and processing, along with promoting proven management practices to reach the set targets. Linking local firms to the global value chains of multinational corporations that have adopted sustainability standards helps leverage international market pressures (box 3.7).

Finally, a better financial infrastructure could significantly boost green technology absorption. In a study on adopting efficient stoves, small biogas plants, and efficient tobacco barns for commercial farmers in Malawi, Rwanda, and Tanzania, financing emerged as the main stumbling block for all projects because of high start-up costs (Barry and others 2011). A study of low-income countries finds that higher financial intermediation significantly helps non-hydroelectric renewable energy generation per capita, because investment in renewable energy is constrained in environments where access to long-term loans is limited (Brunschweiler 2010). Regarding China, a study cites access

---

BOX 3.7   Voluntary standards support the sustainable management of South African deep-sea fishing and Indonesian palm oil

A highly visible and credible certification that deep-sea hake fishing was sustainably managed by the international nongovernmental standards organization (the Marine Stewardship Council) constrained local regulators in South Africa from allowing excessive new entry of fishers, which would have depleted stocks. It also led to restructuring of the equity structures of companies to meet the country's Black Economic Empowerment goals.

For palm oil there was no comprehensive, agreed-upon sustainability standard that producers could adopt, despite the crop's impact on deforestation and biodiversity loss. On top of environmental and social risks, this uncertainty raised the cost of World Bank loan preparation and monitoring and

added potential reputation risk issues, affecting the availability and pricing of Bank financing. Thanks to guidelines issued by the Roundtable on Sustainable Palm Oil (RSPO)—supported by the Indonesia Palm Oil Producers Association, Unilever, the Hong Kong and Shanghai Banking Corporation, the World Wildlife Federation, Oxfam, the International Finance Corporation, and other key members—the share of RSPO-certified palm oil has risen to 11 percent of the total market. To raise this share to the next level, broader government support in the consuming countries is needed to complement achievements driven by consumer activism.

Source: Levy and others 2011; IFC 2010; RSPO 2012.

---

to financial credit and quality of after-sales service as key barriers to adopting solar home systems (D'Agostino and others 2011). And a study on Europe's reconstruction after World War II emphasizes that the largely bank-based, relationship-based financial systems provided vital support for lower-risk technology absorption by firms (Wolf 2011).

Green industrial policies: Ensuring that the standard caveats apply

Many countries include green industrial policies that target industries, firms, or technology-specific innovation and production in their environmental policy mix, from feed-in tariffs for PV solar energy to tax breaks for innovative firms in specific environmental industries and green procurement (box 3.8). But given that this approach is vulnerable to powerful lobbies, rent-seeking behavior, and costly mistakes caused by information asymmetries, there is no consensus on whether it is desirable.

Moreover, while industrial policies can transform an economy's structure, the debate over whether they are effective instruments for accelerating growth continues. Some argue that industrial policies played a key

role in the rise of Japan and other Asian countries (Chang 2006); others consider this catch-up a consequence of large investments (and a catch-up in capital intensity) in countries with high levels of education and institutional capacity (Krugman 1994). Whatever the case, it is critical to not blindly apply the lessons from East Asia to countries with very different characteristics, including low education levels and weaker institutions.

Whether even Asia's industrial policies would have passed a cost-benefit analysis is unclear (Harrison and Rodríguez-Clare 2009; Noland and Pack 2003). But because green industrial policies offer environmental benefits, they could be desirable even with no net positive impact on growth or job creation. For instance, whether or not Brazil's ethanol policy accelerated economic growth or created jobs, there is little doubt that it led to the creation of a dynamic biofuel sector that would, in the absence of that policy, probably not exist (or would at least be much smaller; Karp and Stevenson 2012). For their part, the biofuel policies of Europe and the United States can be considered examples of green industrial policies that failed to generate even an environmental benefit, as they are generally considered to have harmed the environment.

BOX 3.8   The role of green procurement

When governments look for ways to influence the economy to achieve greener growth, public procurement stands out as a viable tool. For this reason, both industrial and developing countries are now pursuing green public procurement. In recent years many countries—Brazil, China, the Republic of Korea, Turkey—have implemented green initiatives to protect the environment and mitigate emissions (OECD 2010; Thomson and Jackson 2007). Green procurement is estimated to have accounted for 6 percent (Korea) to 60 percent (Sweden) of total public procurement in 2005 (OECD 2007).

The preferences of governments for green products in the early stages can help firms reduce production costs. They can also have dynamic effects in relevant markets. New companies can be motivated to enter the market, leading to further market development. If the market evolves rapidly, private users of similar products will also be educated to use greener products. In addition, the dynamic market development may lead to significant economic competitiveness in such technological domains. For instance, a French company that invested in R&D to develop an environment-friendly paint for public road signs also developed other paint products that now lead the market (OECD 2007).

Governments can take advantage of standard-raising demonstration effects and the provision of a guaranteed demand to foster markets of green products, change technological standards, generate green jobs, adapt public assets (such as buildings and infrastructure), and take a lead in educating consumers and firms to engage in more sustainable consumption and production. From a global welfare and climate change perspective, such procurement should not discriminate against foreign suppliers.

Whether green environmental policies are desirable, many countries, mostly middle and high income, are actively engaged in policies that support specific industries. Some of these policies aim to provide direct environmental benefits (biofuel production in Brazil, concentrated solar power in Morocco). Others aim to produce related upstream goods and services (solar PV panels in China, high-speed trains in Europe). It is worth exploring the motivations for green industrial policies and the lessons from past experience with standard industrial policies.

What role for green industrial policies?

Green industrial policies can be implemented for multiple reasons. All these reasons are linked to different market failure or policy objectives.

Compensate for the uncertainty in future environmental policy and promote new industries and technologies. Most countries that adopt green industrial policies claim to do so to take advantage of a latent comparative advantage, create jobs, and pursue new sources of growth. The underlying argument is that prices are not enough to address the standard market failures that hamper new industries (such as increasing returns, coordination failures, and underdeveloped financial markets).

Even if prices were to fully reflect the environmental externality, current and new green industries would face many challenges. Pricing policies are politically vulnerable, and the lack of credible long-term commitments and regulatory uncertainty discourages the private sector from making long-term investments in green industries. Witness the European carbon emission trading scheme, which effectively created a carbon price but did little for environmental innovation (Borghesi and others 2012; Rogge and others 2011). When long-term innovation, deployment, and production scale-up is needed, pricing policies may need to be complemented by innovation and more targeted industrial policies (Vogt-Schilb and Hallegatte 2011), as with PV solar energy in Germany and China (box 3.9).

Level the playing field. The risk of pollution leakage from countries with strict environmental regulations to laxer countries has been used to justify green trade-based industrial policies.[12] The fear is that

BOX 3.9   Comparison of photovoltaic support policies in Germany and China

Germany and China are emerging as leaders in the global photovoltaic (PV) market, thanks to developing a dual industry composed of vertically integrated firms and segment specialists (Grau and others 2011). Public support aims to trigger cost reductions through economies of scale and additional technological innovation. It is directed at three activities:

- *Direct R&D to support innovation.* Both China and Germany provide support to R&D, especially to promote radical innovation that is not the usual focus of the private sector. But this support remains limited, with only 1 percent (in China) and 3 percent (in Germany) of the total support these countries provide to PV panel production (Grau and others 2011).
- *Standard environmental policies to support deployment.* Both China and Germany are using feed-in tariffs to support the large-scale deployment of PV modules. The German example points to the inherent risks resulting from a stable, long-term commitment to buy electricity from PV. When the price of PV modules dropped in 2009, the sudden surge in profitability led to a rush to install PV modules, inflating the total cost of the program and jeopardizing its existence.
- *Investment to support manufacturing plants.* Investment to support manufacturing plants embraces direct subsidies, reduced taxes, public guarantees, and reduced-interest loans. Neither

China nor Germany links investment support to specific innovation requirements.

Striking the right balance among the three forms of support is critical for reducing costs. But support schemes are further complicated by information asymmetries between the industry and the government and by market power exerted by different actors in the industry.

Has public support made a big difference? There is little doubt that it helped achieve the large reduction in solar panel costs, which yielded global benefits. But there are growing concerns that this support is increasingly focused on the interests of domestic producers rather than global welfare objectives.

In Germany the issue is whether hefty feed-in tariffs mainly benefit Chinese PV manufacturers who export to Germany. But Chinese producers are concentrated in the downstream segments of the PV panel supply chain, which are highly labor-intensive and are where the country has a comparative advantage (de la Tour and others 2011). These downstream segments have limited margins and small profits compared with upstream segments, such as silicon production, where industrial countries, including Germany, still dominate. (Germany also manufactures some of the machinery used in China for PV production.) In China the issue is whether the policy leads to the import of mature technology, thus preventing the takeoff of an internal innovation capacity for more radical technology changes.

stricter environmental regulations in one country may cause "dirty" industries to move to pollution havens rather than adopt cleaner processes. There is little support for this argument in the current context. Pollution abatement costs represent only a small fraction of production costs for most industries. And while environmental regulation may cause firms to move from a particular location, the destination location chosen likely has other draws (skilled labor, good business environment, and a well-developed financial sector).

And studies show that the impact of current environmental regulations on firm

competitiveness remains limited. Quirion and Hourcade (2004) calculate that in the European Union, a €20-per-ton CO_2 tax has a lower impact on marginal cost than interannual exchange rate variations, even in energy-intensive industries and without tax revenue recycling. Econometric studies found no negative impact of the EU Emissions Trading System (ETS) on net imports in the aluminum, steel, and cement industries (Ellerman and others 2010; Quirion 2011; Sartor 2012). Anger and Oberndorfer (2008) reach the same conclusion on German firms and the EU ETS. Panel data from the U.K. production census suggest that the climate change levy (an energy tax) had a significant impact on energy intensity but no detectable effects on economic performance or on plant exit (Martin and others 2009).

Empirical evidence fails to support the notion of "pollution havens" (Copeland 2012), though this could change if environmental policies, such as carbon taxes, become much stricter. Should this happen, trade policies may become an important complement to environmental policies: specific trade policies—from bilateral and multilateral agreements on environmental regulation to border tax adjustments, with or without revenue transfers to the exporting country—can help level the competitiveness playing field.

Smooth the transition. Countries may opt to use industrial policies to support ailing industries to facilitate the political economy of a green transition. Japan supported declining traditional industries to make the transition toward high-productivity, high-skill industries more acceptable for the population. In the same manner a green strategy may need to include some transitional support to (declining) energy-intensive industries. This component of the green growth package can be a requirement for its political acceptability, despite its cost. The aim of such support would be to smooth the transition, help businesses adjust their production technologies, and help workers adapt by moving to other industries—while ensuring that any public support remains transitory, with clear sunset clauses.

Heeding the lessons of the past

The desirability of innovation and industrial policies—green or not—cannot be assessed without analyzing a country's economic situation, the benefits it can expect from these policies, and its ability to avoid capture by vested interests. Experiences around the world with these policies show that the following six lessons are key.

First, the relevant policy intervention depends on what market failure needs addressing (Baldwin 1969). Designing industrial policies requires that the government be able to identify and analyze market failures (Pack and Saggi 2006). To do so, the government may need information on which firms and industries generate knowledge spillovers or benefit from economies of scale and dynamics effects (for example, learning by doing). Without a clear understanding of the market failures that need to be corrected, innovation and industrial policies will be inefficient or detrimental, particularly if they are used as a substitute for an enabling business environment.

Second, horizontal (or output-based) policies should be favored over vertical policies ("picking winners" or at least the winning technology) when possible. Vertical policies should be contemplated only when technologies or solutions have been demonstrated in other contexts or are justified by industry or technology-specific characteristics.

But applying this recommendation to green growth policies may be challenging. For example, absolute technology neutrality hardly applies as a guiding principle of climate policy (Azar and Sanden 2011). An example is feed-in tariffs (payments of a cost-based rate to energy producers for the electricity they generate from renewable resources), which can be designed to offer the same premium for any low-carbon electricity, thereby freeing electricity producers to choose the technology. But in the presence of learning-by-doing, a higher feed-in tariff may be desirable for the technology whose potential is estimated to be larger (del Rio Gonzalez 2008; Johnstone and others 2010).

In the early 2000s, advocates of feed-in tariffs to support PV electricity production (rather than other carbon-free technologies, such as wind power) pointed to the large potential of this technology, its fairly high initial cost, and the improvements expected from learning-by-doing, which made it unlikely to be picked up under horizontal support to any carbon-free electricity production technology.

Fortunately, picking winning technologies may be less risky for developing countries implementing green growth, as they may be able to choose environmental technologies already developed and tested in high-income countries. This fact may partly explain why developing countries adopt environmental regulations at earlier stages of development and at lower cost than developed countries (Lovely and Popp 2011). Examples include technologies with large potential for economies of scale (such as solar PV) and technologies broadly used in industrial countries (such as low-sulfur fuels or wastewater treatment technologies). Technology support may also be less risky when a latent (that is, future rather than current) comparative advantage can be observed in an objective manner—for instance, renewable energies that depend on natural endowments, such as the potential for solar energy in North Africa and hydropower in Central Africa.

Third, the desirability of innovation and industrial policies depends on the balance between market failure and government failure. These policies need strong institutions, because they are vulnerable to capture and rent seeking and to inefficient micromanagement of the innovation and investment process (Laffont 1999; Rodrik 2005). In climate policy, rent-seeking behavior is likely to influence policies even in countries with high institutional capacity and appropriate "checks and balances" (Anthoff and Hahn 2010; Helm 2010). Neven and Röller (2000) identify factors that make such problems more likely: sharply partisan political systems, weak governments, and absence of transparency. But rent capture remains possible even in the most efficient, balanced, and transparent country, because industrial lobbies are powerful actors in any economy (box 3.10).

Fourth, successfully using innovation and industrial policies requires the capacity to remove support when it is no longer justified, especially if one technology proves less promising than expected. Regardless of their ability to "pick the winner," there are plenty of political economy reasons to explain why governments find it difficult to interrupt support when a project or business fails. One option is to make support conditional on some market test. East Asian countries used export competitiveness, an indicator difficult to manipulate by local firms. They were fairly ruthless in terminating support to underperformers and made continued protection in the domestic market contingent on export performance (World Bank 1993).

Subjecting green policies to a market test is more challenging than with standard industrial policies (Karp and Stevenson 2012). When the market does not price the environmental externality—that is, in the absence of complementary price policies—a market test cannot be used to decide whether the supported technology is the appropriate one. For instance, R&D subsidies or feed-in tariffs that help the solar panel industry reach scale and technology maturity may need to be permanent to make the industry competitive in the absence of a carbon price. The profitability of the low-sulfur refining industry will depend on permanent subsidies in the absence of regulations on vehicle sulfur emissions. Contrary to classical industrial policies, which are supposed to be temporary because they correct temporary market failures (such as increasing returns to scale), green industrial policies may need to be permanent if they are supposed to correct permanent market failures (such as an environmental externality). To avoid this issue it is preferable to use price-based instruments to correct permanent environmental externalities and industrial policies to cope with transient externalities.

Fifth, the benefits from innovation and industrial policies vary depending on the scale of assessment. When these policies make it possible to create a domestic industry with significant market share, local benefits can be large in terms of jobs and income. But the assessment can be completely different at the global scale if market shares are gained thanks to public support at the expense of more efficient foreign producers. The desirability of these policies should be evaluated in view of trade-offs, especially if ambitious

---

BOX 3.10 Lessons from a "green" industrial policy: U.S. biofuels

In recent decades, concerns about national energy security, dwindling reserves of easily recoverable petroleum (and oil price hikes), and health and safety have prompted many industrial countries to look for renewable energy alternatives, including biofuels. The U.S. biofuels program offers useful lessons on green industrial policies—two of which appear particularly relevant for developing-country policy makers.

First, biofuel industrial policies have mixed consequences for competition among technologies. The relationship between first-generation (ethanol, primarily from corn and sugar) and second-generation (or cellulosic) biofuels, which are being developed to prevent higher food prices and land use changes, has long been viewed as a cooperative process. By developing an infrastructure for handling large volumes of biomass and constraining fuel refiners to blend increasing quantities of biofuels in fossil fuels, producers of first-generation biofuels would naturally pave the way for a new generation of biofuels. But a recent study suggests that first-generation biofuels would be a tough competitor for the nascent industry of next-generation biofuels (Babcock and others 2011). And the difficulty of the nascent technology is heightened by the fact that "declining industries are generally more successful in forming lobby groups and securing policy concessions from governments" (Damania 2002).

Second, the reversibility of a policy (and thus the risk from capture) depends on the instrument used. Producers of biofuels used to be supported through subsidies (or, equivalently, tax breaks).

In the United States the corn-based ethanol tax credit has been complemented by an import tariff on all sources of ethanol, with the tax credit working with federally mandated blending minimums to ensure a domestic market for ethanol. U.S. ethanol subsidies are estimated to have cost taxpayers $6 billion in 2009 (Karp and Stevenson 2012). They likely imposed significant costs on developing-country suppliers that are more efficient—such as Brazil, which uses sugar cane as a feedstock (though in 2009/10, Brazil imported small amounts of ethanol from the United States due to high food demand for sugar and competing crops worldwide). The subsidies sharply pushed up corn prices, though part of that increase could have been avoided if the U.S. market had been open.

The phasing out of the U.S. tax credit (and tariff) at the end of 2011 marked the end of the taxpayer's support to biofuels. But the support by the consumer still remains, through the blending requirement of increasing amounts of ethanol. What is worrisome is that the consumption mandates appear far more difficult to reverse than direct subsidies—which were subject to annual review by legislative bodies in the United States and in most European Union member states. With consumption mandates, biofuel policies are less susceptible to public finance pressure. Although the amounts at stake are substantial, the fact that the burden is spread across millions of consumers reduces the political pressure to relieve it. Indeed, substantial coordination would be needed on the consumer side to stand up against the mandates if warranted from a cost-benefit perspective.

---

policies in a few countries lead to escalating support globally, beyond what is justified by market failures.

Sixth, green growth is about synergies between economic growth and environmental protection. And more targeted innovation and industrial policies represent a way to capture these synergies. Indeed, if and where these policies can promote growth cost-effectively and provide environmental benefits, it is possible that they can be developed to generate synergies between economic and environmental objectives.

In sum, a balanced view of costs, potential benefits, side-effects, and risks is needed to analyze the desirability of green innovation and industrial policies. The fact that these policies have influenced the structure of several economies suggests that they are options for transforming economies and bringing them toward more environment-friendly patterns. But the potential for costly failure and waste of scarce public resources always needs to be factored into any policy decision. In the following three chapters, we explore the three key inputs in a greener production function—human, natural, and physical capital—beginning with labor markets and whether green growth creates jobs.

Notes

1. This section is based on Dutz and Sharma (2012), a background paper produced for this report.
2. Indicators of technological sophistication (R&D personnel per capita) as well as the scale of the R&D sector (total R&D personnel) were considered in making this distinction.
3. Hausmann and Klinger (2006) show that as countries change their export mix, there is a strong tendency to move toward related goods rather than to goods that are farther away, where "relatedness" or "proximity" of products is defined at the global level.
4. See Popp (2012), who highlights the work of Lewis (2007) documenting how both countries went from having no wind turbine manufacturing capacity to having almost complete local production in fewer than 10 years. Sauter and Watson (2008) highlight this as a case study of "environmental leapfrogging," explaining how the adoption of cutting-edge technologies was facilitated by the creation of learning networks.
5. See Popp (2012), who highlights international mobility of workers as a more important source of information than foreign direct investment or licensing, and de la Tour and others (2011) for the underlying analysis.
6. The initiative, led by the Commission for Environmental Cooperation, established by the North American Free Trade Agreement, included the environmental authority of the state of Queretaro and the Global Environmental Management Initiative, a nonprofit organization of leading U.S. multinational corporations focused on environmental sustainability. It is a 10-week eco-efficiency educational training program emphasizing learning-by-doing with a commitment by participating small and medium-size enterprises to generate and implement pollution prevention projects, with recommendations for change made by the participants themselves. Investments related to the implementation of the improvement projects were provided by individual participants, who became convinced of their value. Lyon and van Hoof (2010) find that the average participant generated a project with a net present value of more than $150,000, saved 1,900 cubic meters of water and 42,000 Kwh per year of electricity a year, reduced CO_2 emissions by 61 tons a year, and cut waste disposal by 1,455 tons.
7. Chapter 4 addresses the labor market–related questions concerning skills.
8. See chapter 4 of Zhang and others (2009) for an overview and recommendations of policies to strengthen the ecosystem for the venture capital industry in China, and see chapter 7 of Dutz (2007) for India.
9. Regression results (based on comprehensive deal-level data on high-growth financing and enterprises seeking investment in the clean-tech sector over 2005–10 in 26 countries including Brazil, China, the Czech Republic, and India) suggest that deployment policies such as feed-in tariffs and tradable certificates, government R&D, and firm-level patenting are associated with higher levels of investment in clean-tech industries than short-term fiscal policies such as tax incentives and rebates. No significant correlation is found between public investment loans or public financing of venture capital and the amount of private financing of innovative ventures (Criscuolo and Menon 2012).
10. Henry and Stiglitz (2010) document how the United States used the threat of a compulsory license to manufacture Cipro during the anthrax scare following September 11, 2001.
11. The assessment is based on first-round approximations rather than full general equilibrium effects.
12. This is a different issue from the rise in imported emissions to high-income countries from developing countries, which is associated with their general deindustrialization. In 2008, China emitted about 1,400 $MtCO_2$ through its production of exported goods; the United States imported goods amounting to about 600 $MtCO_2$ of emissions.

References

Ambec, S., M. A. Cohen, S. Elgie, and P. Lanoie. 2011. "The Porter Hypothesis at 20: Can Environmental Regulation Enhance Innovation and Competitiveness?" Discussion Paper 11-01, Resources for the Future, Washington, DC.

Anger, N., and U. Oberndorfer. 2008. "Firm Performance and Employment in the EU Emissions Trading Scheme: An Empirical Assessment for Germany." *Energy Policy* 36: 12–22.

Anthoff, A., and R. Hahn. 2010. "Government Failure and Market Failure: On the Inefficiency of Environmental and Energy Policy."*Oxford Review of Economic Policy* 26 (2): 197–224.

Azar, C., and B. A. Sanden. 2011. "The Elusive Quest for Technology-Neutral Policies." *Environmental Innovation and Societal Transition* 1: 135–9.

Babcock, B. A., S. Marette, and D. Tréguer. 2011. "Opportunity for Profitable Investments in Cellulosic Biofuels." *Energy Policy* 39: 714–9.

Baldwin, R. E. 1969. "The Case against Infant Industry Protection." *Journal of Political Economy* 77 (5–6): 295–305.

Baldwin, R. E., and P. R. Krugman. 1988. "Industrial Policy and International Competition in Wide Bodied Jet Aircraft." In *Trade Policy Issues and Empirical Analysis*, ed. R. E. Baldwin, 45–78. Chicago: University of Chicago Press.

Barry, M.-L., H. Steyn, and A. Brent. 2011. "Selection of Renewable Energy Technologies for Africa: Eight Case Studies in Rwanda, Tanzania, and Malawi." *Renewable Energy* 36: 2845–52.

Barton, J. H. 2007. "Intellectual Property and Access to Clean Energy Technologies in Developing Countries." ICTSD Issue Paper 2, International Centre for Trade and Sustainable Development, Geneva.

Borghesi, S., G. Cainelli, and M. Mazzanti. 2012. "Brown Sunsets and Green Dawns in the Industrial Sector: Environmental Innovations, Firm Behavior and the European Emission Trading." Nota di Lavoro 3.2012, Fondazione Eni Enrico Mattei, Milan, Italy.

Brunschweiler, C. N. 2010. "Finance for Renewable Energy: An Empirical Analysis of Developing and Transition Economies." *Environment and Development Economics* 15: 241–74.

CEDEFOP (European Centre for the Development of Vocational Training). 2009. *Future Skill Needs for the Green Economy.* Luxembourg: Publications Office of the European Union.

Chang, H.-J. 2006. *The East Asian Development Experience: The Miracle, the Crisis, and the Future.* London: Zed Press.

Copeland, B. R. 2012. "International Trade and Green Growth." Paper presented at the Green Growth Knowledge Platform inaugural conference, Mexico City, January 12–13.

Copenhagen Economics. 2009. "Are IPRs a Barrier to the Transfer of Climate Change Technology." Report commissioned by the European Commission (DG Trade), Brussels.

Criscuolo, C., and C. Menon. 2012. "The Role of Government Policies, Local Knowledge Stocks and Firms Patenting Activity for High-Growth Financing in Clean Technologies." STI Working Paper, Organisation for Economic Co-operation and Development, Paris.

D'Agostino, A. L., B. K. Sovacool, and M. J. Bambawale. 2011. "And Then What Happened? A Retrospective Appraisal of China's Renewable Energy Development Project (REDP)." *Renewable Energy* 36: 3154–65.

Damania, R. 2002. "Influence in Decline: Lobbying in Contracting Industries." *Economics & Politics* 14: 209–23.

de la Tour, A., M. Glachant, and Y. Ménière. 2011. "Innovation and International Technology Transfer: The Case of the Chinese Photovoltaic Industry." *Energy Policy* 39 (2): 761–70.

Dechezleprêtre, A., and M. Glachant. 2011. "Does Foreign Environmental Policy Influence Domestic Innovation? Evidence from the Wind Industry." Working Paper 44, Grantham Research Institute on Climate Change and the Environment, London, UK.

Dechezleprêtre, A., M. Glachant, I. Hascic, N. Johnstone, and Y. Ménière. 2011. "Invention and Transfer of Climate Change Mitigation Technologies: A Global Analysis."*Review of Environmental Economics and Policy* 5 (1): 109–30.

Dechezleprêtre, A., M. Glachant, and Y. Ménière. 2009. "Technology Transfer by CDM Projects: A Comparison of Brazil, China, India and Mexico." *Energy Policy* 37 (2): 703–11.

del Rio Gonzalez, P. 2008. "Policy Implications of Potential Conflicts between Short-Term and Long-Term Efficiency in CO_2 Emissions Abatement." *Ecological Economics* 65 (2): 292–303.

Dutz, M. A. 2007. *Unleashing India's Innovation: Toward Sustainable and Inclusive Growth.* Washington, DC: World Bank.

Dutz, M. A., and S. Sharma. 2012. "Green Growth, Technology and Innovation." Policy Research Working Paper 5932, World Bank, Washington, DC.

Ellerman, A. D., F. Convery, and C. de Perthuis. 2010. *Pricing Carbon.* Cambridge, UK: Cambridge University Press.

Financial Times. 2011. "How Green Were Their Ventures." November 5.

Grau, T., M. Huo, and K. Neuhoff. 2011. *Survey of Photovoltaic Industry and Policy in Germany and China.* Berlin: Climate Policy Initiative.

Hall, B. H., and C. Helmers. 2010. "The Role of Patent Protection in Clean/Green Technology Transfer." *Santa Clara High Technology Law Journal* 26 (4): 487–532.

Harrison, A., and A. Rodríguez-Clare. 2009. "Trade, Foreign Investment, and Industrial Policy for Developing Countries." In *Handbook for Development Economics,* ed. D. Rodrik and M. Rosenzweig, vol. 5, 4039–214. Amsterdam: North Holland.

Hausmann, R., and B. Klinger. 2006. "Structural Transformation and Patterns of Comparative Advantage in the Product Space." Working Paper RWP06-041, Harvard University, John F. Kennedy School of Government, Cambridge, MA.

Helm, D. 2010. "Government Failure, Rent-Seeking, and Capture: The Design of Climate Change Policy." *Oxford Review of Economic Policy* 26 (2): 182–96.

Helpman, E., and P. R. Krugman. 1989. *Trade Policy and Market Structure.* Cambridge, MA: MIT Press.

Henry, C., and J. E. Stiglitz. 2010. "Intellectual Property, Dissemination of Innovation and Sustainable Development." *Global Policy* 1 (3): 237–51.

IEA (International Energy Agency). 2008. *Deploying Renewables: Principles for Effective Policies.* Paris: IEA.

IFC (International Finance Corporation). 2010. *Telling Our Story: Renewable Energy.* Washington, DC: IFC.

Johnstone, N., I. Haščic, and D. Popp. 2010. "Renewable Energy Policies and Technological Innovation: Evidence Based on Patent Counts." *Environmental and Resource Economics* 45: 133–55.

Karp, L., and M. Stevenson. 2012. "Green Industrial Policy: Trade and Theory." Paper presented at the Green Growth Knowledge Platform inaugural conference, Mexico City, January 12–13.

Khan, M. H. 2009. "Learning, Technology Acquisition and Governance Challenges in Developing Countries." Research Paper Series on Governance for Growth, University of London, School of Oriental and African Studies, London.

Krugman, P. 1994. "The Myth of Asia's Miracle." *Foreign Affairs* 73 (6): 62–78.

Laffont, J.-J. 1999. "Political Economy, Information, and Incentives." *European Economic Review* 43: 649–69.

Lee, H., and D.-S. Moon. 2005. "Next Generation of Korea Train Express (KTW): Prospect and Strategies." *Proceedings of the Eastern Asia Society for Transportation Studies* 5: 255–62.

Lerner, J. 2009. *Why Public Efforts to Boost Entrepreneurship and Venture Capital Have Failed—and What to Do about It.* Princeton, NJ: Princeton University Press.

Levy, B., A. de Jager, B. Meehan, and T. Leiman. 2011. *Regulatory Efficacy in a Changing Political Environment: A Tale of Two South African Fisheries.* Washington, DC: World Bank.

Lewis, J. I. 2007. "Technology Acquisition and Innovation in the Developing World: Wind Turbine Development in China and India." *Studies in Comparative International Development* 42 (3–4): 16–35.

Lovely, M., and D. Popp. 2011. "Trade, Technology and the Environment: Does Access to Technology Promote Environmental Regulation?" *Journal of Environmental Economics and Management* 61 (1): 16–35.

Lyon, T. P., and B. van Hoof. 2010. *Evaluating Mexico's Green Supply Chains Program.* Ann Arbor, MI: University of Michigan, Ross School of Business.

Martin, R., U. J. Wagner, and L. B. de Preux. 2009. "The Impacts of the Climate Change Levy on Business: Evidence from Microdata." CEP Discussion Paper, Centre for Economic Performance, London School of Economics, London.

Murphy, K. M., A. Shleifer, and R. W. Vishny. 1989. "Industrialization and the Big Push." *Journal of Political Economy* 97 (5): 1003–26.

Neven, D. J., and L.-H. Röller. 2000. "The Political Economy of State Aids: Econometric Evidence for the Member States." In *The Political Economy of Industrial Policy: Does Europe Have an Industrial Policy?* ed. D. J. Neven and L.-H. Röller. Berlin: Edition Sigma.

Noland, M., and R. Pack. 2003. *Industrial Policy in an Era of Globalization.* Washington, DC: Petersen Institute for International Economics.

OECD (Organisation for Economic Co-operation and Development). 2007. "Improving the

Environmental Performance of Public Procurement: Report on Implementation of the Council Recommendation." Working Party on National Environmental policies, ENV/EPOC/WPNEP(2006)6/Final, OECD, Paris.

———. 2009. *Learning for Jobs: OECD Policy Review of Vocational Education and Training: Initial Report.* Paris: OECD Publishing.

———. 2010. "Interim Report of the Green Growth Strategy: Implementing Our Commitment for a Sustainable Future." Meeting of the OECD Council at Ministerial Level, C/MIN(2010)5, OECD, Paris.

———. 2011. *Skills for Innovation and Research.* Paris: OECD Publishing.

Okuno-Fujiwara, M. 1988. "Interdependence of Industries, Coordination Failure, and Strategic Promotion of an Industry." *Journal of International Economics* 25 (1/2): 25–43.

Pack, H., and K. Saggi. 2006. "Is There a Case for Industrial Policy? A Critical Survey." *World Bank Research Observer* 21 (2): 267–97.

Pack, H., and L. E. Westphal. 1986. "Industrial Strategy and Technological Change" *Journal of Development Economics* 22 (1): 87–128.

Popp, D. 2012. "The Role of Technological Change in Green Growth." Paper presented at the Green Growth Knowledge Platform inaugural conference, Mexico City, January 12–13.

Prahalad, C. K., and R. A. Mashelkar. 2010. "Innovation's Holy Grail." *Harvard Business Review* (July–August): 132–41.

Quirion, P. 2011. "Les quotas échangeables d'émission de gaz à effet de serre: éléments d'analyse économique." Mémoire d'habilitation à diriger les recherches, Ecole des Hautes Etudes en Sciences Sociales, Paris.

Quirion P., and J.-C. Hourcade. 2004. "Does the CO$_2$ Emission Trading Directive Threaten the Competitiveness of European Industry? Quantification and Comparison to Exchange Rate Fluctuations." Paper presented at the Conference of the European Association of Environmental and Resource Economists, Budapest, June.

Rodenstein-Rodan, P. N. 1943. "Problems of Industrialization of Eastern and Southeastern Europe." *Economic Journal* 53: 202–11.

Rodrik, D. 2004. "Industrial Policy for the Twenty-First Century." CEPR Discussion Paper 4767, Center for Economic Policy Research, Washington, DC.

———. 2005. "Growth Strategies." In *Handbook of Economic Growth*, ed. P. Aghion and S. Durlauf. Amsterdam: North-Holland.

Rogge, K. S., M. Schneider, and V. H. Hoffmann. 2011. "The Innovation Impact of the EU Emission Trading System: Findings of Company Case Studies in the German Power Sector." *Ecological Economics* 70 (3): 513–23.

RSPO (Roundtable on Sustainable Palm Oil). 2012. "2011 RSPO CSPO Growth Interpretation Narrative." RSPO Secretariat, Kuala Lumpur, Malaysia.

Sartor, O. 2012. "Carbon Leakage in the Primary Aluminium Sector: What Evidence after 6 ½ Years of the EU ETS?" CDC Climate Research Working Paper 2012–12, Caisse des Dépôts et des Consignations, Paris.

Sauter, R., and J. Watson. 2008. "Technology Leapfrogging: A Review of the Evidence." Sussex Energy Group, University of Sussex, Brighton, UK.

Thomson, J., and T. Jackson. 2007. "Sustainable Procurement in Practice: Lessons from Local Government." *Journal of Environmental Planning and Management* 50: 421–44.

Thorncroft, C. 2011. "African Monsoon Multidisciplinary Analysis." University of Albany, Department of Atmospheric and Environmental Sciences, Albany, NY.

Trindade, V. 2005. "The Big Push, Industrialization, and International Trade: The Role of Exports." *Journal of Development Economics* 78 (October): 22–48.

Vogt-Schilb, A., and S. Hallegatte. 2011. "When Starting with the Most Expensive Option Makes Sense: Use and Misuse of Marginal Abatement Cost Curves." Policy Research Working Paper 5803, World Bank, Washington, DC.

Wolf, H. 2011. "Relationship-Based and Arms-Length Financial Systems: A European Perspective." Policy Research Working Paper 5833, World Bank, Washington, DC.

World Bank. 1993. *The East Asian Miracle: Economic Growth and Public Policy.* Oxford, UK: Oxford University Press.

———. 2008. *International Trade and Climate Change: Economic, Legal and Institutional Perspectives.* Washington, DC: World Bank.

———. 2012. *Doing Business 2012: Doing Business in a More Transparent World.* Washington, DC: World Bank.

World Economic Forum. 2011. *Redefining the Future of Growth: The New Sustainability*

Champions. Geneva: World Economic Forum.

Yusuf, S., K. Nabeshima, and S. Yamashita. 2008. *Growing Industrial Clusters in Asia: Serendipity and Science*. Washington, DC: World Bank.

Zhang, C., D. Z. Zeng, W. P. Mako, and J. Seward. 2009. *Promoting Enterprise-Led Innovation in China*. Directions in Development. Washington, DC: World Bank.

Human Capital: Implications of Green Growth Policies for Labor Markets and Job Creation | 4

Key Messages

- Green growth cannot substitute for good growth policies, and employment is no exception: shortcomings in labor markets will not disappear with the adoption of environmental policies.
- But even if green jobs will not be a panacea, environmental regulation need not kill jobs either, and the net balance can be positive.

- To smooth the impacts on labor markets of the transition to green growth, policy makers need to tackle potential skill shortages and impediments to worker mobility—both of which have constituted barriers to other types of economic adjustment, such as trade liberalization.

For many countries the promise of new sources of growth and job creation is what lies behind the attractiveness of green growth. They look at Brazil, China, Denmark, India, and Japan—world leaders in exports of green products, who created entirely new industries in wind, solar, and biofuels. They hear about the promised double dividend of a green fiscal stimulus that can create jobs in the short run while laying the foundations for a more sustainable future.

For others the fear of diminished competitiveness and job losses remains one of the main barriers to pursuing green growth. They worry that tightening environmental policies could lead to industries relocating in countries with laxer environmental policies (so-called "pollution havens")—and that these policies will lead to trade wars.

Yet, to some extent, this is an old debate—one that centers on the complex relationships between environmental regulation and competitiveness, and the ensuing job impacts. The topic of "green jobs" is just the latest round, prompted by global economic worries.

This chapter is based on Bowen (2012), except section "... and Learn from the Lessons of Trade Adjustment," which draws from Porto (2012).

For example, a study of the impact of carbon price policies on U.S. industry considers outcomes along four time scales (Ho and others 2008):

- The very short run, where firms cannot adjust prices and profits fall accordingly.
- The short run, where firms can raise prices to reflect the higher energy costs, with a corresponding decline in sales as a result of product or import substitution.
- The medium run, when in addition to the changes in output prices, the mix of inputs may also change, but capital remains in place, and economy-wide effects are considered.
- The long run, when capital may be reallocated and replaced with more energy-efficient technologies.

It concludes that employment consequences of green policies differ strongly, depending on the time horizon. Short-term employment losses mirror output declines and are substantial in energy-intensive sectors, but gains in other industries would fully offset those losses in the longer term.

But few studies account for labor market rigidities and other obstacles to job creation, and yet they may impair any positive effect of green policies. As the World Bank study on South Africa (World Bank 2011a) noted, green policies cannot correct all the problems holding back job creation—such as skill mismatches and the dualism (insider-outsider) of the job market. Thus, the scope for green job creation is limited in the absence of parallel economic policy changes.

Evaluating the impact of green policies on jobs: Gross versus net job creation

What is the overall job creation impact of green policies in developing countries? Few studies have explicitly focused on this, and those that have suffer from many definitional issues, making comparisons difficult.[4] They also fail to look at economy-wide effects. That said, the few that do exist suggest that climate-change policies in general and renewable energy policies in particular can generate considerable extra employment:

- In South Africa, a study finds that an "energy revolution" scenario—that is, a scenario with a strong transition toward renewable energy—creates 27 percent more jobs than the International Energy Agency's business-as-usual scenario and 5 percent more than the growth-without-constraints scenario (Rutovitz 2010).
- In India, a study finds that low-carbon employment is one of the key co-benefits of promoting the renewables sector. It notes that solar power is more labor-intensive than wind power and better able to meet India's requirements for small-scale, off-grid power. Biomass, green transport, and public works in water and forest management are also attractive ways of achieving both employment and environmental objectives (GCN 2010).
- In China, a study emphasizes the possible employment losses from the planned sharp reduction in the energy intensity of Chinese industry, but notes that this could be outweighed by increased employment in renewables and—quantitatively, much more important—the shift of the Chinese economy toward services and away from heavy industry (GCN 2010).
- In Brazil, a study argues that renewable energy sources have a stronger potential in Brazil than is envisioned in official studies and government policies, both in contributing to CO_2 mitigation and generating jobs (GCN 2010).

What is the record of green fiscal stimuli on job creation in developing countries? The evidence is scant, but a few studies do show some job creation, with substantial variation in jobs created per dollars spent.

- In the Republic of Korea, forest restoration generated nearly eight times as many jobs per dollar as the least labor-intensive green objective, "vehicles and clean energy" (Barbier 2009).
- In China, biomass spending was found to be nearly 30 times more effective in generating jobs per dollar than wind

power (UNEP 2008). That suggests that the focus on renewable energy and low-carbon manufacturing prevalent in studies for Europe and the United States may miss the opportunities for employment creation from changes in land management and agriculture in developing countries, where these economic sectors are fairly more important.

- In Latin America, water network rehabilitation and expansion in Honduras is much more effective (by a factor of more than 10) in creating jobs than hydroelectric schemes in Brazil, with rural electrification in Peru falling in between (Schwartz and others 2009).

While useful, these studies have limitations. They do not discuss the capital constraints that may hamper the (public or private) investments needed to create the green jobs. They assume people will move seamlessly from one sector to another and ignore labor market rigidities. They tend to focus narrowly on the energy sector when green growth options (even when limited to climate change concerns) exist in other sectors that may be more labor-intensive. And they do not always distinguish between substitution (using more labor and less capital, energy, and other inputs) and lower productivity (using more inputs to produce the same amount of output). This distinction matters because capital-labor substitution is desirable, at least for countries with excess labor supply, large unemployment, and limited access to capital; lower productivity is not.

Another question worth asking is whether green spending is a good way of creating short-term employment during a crisis. The argument in favor of green fiscal stimuli is that they can both create jobs and lay the foundations for more sustainable growth. But experience suggests the need to look across the range of possible green works (from renewable energy to reforestation) as not all are equally labor-intensive and "shovel-ready."

To begin with, if employment creation is the objective, higher spending in sectors with lower capital intensities than either conventional or renewable energy—such as reforestation programs or even education and health services—may be more effective. But there may be tradeoffs between rapid employment creation and "greenness." Road building, for example, is fairly labor-intensive and can help to provide valuable infrastructure, but it is not particularly green. And some sectors, such as energy, will not top the list for sustainable rapid job creation, given that they require a long lead time for replacing capital.

And programs that yield larger employment effects tend to lead to more employment gains for largely lower skilled workers, so that the long-term growth effects are fairly small. Long-term development, including sustainable development, requires more of a focus on growth-enhancing infrastructure investment, which is not necessarily labor-intensive.

More analysis is needed of how global markets will affect job creation—leakages of green jobs and spending to other countries depend on endowments of skills, existing industry structure, the nature of the technologies newly deployed, and the ways that comparative advantage is exploited (GCN 2010).

The last point is a useful reminder that general equilibrium effects matter. Yet these are largely ignored in the green jobs literature. That may be particularly misleading for developing countries, as the next section discusses.

The effect of green policies on employment depends on labor market structure and the specific policy considered

The problem with studies that discuss job markets is that they tend to either model them as perfectly competitive, and thus adapting instantly to all shocks with no involuntary unemployment (the neoclassical model)—or as having involuntary unemployment that could be cleared with a fiscal stimulus (the Keynesian model). The first set of assumptions implies that green jobs are likely to displace as many jobs elsewhere in the economy.[5] The second, that there will be no crowding out of jobs by green fiscal stimuli.

Neither approach is realistic. Most developing countries have surplus labor economies, so estimates limited to direct employment creation in the green jobs literature might be less misleading for developing countries than for industrial economies closer to full employment. But it is more complicated in "dual" economies with modern and traditional sectors or in three-sector economies with a traditional rural sector and both formal and informal urban sectors characteristic of many developing countries (Harris and Todaro 1970; Mazumdar 1976). In that case the (skilled) formal urban labor market is often very shallow and green job creations can have crowding-out effects on other activities.

So knowing how best to model how the aggregate labor market works—and, indeed, how the macroeconomy as a whole works—is crucial to properly assess overall (net) job creation. Babiker and Eckaus (2007) illustrate the value of the implicit or explicit macroeconomic framework, showing how climate policy could increase unemployment in the presence of real wage rigidities or barriers to the sectoral reallocation of labor. Guivarch and others (2011) highlight that climate policy costs depend significantly on labor market rigidities and that policy cost estimates are much higher in models with imperfect labor markets. Overall, labor market impacts can also be influenced by how the revenues from other environmental taxes are used, as the literature on the "double dividend" from environmental taxation shows (Fullerton and Metcalf 1997; Sartzetakis and Tsigaris 2007). Studies tend to show that if tax revenues are used to reduce payroll tax—a tax on labor supply—employment will fall by less or even increase.

The key point is that the overall effects of green policies on employment depend on the characteristics of the economy's labor markets and the nature of the policy interventions, including their funding, not just the input requirements of rival energy technologies.

Indeed, underemployment can have multiple causes, and the consequences of green policies will differ depending on these causes. It thus helps to consider the implications of a wider range of theories of underemployment and labor market adjustment in different types of economy (box 4.1).

But environmental regulation need not kill jobs either

A major fear being voiced in the green jobs debate is that environmental regulation—needed to price externalities and encourage firms to change their production processes—will destroy jobs.

A tale of two antithetical hypotheses: the "pollution haven" and "Porter" hypotheses

For the past 20 years the debate on the implications of environmental policies on competitiveness (and jobs) has revolved around two antithetical hypotheses: the "pessimistic" pollution haven hypothesis, which contends that firms will flee locations with strong environmental regulations; and the "optimistic" Porter hypothesis, which argues that environmental regulation will lead to innovation (Porter and van der Linde 1995). In the latter, innovation reduces the cost of regulation (weak Porter hypothesis) and may lead to increased competitiveness and profitability (strong Porter hypothesis).

What is the latest thinking on this issue? As chapter 3 reported, there is no evidence that environmental policies have systematically led to job losses because of an exodus of firms to pollution havens. Tighter environmental regulation may cause firms to relocate, but they will choose locations that are more attractive overall, as pollution abatement costs represent a small share of production costs for most industries (Copeland 2012). Factors such as availability of capital, exchange rates, labor abundance, location, institutions, and agglomeration effects are more important than environmental policy in determining firm location and competitiveness. Empirical evidence from existing

BOX 4.1   A framework to estimate the impacts of green policies on jobs

How can policy makers determine if green policies will create jobs? The following provides a framework to assess labor market consequences, exploring what would happen in an economy with two sectors: a clean one and a dirty one. The products are imperfect substitutes that are produced with many inputs, including labor. The first two cases explore the impact of green growth policies that focus on the demand side, and the rest deal with policies that focus on the supply side.

Case 1. Demand deficit and a green stimulus

In this case the economy is typified by "Keynesian" unemployment—that is, with insufficient overall demand. The green policy involves a fiscal stimulus with spending focused on the clean sector. What would happen? Greater demand for the clean sector's product would stimulate greater employment in the clean sector, in turn pushing up wages in this sector, and thus increasing final demand. Increased demand in the labor market would put upward pressure on wages throughout the economy, possibly causing a slight decline in employment in the dirty sector. Overall, employment would be expected to rise as long as job creation in the clean sector outweighs the (indirect) job losses elsewhere, facilitating a virtuous outcome.

Case 2. A green paradox: demand deficit and a green stimulus meet a skills deficit

Here again we have a Keynesian economy, but there is a skills deficit in the clean sector. The green policy involves a fiscal stimulus with spending focused on the clean sector. Higher demand for the clean sector's products would feed into higher wages across the economy, because employment in the clean sector cannot expand, but overall employment levels would not expand much, and may even decline. Thus, the green fiscal stimulus would be largely ineffectual, generate higher wages, and create little (if any) additional employment. (In an open economy the green stimulus may trigger imports, in which case it would have little impact on employment.)

Case 3. Pollution regulation with virtuous initial conditions

Now the green policy involves a pollution tax to correct a pollution externality in the dirty sector, and there are no wage or price rigidities in the economy. Faced with an emissions tax, the optimum response would be a contraction of output and an investment in pollution abatement. What would happen? The regulations would be expected to destroy jobs in the dirty sector, given that the tax raises production costs with the dirty technology and the price of these goods rises. As a result, demand for the clean substitute good rises and employment in the clean sector increases—imparting incentives to reduce the externality either through new production techniques or end-of-pipe abatement, which would boost jobs in pollution abatement.

This scenario suggests that overall employment would increase when there exists a close and clean substitute produced with more labor-intensive technology or when abatement is feasible and more labor-intensive than dirty production (on the margin). This situation might apply to economies such as Japan's or the Republic of Korea's that are well endowed with labor skills and technology for cleaning up.

Case 4. Pollution regulation with immiserizing initial conditions

This is similar to the previous case but with two key differences: no clean substitute for the dirty good, and pollution abatement is either far too costly or unavailable, or is highly capital intensive. Production and employment in the dirty sector would decline, with little or no offsetting increase in cleaner jobs. This situation most likely applies to economies reliant on extractive industries—such as artisanal mining, where pollution abatement is typically far too costly for the small producers and there is no clean substitute available for the mineral.

Case 5. Renewable resource regulations—restore rents but not necessarily jobs

Here we have a classic open-access common-property resource such as a fishery. Entry occurs until the payoffs from harvesting decline to zero (or to the opportunity cost). If there is a tax or restriction on harvesting, this would lower employment but increase resource stocks and the payoffs. Thus, while employment may decline, economic returns increase and environmental benefits accrue. Conversely, if the policy were accompanied by expenditure on ecosystem restoration, there would be offsetting changes in employment, with ambiguous net impacts.

The bottom line is that the labor market consequences of green policies depend on the policy under consideration, technological parameters, and the state of the economy. There are cases where a given policy can create jobs, and other circumstances when it can destroy jobs.

Box text contributed by Richard Damania.

regulation or environmental taxes confirms this result (Anger and Oberndorfer 2008; Ellerman and others 2010; Martin and others 2011; Morgenstern and others 2002; Quirion 2011; Sartor 2012). But this evidence is based mostly on existing regulations in developed countries, and future research needs to ascertain whether these results extend to developing countries and to more ambitious environmental policies than have been applied to date.

For sectors intensive in natural capital—with which many developing countries are well endowed—the pollution haven hypothesis is even less likely. After all, without sound environmental policies, the increased pressures coming from trade could rapidly deplete natural capital, and then the short-term benefits from increased trade would be wiped out by the subsequent collapse of the resource base of the activity (Copeland 2012).

The reality is that stringent environmental provisions are essential for guaranteeing the long-term sustainability of the economic activities (and jobs) that depend on natural capital. If a natural resource base is well managed, it can be used to create jobs (moving up the value chain by creating a downstream processing sector, for instance) and seize opportunities in global markets.

At the firm level, studies show that the impact of more stringent environmental regulation on productivity and competitiveness is modest and sometimes even positive, thanks to innovation (Ambec and others 2011). The large body of literature triggered by the seminal paper by Porter and van der Linde (1995) supports the weak version of the Porter hypothesis: innovation does reduce costs.

Further, recent studies have found an increasing number of cases where environmental regulation had positive impacts on profits (Ambec and others 2011). This may be due to the fact that regulators have become better at designing smart regulatory policies, as well as that the models used to assess the effects of environmental regulation on innovation and competitiveness were refined to account for the lagged structure of innovation (essentially they wait a few more years to evaluate the impact, giving the firm more time to adapt).

Thus, the overall effect of environmental regulations on jobs is likely to be limited. In the United States, an econometric study of highly regulated industries finds that the impact of stringent environmental regulations on U.S. jobs was negligible in most cases—across all industries, 1.5 jobs were created per $1 million spent in additional environmental spending, with a standard error of 2.2 jobs (Morgenstern and others 2002).

Types of adjustment needed across countries

There is much variation across developing countries in the likely ease of transition to a low-carbon growth pathway. Chapter 3 shows that developing a comparative advantage in the production of equipment for low-carbon electricity depends on the manufacturing base of the country and on whether there are scale and learning economies in the technology. Some countries have a comparative advantage in particular renewable energy sources because of natural endowments. Brazil has the right climatic conditions and soils to give it a substantial cost advantage in biofuels, though other characteristics of the Brazilian economy also help, in addition to being very well endowed in hydroelectric potential (Kojima and Johnson 2005).

Developing countries that produce a high level of greenhouse gas emissions per unit of GDP face a more difficult challenge of structural adjustment. They are the ones in which more labor is likely to have to be reallocated from greenhouse gas–intensive activities, either by switching technologies within an industry or by moving labor between industry sectors. Given the importance of CO_2 emissions from energy production, energy-intensive economies will compose a large part of this group.

Endowments of fossil fuels combined with industrial development strategies that have favored carbon-intensive industry make a transition to low carbon much more challenging (EBRD 2011). If such economies impose a carbon tax, the standard economic policy instrument to internalize the greenhouse gas externality, the relative returns to different factors of production are likely to change. The few empirical studies focusing on how carbon taxation might affect factor returns suggest that the incidence of a carbon tax is likely to be regressive when emission abatement measures are capital-intensive, requiring complementary policies (Fullerton and Heutel 2007, 2010). Countries such as Kazakhstan and Mongolia, with a much larger-than-average proportion of the labor force in mining and energy supply, are more likely to suffer as a result of this adjustment and also from the difficulties of reallocating displaced labor to other sectors. Chapter 3 discusses how industrial and other sector-specific policies can facilitate this transition.

Smoothing the transition to greener growth paths for the labor market

Policy makers need to worry about skills that can limit job creation...

To what extent are the skills needed in the labor force for greener growth being altered? This matters because if the skills required are unavailable, that could place a major obstacle in the way of the transition to green growth.

Overall, "green restructuring" brings with it the usual challenges to policy makers trying to facilitate restructuring and reduce the labor market adjustment costs, including those from a changing skill mix. Many of the expanding industries are likely to be using new products and processes, reflecting the transition to low-carbon technologies, so the generic skill requirements of many of the newly created jobs are likely to be higher than average, as they have to allow for assimilation of unfamiliar tasks and working methods and "learning-by-doing." But a larger proportion of jobs in the renewable energy sector and in energy efficiency are lower skilled than in the fossil fuel energy sector (Pollin and others 2009). Contrary

to the coal industry—which employs many low-skill workers in developing countries—the oil and gas industries tend to have fairly well-paid workers and a large proportion of highly qualified engineers and technicians.

Perhaps the most thorough study of green growth and skills so far is ILO/CEDEFOP (2011), which reports and synthesizes the results of 21 country reviews. It notes that the demand for skills is being affected in three ways by the transition to green growth:

1. Induced structural change across industries increases the demand for skills specific to expanding industries such as renewable energy and reduces the demand for skills such as those for coal mining.
2. Some new occupations are emerging—such as photovoltaic (PV) fitters and carbon-footprint assessors—though there appear to be fairly few unique green skills.
3. The content of many jobs in current industries is changing, as companies focus on achieving better energy efficiency, switching from fossil fuel sources to renewable energy, and producing capital equipment for expanding green industries. In agriculture, low- and no-till agriculture and reduced use of fertilizers and pesticides will entail changes in farmers' practices, as will increased production of biofuel crops and efforts to increase forest cover—a development likely to have the most pervasive effects on labor markets, particularly in developing countries.

What is worrisome is that skill shortages may already be impeding the transition to green growth (box 4.2). In 2011 the OECD (2011a) drew attention to widespread skill shortages in energy-efficient construction and retrofitting, renewable energy, energy and resource efficiency, and environmental services. Many countries have reported specific bottlenecks, such as the shortage of skilled PV workers in Germany and the lack of design engineers for smart grids in the United Kingdom. Karp and Stevenson (2012) identify similar shortages in developing countries. In India, maintaining and operating the

---

BOX 4.2   Shortage of skills and inadequate training provisions can undermine green programs

The problems that can arise when training provision is not up to the challenge of the induced structural change are illustrated by Australia's experience with a new Home Insulation Program introduced in February 2009 as a key part of the government's fiscal stimulus.

The program was designed partly to generate jobs for lower skilled workers in the housing and construction industries. At the start of the program only supervisors were required to satisfy one of three minimum competences—prior experience in the insulation industry, qualifications in an approved trade, or insulation-specific training. The program proved popular. At its peak, demand was running at almost 2.5 times the anticipated level and some 1.1 million roofs of 2.7 million eligible were insulated. But fires,

fitters' deaths, and reports of fraud undermined public confidence, and the program was canceled in February 2010. A subsequent sample of inspections revealed that nearly 30 percent of installations had some level of deficiency. Investigations showed that low skill levels in the industry, inadequate provision of training, and poor management of the program were among the factors responsible.

The importance of competent project management and national policy making in this case is a reminder of the key role of higher level management and planning skills in a policy-induced transition to green growth that is likely to take sustained effort and policy credibility over a long period.

Source: Australian National Audit Office 2010.

---

renewable energy systems deployed by the Remote Village Electrification is complicated by the lack of skilled workers (IEA 2010).

In 2001 China started the Township Electrification Program to bring electricity to rural communities using solar PV, small hydro, and wind. While installation appears to be working well, there are problems with maintenance and operation, partly because of a lack of qualified electricians. Reasons for these reported shortages include the underestimation of the growth of certain green sectors, the general shortage of scientists and engineers, the low reputation and attractiveness of some sectors important for the green transition such as waste management, and a shortage of teachers and trainers in environmental service (ILO/CEDEFOP 2011).

Many of the skill shortages already reported in connection with green growth strategies appear to result from generic failings in education and training. And they reflect long-standing issues such as the lack of functioning universities and research centers, the mismatch between students' choices of discipline and the needed skills, the lack of incentives for employers to invest

in developing the transferable skills of their workforces, the lack of access for the disadvantaged to time and finance for training, and the stickiness of relative pay rates.

Fortunately, there is a potential for synergies between green policies aimed at skill development and growth policies aimed at increasing labor capital, worker education, and labor productivity. Figure 4.1 shows that many developing countries need to increase their enrollment in technical tertiary education. Such an increase would accelerate growth and help with skill limitations created by green policies.

...and learn from the lessons of trade adjustment

Green growth is about transforming our production and consumption processes from a dirty, environmentally unsustainable model to a sustainable one. Like any structural transition it inevitably entails transition costs, which green growth policies must seek to minimize. As such, the trade literature, which has extensively documented adjustment costs associated with trade liberalization, offers interesting insights.

Adjustment costs, whether stemming from trade shocks or a transition to green growth, are fundamentally driven by factor immobility—sluggishness in capital or labor market adjustments.[6] These costs would be zero were workers able to adjust instantly to the changing demand for skills (moving instantly from one industry to another) and were firms able to instantly modify their fixed capital following changes in carbon prices or pollution standards.

In the real world, labor markets are sluggish, as experience with trade liberalization shows. Trade liberalization creates and destroys jobs within industries. But the flow of labor across sectors—from shrinking to expanding ones—is slow. In Brazil it took several years for workers displaced from de-protected industries to be absorbed by sectors with comparative advantages (Muendler 2010). In addition, large wage differences persist among workers with similar qualifications and status across industries, suggesting limited mobility of workers across industries (if workers were mobile, they would switch to the highest paying industry until wages equalized). This "industry-effect" explains a large fraction of wage differences across workers, and prevails in both developed and developing countries, for skilled and unskilled workers (Krueger and Summers 1989).

What does this sluggishness stem from? Slow labor market adjustments reflect demand-side (industries requiring specific skills) and supply-side (worker characteristics) factors. Whether sector-specific knowledge and training are a bigger impediment to mobility than labor market frictions (the time and costs associated with search and matching) depends on the extent to which worker experience is specific to each sector (Cosar 2010; Dix-Carneiro 2010). And there appears to be significant variation in the mobility of different types of workers, with lower adjustment costs for younger workers and skilled workers. The policies needed to help transition may thus differ by country (depending on the nature of the adjustment) or by affected worker categories (depending on age, skill, and so on).

FIGURE 4.1 Many developing countries need to increase their enrollment in technical tertiary education
(enrollment in engineering, manufacturing, and construction in tertiary education as a percentage of the total population, 2009)

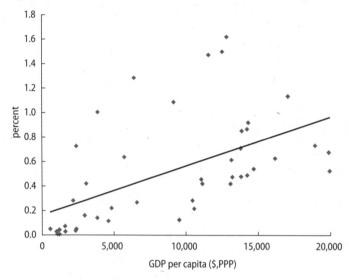

Source: Authors based on UNESCO Institute for Statistics, http://stats.uis.unesco.org/unesco/ReportFolders/ReportFolders.aspx (accessed March 18, 2012); World Bank 2011b.
Note: PPP = purchasing power parity.

As for capital stocks, a shift toward greener production processes is likely to require substantial changes, as firms may need to invest in new product lines, machines, and equipment. Yet, as experience with trade adjustment shows, the process may be quite costly—for example, following Argentina's trade reform, the required capital adjustment averaged 14.5 percent of firms' capital stock (Bet and others 2011). Thus, the capacity of economies to adjust to green policies may be limited by capital constraints, which could affect labor demand.

Because adjustment costs are a direct function of factor immobility, efforts to increase labor or capital mobility will be critical. And support policies should be targeted to facilitating the transition rather than cushioning potential losses. Simple unemployment insurance tends to hamper reallocation and skill formation. But employment subsidies can be useful if made conditional on working in the export-oriented (or green) sector (a form of industrial policy; see chapter 3).

Ultimately, the cost of the transition will depend on the overall economic policy framework and the extent to which it facilitates the emergence and growth of new sectors and firms. So the ability to carry out and reap the benefits of a green growth policy will depend on good economic policy.

In sum, fears that environmental regulations will lead to massive job losses or loss of competitiveness are probably as unfounded as the hope that green jobs will single-handedly solve countries' employment problems. That said, it is vital to invest in human capital to accelerate growth and to green growth. This is one of the inputs to economic production. Natural capital is another critical input, and the next chapter will look at why it is important to invest in this domain, too.

Notes

1. UNEP also includes a provision that "green jobs need to be decent jobs" (UNEP 2008).
2. At the same time developed countries are responsible for, by far, the largest share of the stock of greenhouse gases in the atmosphere. They have also probably made a disproportionate contribution to long-lived solid waste. So some of the green jobs reflect the unsustainability of developed-country economies.
3. See Kammen and others (2004) and Wei and others (2010) for a review.
4. Further, studies use a range of methods, reflecting the different definitions of green job creation discussed above, differ in coverage of countries and sectors and as to whether they include gross or net effects and whole value chain effects, and make varying assumptions concerning economic growth and business-as-usual scenarios (Bacon and Kojima 2011; Fankhauser and others 2008; GCN 2010; GHK 2009; Kammen and others 2004; Wei and others 2010). The few studies of developing countries conclude to significant job creation, but offer no analysis of the net impact (see box 4.2).
5. In such models implementing carbon pricing will tend to both redistribute labor to low-carbon activities and reduce overall labor supply due to the higher relative price of carbon-intensive goods and services. There can be net job destruction, depending on how the revenues from carbon pricing are used as in a study of the potential implications of a cap-and-trade system for the United States, which found significant reductions in labor input in 29 of 35 U.S. industries without revenue recycling (Goettle and Fawcett 2009).
6. For instance, Guivarch and others (2011) model economic transaction costs due to a climate policy with different levels of rigidity in the labor market, finding that mitigation costs are much larger when labor market imperfections are considered.

References

Ambec, S., M. A. Cohen, S. Elgie, and P. Lanoie. 2011. "The Porter Hypothesis at 20: Can Environmental Regulation Enhance Innovation and Competitiveness?" Discussion Paper 11-01, Resources for the Future, Washington, DC.

Anger, N., and U. Oberndorfer. 2008. "Firm Performance and Employment in the EU Emissions Trading Scheme: An Empirical Assessment for Germany." *Energy Policy* 36: 12–22.

Australian National Audit Office. 2010. "Report on the Home Insulation Program." Auditor General Report 12, 2010–11, Canberra.

Babiker, M. H., and R. S. Eckaus. 2007. "Unemployment Effects of Climate Policy." *Environmental Science & Policy* 10: 600–9.

Bacon, R., and M. Kojima. 2011. "Issues in Estimating the Employment Generated by Energy Sector Activities." Background paper for the World Bank Group energy sector strategy, World Bank, Washington, DC.

Barbier, E. B. 2009. "A Global Green New Deal." Policy Brief, United Nations Environment Programme, Geneva.

Bet, G., I. Brambilla, and G. Porto. 2011. "Trade Reforms, Wages and Employment with Labor Mobility and Capital Adjustment Costs." Working Paper, Universidad Nacional de La Plata, Buenos Aires.

Bowen, A. 2012. "Green Growth, Green Jobs, and labor Markets." Policy Research Working Paper 5990, World Bank, Washington, DC.

CCICED (China Council for International Cooperation on Environment and Development). 2011. "Development Mechanism and Policy Innovation of China's Green Economy." CCICED Task Force Report, CCICED Annual General Meeting, November 15–17.

Copeland, B. R. 2012. "International Trade and Green Growth." Paper presented at the Green Growth Knowledge Platform inaugural conference, Mexico City, January 12–13.

Cosar, A. K. 2010. "Adjusting to Trade Liberalization: Reallocation and Labor Market Policies." University of Chicago, Booth School of Business, Chicago.

Dix-Carneiro, R. 2010. "Trade Liberalization and Labor Market Dynamics." CEPS Working Paper 212, Princeton University, Department of Economics, Center for Economic Policy Studies, Princeton, NJ.

EBRD (European Bank for Reconstruction and Development). 2011. *Special Report on Climate Change: The Low Carbon Transition.* London: EBRD.

Ellerman, A. D., F. Convery, and C. de Perthuis. 2010. *Pricing Carbon.* Cambridge, UK: Cambridge University Press.

European Commission. 2007. *Facts and Figures: Links between EU's Economy and Environment.* Luxembourg: Office for Official Publications of the European Communities.

Fankhauser, S., F. Sehlleier, and N. Stern. 2008. "Climate Change, Innovation and Jobs." *Climate Policy* 8: 421–9.

Fullerton, D., and G. Heutel. 2007. "Who Bears the Burden of a Tax on Carbon Emissions in Japan?" *Environmental Economics and Policy Studies* 8: 225–70.

———. 2010. "Analytical General Equilibrium Effects of Energy Policy on Output and Factor Prices." NBER Working Paper 15788, National Bureau of Economic Research, Cambridge, MA.

Fullerton, D., and G. E. Metcalf. 1997. "Environmental Taxes and the Double-Dividend Hypothesis: Did You Really Expect Something for Nothing?" NBER Working Paper 6199, National Bureau of Economic Research, Cambridge, MA.

GCN (Global Climate Network). 2010. "Low-Carbon Jobs in an Interconnected World." Discussion Paper 3, GCN, London.

GHK. 2009. "The Impacts of Climate Change on European Employment and Skills in the Short to Medium-Term: A Review of the Literature." Final Report to the European Commission Directorate for Employment, vol. 2, Social Affairs and Inclusion Restructuring Forum, London.

Goettle, R. J., and A. A. Fawcett. 2009. "The Structural Effects of Cap and Trade Climate Policy." *Energy Economics* 31 (Special Supplement 2): 244–53.

Guivarch, C., R. Crassous, O. Sassi, and S. Hallegatte. 2011. "The Costs of Climate Policies in a Second Best World with Labour Market Imperfections." *Climate Policy* 11: 768–88.

Harris, J. R., and M. P. Todaro. 1970. "Migration, Unemployment, and Development." *American Economic Review* 60: 126–42.

Ho, M. S., R. D. Morgenstern, and J-S Shih. 2008. "Impact of Carbon Price Policies on U.S. Industry." Discussion Paper 08-37, Resources for the Future, Washington, DC.

IEA (International Energy Agency). 2010. *Comparative Study on Rural Electrification Policies in Emerging Economies: Keys to Successful Policies.* Paris: IEA.

ILO/CEDEFOP (International Labour Organization and European Centre for the Development of Vocational Training). 2011. *Skills for Green Jobs: A Global View.* Geneva: ILO.

Kammen, D. M., K. Kapadia, and M. Fripp. 2004. "Putting Renewables to Work: How Many Jobs Can the Clean Energy Industry Generate?" Report of the Renewable and Appropriate Energy Laboratory, University of California, Berkeley.

Karp, L., and M. Stevenson. 2012. "Green Industrial Policy." Paper presented at the Green Growth Knowledge Platform inaugural conference, Mexico City, January 12–13.

Kojima, M., and T. Johnson. 2005. "Potential for Biofuels for Transport in Developing Countries." Energy Sector Management Assistance Programme, World Bank, Washington, DC.

Krueger, A., and L. Summers. 1989. "Efficiency Wages and the Inter-Industry Wage Structure." *Econometrica* 56: 259–93.

Martin, R., U. J. Wagner, and L. B. de Preux. 2011. "The Impacts of the Climate Change Levy on Manufacturing: Evidence from Microdata." NBER Working Papers 17446, National Bureau of Economic Research, Cambridge, MA.

Mazumdar, D. 1976. "The Rural-Urban Wage Gap, Migration, and the Shadow Wage." *Oxford Economic Papers* 28 (3): 406–25.

Michaels, R., and R. P. Murphy. 2009. "Green Jobs: Fact or Fiction? An Assessment of the Literature." Institute for Energy Research, Houston, TX.

Morgenstern, R. D., W. A. Pizer, and J.-S. Shih. 2002. "Jobs versus the Environment: An Industry-Level Perspective." *Journal of Environmental Economics and Management* 43 (3): 412–36.

Morriss, A. P., W. T. Bogart, A. Dorchak, and R. E. Meiners. 2009. "Green Jobs Myths." Law & Economics Research Paper LE09-001, University of Illinois, Champaign, IL.

Muendler, M. 2010. "Trade Reform, Employment Allocation and Worker Flows." In *Trade Adjustment Costs in Developing Countries: Impacts, Determinants and Policy Responses*, ed. G. Porto and B. M. Hoekman, 103–42. Washington, DC: World Bank.

OECD (Organisation for Economic Co-operation and Development). 1999. *The Environmental Goods and Services Industry: Manual for Data Collection and Analysis*. Paris: OECD Publishing.

———. 2011a. "Labor Markets in the Transition to Green Growth: Challenges and Policy Responses." OECD, Paris.

———. 2011b. *Towards Green Growth: A Summary for Policy Makers*. Paris: OECD Publishing.

Pollin, R., H. Garrett-Peltier, J. Heintz, and H. Scharber. 2008. "Green Recovery: A Program to Create Good Jobs and Start Building a Low-Carbon Economy." University of Massachusetts Political Economy Research Institute and the Center for American Progress, Amherst, MA, and Washington, DC.

Pollin, R, J. Heintz, and H. Garrett-Peltier. 2009. "The Economic Benefits of Investing in Clean Energy." University of Massachusetts Political Economy Research Institute and the Center for American Progress, Amherst, MA, and Washington, DC.

Porter, M., and C. van der Linde. 1995. "Towards a New Conception of the Environment-Competitiveness Relationship." *Journal of Economic Perspective* 9 (4): 97–118.

Porto, G. 2012. "The Cost of Adjustment to Green Growth Policies: Lessons from Trade Adjustment Costs." Paper prepared for the Green Growth Knowledge Platform inaugural conference, Mexico City, January 12–13.

Quirion, P. 2011. "Les quotas échangeables d'émission de gaz à effet de serre: éléments d'analyse économique." Mémoire d'habilitation à diriger les recherches, École des Hautes Études en Sciences Sociales, Paris.

Rutovitz, J. 2010. "South African Energy Sector Jobs to 2030" Paper prepared for Greenpeace Africa by the Institute for Sustainable Futures, University of Technology, Sydney, Australia.

Sartor, O. 2012. "Carbon Leakage in the Primary Aluminium Sector: What Evidence after 6½ Years of the EU ETS?" CDC Climate Research Working Paper 2012-12, Caisse des Dépôts et des Consignations, Paris.

Sartzetakis, E. S., and P. D. Tsigaris. 2007. "Uncertainty and the Double Dividend Hypothesis." Nota di Lavoro 99.2007, Fondazione Eni Enrico Mattei, November.

Schwartz, J. Z., L. A. Andres, and G. Draboiu. 2009. "Crisis in Latin America. Infrastructure Investment, Employment and the Expectations of Stimulus." Policy Research Working Paper 5009, World Bank, Washington, DC.

UNEP (United Nations Environment Programme). 2008. *Green Jobs: Towards Decent Work in a Sustainable, Low-Carbon World*. Washington, DC: Worldwatch Institute.

———. 2011. *Towards a Green Economy: Pathways to Sustainable Development and Poverty Eradication—A Synthesis for Policy Makers*. Geneva: UNEP. http://www.unep.org /greeneconomy.

Wei, M., S. Patadia, and D. M. Kammen. 2010. "Putting Renewables and Energy Efficiency to Work: How Many Jobs Can the Clean Energy Industry Generate in the US?" *Energy Policy* 38: 919–31.

World Bank. 2011a. *South Africa Economic Update—Focus on Green Growth*. Washington, DC: World Bank.

———.2011b. *World Development Indicators*. Washington, DC: World Bank.

World Bank and DRC (Development Research Center of the State Council, China). 2012. "Seizing the Opportunity of Green Development in China." Supporting Report 3 for *China 2030: Building a Modern Harmonious, and Creative High-Income Society*. Washington, DC: World Bank.

Natural Capital: Managing Resources for Sustainable Growth | 5

Key Messages

- Sustainable management of natural capital underlies green growth in key sectors—such as agriculture, manufacturing, and energy—and is vital for resilience and welfare gains.
- Different resources require different types of policies. For extractable but renewable resources, policy should center on defining property rights and helping firms move up the value chain. For cultivated renewable resources, policy should focus on innovation, efficiency gains, sustainable intensification, and "integrated landscape" approaches.
- The elements of natural capital cannot be regarded in isolation. Integrated landscape approaches can increase production of both "regulating" and "provisioning" services of natural capital.
- In some cases, growth and green outcomes—such as cleaner air, cleaner water, less solid waste, and more biodiversity—will involve tradeoffs. But not all of these tradeoffs are inevitable: innovation, which can be supported through smart subsidies, can help minimize or eliminate some of them.

Meeting peoples' needs for food, fuel, and fiber depends on sound management of the natural capital—agricultural lands, forests, water, fisheries—on which production of these goods depends. Manufactured goods also depend on sustained production from natural capital, such as subsoil assets.

But what exactly is natural capital? The term refers to the stock of natural resources that provides flows of valuable goods and services. Major types of natural capital include agricultural lands; subsoil assets (oil, gas, coal, and minerals); forests; water; fisheries; and the atmosphere.[1] Goods and services provided by natural capital underpin conventionally measured economic growth by providing inputs to agriculture, manufacturing, and services and by increasing the productivity of agriculture and the reliability of infrastructure services through climate control.

Complementing natural capital with human, physical, and social capital greatly increases its productive capacity. But the extent to which other forms of capital can substitute for natural capital is bounded, because people require water, food, and air to live, and demand for water and food will increase as population and incomes rise.

How can better management of natural capital lead to green growth? Sustainable management of capture fisheries can increase economic returns. Restoration and enhancement of watershed services can enhance agricultural productivity. Conservation of biodiversity can generate economic returns through nature-based tourism and bioprospecting. Rents accrued from mineral extraction can be invested in infrastructure and human capital, thus generating economic returns.

But achieving these outcomes is not easy, given the myriad market and institutional failures at play. What is needed, therefore, is a package of measures encompassing both price and nonprice interventions to enhance the management of natural capital. Reaping higher economic returns from natural forests, for example, requires aligning policies, incentives, capacity, and governance. Reaping higher returns from mineral extraction requires policies that increase production efficiency, fiscal policies that are fair to both the government and investors, and public expenditure policies that encourage the reinvestment of income for broader development gains.

This chapter explores how better managing natural capital can promote green growth. It looks at four broad categories: (1) extractable renewable resources (capture fisheries, natural forests, soil, and water); (2) cultivated renewable resources (crops, livestock, aquaculture, and forest plantations; (3) nonrenewable resources (oil, gas, coal, and minerals); and (4) ecosystems that provide regulating services (watershed management, climate regulating services, and nature-based tourism). The first three categories provide "provisioning" services (those that directly produce goods and services, such as food and water); the fourth embraces "nonprovisioning" services (those that provide regulating services, supporting services, and cultural services).[2]

The key finding is that sustainable management of natural capital is essential for green growth in key sectors—such as agriculture, manufacturing, and energy—and is vital for resilience and welfare gains. The type of measure (both price and nonprice) needed will vary with the type of resource being targeted:

- For extractable but renewable resources, policy should center on defining property rights and helping firms move up the value chain.
- For cultivated renewable resources, policy should center on innovation, efficiency gains, sustainable intensification, and "integrated landscape" approaches that can lead to productivity gains without damaging the environment.[3]
- For nonprovisioning services, efforts should concentrate on increasing knowledge of the economic value of these services and incorporating these values in policy decisions.
- For nonrenewable resources, the focus should be on minimizing environmental damage and recovering and reinvesting rent optimally for broader economic development.

Second, the elements of natural capital cannot be regarded in isolation. Integrated landscape approaches can increase production of both "regulating" and "provisioning" services of natural capital—for example, by integrating the production of crops, trees, and livestock on the same land area or by managing animal waste to enhance soil fertility and produce energy rather than contributing to pollution. But solutions need to be adapted to local circumstances and need to include the right policy measures to provide incentives for innovation and adoption.

Third, in some cases, growth and green outcomes—such as cleaner air, cleaner water, less solid waste, and more biodiversity—will involve tradeoffs. These tradeoffs are most common in current cultivation practices in agriculture, livestock, aquaculture, and plantation forests. But not all of these tradeoffs are inevitable: innovation, which can be supported through smart subsidies, can help minimize or eliminate some of them.

Extractable renewable resources: Defining property rights and moving up the value chain

Extractable renewable resources (capture fisheries, natural forests, soil, and water) are often, though not always, common property resources—goods from which it is difficult to exclude potential users, whose consumption precludes consumption by others. The inability to exclude users often leads these resources to be managed under open access property rights regimes, under which no economic returns or rents accrue to the scarce natural capital. Under such a scenario, more factors of production are employed in the extraction of the resource than is efficient, and more of the resource is extracted, accelerating its depletion.

If property rights were established, total output would increase (perhaps after a lag during which the resource regenerates itself), and rents would accrue to the scarce natural resource. Some factors of production, such as labor, could, however, be worse off once property rights were established, unless the rents were redistributed (Weitzman 1974). The fact that establishment of property rights can reduce the returns to labor may explain the resistance to introducing such rights. These potential losses should be weighed against enhanced productivity, which can improve overall economic welfare and, with a supportive policy environment, can enhance opportunities for moving up the value chain (by shifting from extraction alone to downstream processing), providing new job opportunities.

Capture fisheries

Globally, capture fisheries added $80 billion in gross value and provided direct and indirect employment to more than 120 million people in 2004 (World Bank and FAO 2009). But because fish are mobile, marine capture fisheries are very difficult to manage: only a handful of fisheries are being managed reasonably efficiently.

The open access nature of capture fisheries has led to overcapitalization, rent loss,

and overexploitation. Because of a shrinking resource base, the growing number of fishers and fishing overcapacity, the catch per fisher and per vessel has been declining globally—despite significant technological change and investments in vessel capacity (figure 5.1). The prevalence of subsidies has reduced the cost of fishing below its economic cost and has contributed both to overfishing and resource depletion and to the economic waste associated with overcapacity (World Bank and FAO 2009).

The good news is that well-managed fisheries could accrue rents as high as $50 billion (World Bank and FAO 2009), which could be used to build wealth or increase productivity. Establishing property rights would help unlock the potential economic value of fisheries. But defining and enforcing these rights remains a challenge. High-sea capture fisheries (beyond the exclusive economic zone) are dominated by large commercial vessels, which are often largely unregulated, overcapitalized through subsidies, or both.[4]

For their part, inshore capture fisheries have long been used as a safety net

FIGURE 5.1 Current fishery practices are not sustainable
(productivity of global fishing fleet, 1970–2005)

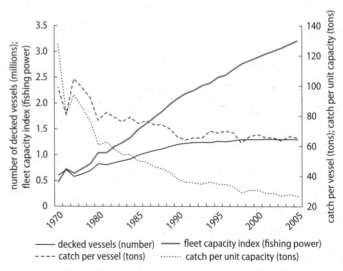

Source: World Bank and FAO 2009.
Note: The fleet capacity index is the relationship between the capacity of a fishing fleet to catch a particular quantity of fish and the quantity of fish it actually catches.

for the rural unemployed; for this reason, policy makers resist altering the status quo. Success stories suggest that policy interventions that directly address the job loss associated with defining property rights can make green growth politically feasible (box 5.1). In addition, moving up the value chain can help create jobs that are more productive. However, such "industrial" policies may not reflect the country's comparative advantage and would need to be justified on a case-by-case basis (Hausmann and others 2008).

Natural (including managed) forests

Natural forests (including natural forests that are actively managed) provide a range of extractable commodities (from timber to wood fuel to various nontimber forest products) and a range of ecosystem services (from regulation of soil, water, and the climate to sequestration of carbon and provision of habitats). In Africa alone, forests account for 65 percent of the total primary energy supply. Nontimber forest products (fruit, nuts, medicinal plants, and game) are an important source of rural livelihoods.

Global demand for industrial wood was about 1.8 billion cubic meters in 2010, and

it is projected to rise to 2.6 billion cubic meters by 2030, with most of the increase coming from Asia and Eastern Europe (FAO 2011).[5]

How will this growing demand be met given that natural forests are often not well managed? The global rate of deforestation remains high, especially in tropical regions, with deforestation averaging about 1 percent a year in Latin America and Africa over the 1990–2010 period. The encouraging news is that the rate of deforestation has been declining since 2000 (FAO 2011), with impressive declines in some key countries such as Brazil. Moreover, some areas—such as temperate and boreal zones and some emerging economies—have witnessed increases in forest area through both natural forest recovery and reforestation. Indeed, more than 80 percent of traded timber is produced in temperate countries.

A problem for the world's forests—80 percent of which are publicly owned—is poorly defined property rights. In many developing countries, forests are often treated as de facto open access areas. Significant progress has been made in recent years toward devolving full or partial forest management to local communities to deal with the problems associated with open access

---

BOX 5.1 Job creation and revenue generation from off-shore capture fisheries in Namibia

Soon after gaining independence from South Africa in 1990, the new Namibian government declared an extended economic zone, established a coherent fisheries policy, and enacted comprehensive fisheries legislation based on long-term fishing rights (rights-based management) and payments for these rights. At the same time, it focused on the "Namibianization" of the processing sector. Before independence, all fish were exported (or transshipped at sea) whole and frozen for later processing into value-added products abroad. By investing in local processing capacity, Namibia created many jobs and increased the industry's

value added (although it also created considerable processing overcapacity).

With an average catch of 500,000–800,000 tons a year (in 2003 the total catch was about 636,000 tons), the fisheries sector's contribution to gross domestic product rose from about 4 percent at independence to 10.1 percent in 1998. About 95 percent of Namibia's total fish production is exported, yielding about $375 million in foreign exchange in 2005. About 14,000 people were employed in the fisheries sector in Namibia in 2003, about half of them in onshore processing.

Source: http://www.fao.org/fishery/countrysector/FI-CP_NA/en.

BOX 5.2   Reform of forest tenure in Albania and China

In Albania serious degradation of the forests and pastures was observed in the early transition years. To address the problem, the government reformed and decentralized national institutions and increased support to pasture and forest management at the local level. Reforms transferred management rights of forests and pastures to local communities. To deal with fire management and control illegal logging, the government adopted a cross-sectoral approach. It provided local investment support for the restoration of watersheds, forests, and pasture land using participatory planning approaches. This support included small-scale investments in the planting of forests and orchards in degraded lands, the thinning and cleaning of degraded forests and pastures, and measures to control erosion and grazing. This mix of policy, social, and natural capital investments enhanced resilience (erosion control and soil restoration), yielded environmental benefits (carbon sequestration), increased efficiency (greater

pasture and forest productivity), created jobs, and reduced poverty.

In China, the government has made substantial investments in tree planting across the country over the past 25 years to restore environmental balance and secure supplies of raw materials. It has also reformed forest user rights to collective forests (forests under the control of provinces and other subnational authorities). Like reforms to property rights of agricultural lands, these reforms sought to harness the productive energies of rural households and communities. They amount to the largest transfer of forest wealth ever recorded. Most reforms involve provisions that offer individual households a large degree of economic autonomy and independence to manage the forests, with households and farmers' groups receiving certificates of use rights.

Source: World Bank 2010b, 2010c.

---

regimes (box 5.2). But there have been few assessments of the impact of changes in forests management regimes on the rate of deforestation or the productivity of forests. A review of 42 studies on community forest management concludes that little is known about the effect of community forest management on improving the productivity of forests or reducing poverty (Bowler and others 2010).

Another problem is that assessments of the economic value of forests are rare, especially in developing countries, particularly when it comes to valuing the economic contribution of nontimber forest products. These products are undervalued because, in many countries, they are not reflected in national accounts systems, in part because they are produced informally. For example, in Europe, where these products are economically marginal, they were valued at $7 billion in 2010. In contrast, in Africa, where they are much more important economically, they totaled only an estimated $0.5 billion (FAO 2011).

Where these assessments do exist, they suggest that a number of factors limit the value added from these resources. A meta-study of 61 case studies of production of and trade in nontimber forest products in Africa, Asia, and Latin America finds that, by and large, commercialization has not helped reduce poverty, for four reasons:

- Resources are often collected under open access regimes, where overexploitation is common, leading to rent dissipation.
- Access to markets tends to be poor, limiting economic returns.
- Fluctuations in quantity and quality make commercialization of nontimber forest products difficult.
- Middlemen often capture the bulk of added value (Belcher and others 2005).

As with capture fisheries, increasing the economic returns from natural forests sustainably requires a package of measures that includes strengthening property rights; assessing the economic value of forests; and adopting measures, such as better market access and improved product quality, that increase economic returns and reflect the full value of the service.

Soil

Soil quality reflects how well a soil performs the functions of maintaining biodiversity and productivity, supporting plants and other structures, and providing a slew of other nonprovisioning ecosystem services. Land degradation includes deterioration of soil quality, vegetation, and water resources (Nkonya and others 2011). It is a process that affects all agroecological zones, potentially reducing GDP (table 5.1). A quarter of the world's agricultural land is estimated to be seriously degraded (Bai and others 2008).

Factors leading to land degradation include poor agricultural and grazing practices and forest degradation as well as factors outside the renewable natural resource sector, including poorly designed infrastructure and mining activities. Land degradation can, in turn, affect the operation of infrastructure installations by silting up key facilities such as ports and hydroelectric power generation facilities.

Land users need to be given the right economic incentives to invest in preventing or mitigating land degradation. The strength of these incentives depends on the nature of land tenure regimes (Deininger and Feder 2001; López 2002) and on the way costs and benefits are shared. Costs, for example, are often borne only by the farmer, whereas environmental benefits accrue to society as a whole.

Well-defined, transparent, and secure land tenure systems are essential if farmers are to undertake the long-term conservation that underpins agricultural production and investments to improve natural capital and productivity. In Rwanda, for example, land tenure reform led to a rapid doubling of investment in soil conservation, with even larger increases for plots managed by female farmers (Ali and others 2011). Secure land tenure also leads to the development of land markets, which improves overall allocative efficiency and the possibility of using land as collateral in formal credit markets. That said, land registration and tenure systems must be adapted to local conditions and customs (Deininger and Feder 2001). In Africa, approaches to land use rights increasingly recognize that customary and modern systems may exist side by side.

On-site approaches, such as conservation agriculture, can be tapped to foster natural ecological processes to increase agricultural yields and sustainability. This approach, which dates back to the 1930s, is based on three main principles: continuous minimum mechanical soil disturbance; permanent organic soil cover; and diversification of crop species grown in sequences, associations, or both (FAO 2001). Its use yields environmental benefits (decreased nutrient pollution of waterways, increased carbon sequestration in soils), increases the efficiency of production (through the use of lower levels of energy inputs), increases resilience (through frequent crop rotation), and increases long-run agricultural productivity (through decreased erosion and enhanced soil structure). Local conditions should dictate the technology (box 5.3).

Conservation agriculture tends to involve up-front costs (for new machinery necessary for direct seeding or for tree seedlings in

TABLE 5.1   Poor soil quality and land degradation hurt economic growth

Country	Type of degradation	Percentage of GDP lost
Central African Republic	Cropland and soil	1.0
Colombia	Land	0.8
Egypt, Arab Rep.	Soil	1.2
Ghana	Agricultural soils, forests, and savanna woodlands	5.3
Pakistan	Soil salinity and erosion	1.2
Tajikistan	Land, including soil erosion and salinity	3.7

Source: Country Environmental Analyses conducted by the World Bank (World Bank 2005a, 2006a, 2006b, 2007c, 2008b, 2010a).

BOX 5.3   Conservation agriculture in Brazil and Zambia

Conservation agriculture first emerged in the 1930s during the severe dust storms in the United States. It has been gaining momentum worldwide since the 1990s, when it was employed to deal with soil erosion crises in southern Brazil. Its use is now widespread globally. By 2007, for example, zero-tillage practices were in use on about 43 percent of arable land in Latin America (World Bank 2007a).

In Brazil, conservation agriculture relies on a variety of technologies, depending on the region. One approach supports a mixed livestock and crop system, rotating pastures with crops. The zero-tillage system supplies residual nutrients for cheap pasture, thereby reducing pests, weeds, and diseases. The most common rotations are soybeans, cotton, and maize, followed by 1–3 years of pasture. These practices have increased pasture stocking rates and have reduced soil degradation and water runoff.

In Zambia, five basic conservation farming technologies are being used: retaining crop resi-

dues, concentrating tillage and fertilizer application in a permanent grid of planting basins or series of planting rows, completing land preparation in the dry season, weeding aggressively to reduce plant competition, and intercropping or rotating nitrogen-fixing legumes on up to 30 percent of cultivated area.

Many farmers also incorporate nitrogen-fixing trees, which provide fodder and fuelwood. As of 2010, Zambia had restored 300,000 hectares in an effort that involved more than 160,000 households. Conservation agriculture practices doubled maize yields over those achieved with conventional plowing systems, and increased cotton yields 60 percent. A recent study finds returns of $104 per hectare for plots under conservation agriculture in Zambia—5.5 times the $19 per hectare of plots under conventional tillage (FAO 2010a).

Source: Landers 2005; FAO 2010a; Scherr and others 2011.

agroforestry systems) and short-term yield reductions as farm systems are changed. Benefits may materialize only in the medium to long run. Smart subsidies and access to long-term financial markets can help cover short-run costs and increase adoption.

Focusing public support measures on soil fertility can yield impressive results. In Brazil—where state support of agriculture is just 5 percent of aggregated gross farm receipts compared with an average of 18 percent in Organisation for Economic Co-operation and Development (OECD) countries in 2010 (OECD 2011)—the government has concentrated on investments in soil fertility enhancement, land and water management systems, and crop and livestock breeding for varieties adapted to Brazil's climate and ecosystems. Brazil's public support of research and soil fertility has paid off handsomely, helping transform the country from a net food importer into a global food exporter.

Water

The sustainable management of water resources is becoming more urgent than ever as several global trends collide.[6] In developing countries, growing populations are increasing demand for water to produce essential commodities like food and energy. Higher rates of urbanization fuel demand for water for domestic and industrial uses, putting stress on existing raw water sources. Exacerbating matters, climate change increases the risks of greater water variability.

One big worry is water scarcity. Developing countries account for 71 percent of global water withdrawals, and their demand is expected to increase by 27 percent by 2025 (from 2010). In 2010, about 44 percent of the world population lived in areas of high water stress, and projections indicate that an additional 1 billion people will be living in areas with severe water stress by 2030 (OECD 2008). And many countries in Asia and North Africa are exhibiting moderate or extreme scarcity, which is expected to increase in the future.

Another worry is poor water quality, which sets back growth because it degrades ecosystems; causes health-related diseases; constrains economic activities (such as agriculture, industrial production, and tourism); reduces the value of property and assets; and boosts wastewater treatment costs. For example, the annual costs of poor water quality stand at 0.6 percent of GDP in Tunisia and 2.8 percent of GDP in the Islamic Republic of Iran (World Bank 2007b).

Yet another worry is natural hazards—the vast majority of which involve water—which affect almost everyone and retard growth. Kenya, for example, was hit by several disasters over a 3-year period that undid years of economic growth (an extreme flood cost its economy 16 percent of GDP, and extreme drought 11 percent of GDP) (World Bank 2004). And when these natural hazards strike, it is the poor who suffer most, because of their locations, low incomes, insufficient infrastructure, and greater reliance on climate-sensitive sectors like agriculture.

What can policy makers do to better manage water resources? Four green growth water policies—none of them easy to design or implement—can be adopted:

- *Correct distortions in water allocation decisions.* New mechanisms for allocating water resources should embrace economic principles of allocative efficiency to correct for market failures and imperfections. These failures are compounded by the sector's political economy and the fact that more efficient water pricing boosts costs for some elements of society more than others. Decision makers need to devise efficient and flexible ways to allocate water among competing quantity and quality demands for human use (energy, agriculture, fisheries, and urban consumption) and ecosystems health (forests and wetlands) (World Bank 2010d). A study of China finds that improving water allocation could increase per capita income by 1.5 percent a year between 2000 and 2060 (Fang and others 2006).

- *Expand the use of water pricing mechanisms to manage demand.* The price of most water services does not include investment, operation, and maintenance costs or the scarcity value of the resources. Pricing could be used as an effective instrument to ensure the resource's optimal allocation. Most countries fail to use it because of the political and social sensitivities of water management, particularly the need to ensure affordability for the poorest communities. Most countries allocate surface and groundwater by assigning fixed quotas to major sectors and activities. Although far from effective, these quotas have been politically and socially acceptable. In the short term, they seem to be a more realistic option than full cost pricing.

- *Create new markets.* Tradable water rights are an effective water management instrument in the long term but have proven difficult to implement in the short term in most developing countries—partly because success depends greatly on sound design and partly because it takes a long time to establish the necessary institutions (World Bank 2010d). Thus, in the short term, it is imperative to ensure that the proper institutional arrangements and capacities are in place.

- *Strengthen the framework for analyzing the relationship between growth and water.* There have been few attempts to analyze and quantify the relationship between water and economic growth and development because of the complex spatial and temporal dimensions of water and its management. There is a need to strengthen this analytical framework by examining regional differences in growth within a country or group of countries. This information would allow more informed decision-making processes by providing a clear understanding of the economic tradeoffs of policies in different sectors (such as energy, agriculture, urban, land use, environment, and health).

Cultivated renewable resources: Innovation, sustainable intensification, and integrated landscape approaches

Food production will need to increase by 75 percent between 2010 and 2050 to cope with rising demand caused by population and income growth and changes in the structure of demand. As incomes increase, demand for higher-value horticultural and livestock products is likely to increase by more than direct demand for staples; demand for livestock products will likely increase 85 percent between 2010 and 2030 (Foresight 2011). Yet hunger remains a challenge: 800 million people in the world remain food insecure. Improving agricultural productivity and access to food remain core elements of an inclusive growth agenda.

For cultivated renewable resources, the main policy challenges are to support sustainable increases in productivity and resource-efficient production by focusing on innovation, increasing efficiency in input use, regulating pollution, and ensuring that smallholder farming more fully realizes its potential, especially in lower-income developing countries. In the future, a larger share of fish and wood products is likely to come from aquaculture and plantation forestry than from natural forests or wild fisheries, further increasing the importance of sustainable management of cultivated renewable resources in meeting green growth objectives.

Agriculture, including livestock

Agricultural production is strongly affected by how natural capital—especially energy, land, water, forest, marine, and coastal systems—is managed. Agriculture, including livestock, accounts for 70 percent of fresh water consumption and 40 percent of land area. Many agricultural systems depend heavily on fossil fuels for nitrogen fertilizer, crop husbandry, harvesting, transport, and pumping water for irrigation. Thus, food and fossil fuel energy prices are closely linked. There are synergies and tradeoffs between maximizing production of food at low cost and conserving the environment. These synergies need to be maximized and the tradeoffs managed.

Strategies in support of a green growth agenda for agriculture need to differentiate between agriculture-dependent, transitioning, and urbanized economies and between land and water–dependent and land and water–abundant ecosystems and countries. In agriculture-dependent countries, agricultural productivity and inclusive growth are closely related: GDP growth in these sectors is estimated to benefit the poor two to four times as much as GDP growth in other sectors (World Bank 2007a). Four elements may be considered in a green growth strategy for agriculture.

Increasing productivity while improving land and water management. Intensification—producing more with less—has been responsible for the dramatic rise in global cereal yields in recent decades. From 1960 to 2010, rice yields rose 250 percent (from 1.8 to nearly 4.5 tons per hectare [Dobermann and others 2008; International Rice Research Institute data]), while between 1965 and 2000 cultivated land area increased by just 20 percent (from 125 million to 150 million hectares [Khush and Virk 2005]). Attaining the same production increase with no growth in yields would have required increasing the area planted with rice to 300 million hectares, reducing further land availability for wetland or watershed protection functions. Extensive, poorly managed agricultural and grazing systems, often related to poverty and lack of access to finance or knowledge, contribute to the land degradation and loss of soil fertility described above. Sustainable intensification can protect biodiversity, reduce deforestation, save water, and reduce greenhouse gas emissions. By integrating improved land, soil, and water management measures into production systems, such intensive systems can also increase productivity while maintaining and even enhancing the value of natural capital.

In a number of agricultural systems intensification has been accompanied by negative environmental consequences. Excessive and poorly managed fertilizer and agrochemical use has polluted water bodies and soils; runoff has created "dead zones" in coastal areas that cover about 245,000 square kilometers worldwide, mostly in OECD countries.[7] Agricultural run-off from intensive farming is the single greatest water polluter in China and other intensively farmed countries, including Denmark, the Netherlands, and the United States (Chinese National Census of Pollution 2010; Scheierling 1996).

Similar tradeoffs are linked to livestock production. In the United States, for example, production efficiency in the dairy industry soared over the past 60 years. In 2007, producing 1 billion kilograms of milk required just 10 percent of the land, 21 percent of the animals, 23 percent of the feed, and 35 percent of the water used to do so in 1944. But there were plenty of negatives, including the geographical concentration of livestock waste, increased water and air pollution, and reduced animal welfare. These problems could be avoided with the right mix of incentives and regulation to protect water bodies and manage waste. Productivity increases, innovation, and genetic improvements are a "low-hanging fruit": in India, average milk yields are only 3.4 kilograms per day compared with the world average of 6.3 kilograms, and only 20 percent of animals are cross-bred; doubling productivity would halve greenhouse emissions per cow.

But in Colombia, a mix of policies has supported sustainable productivity increases for livestock by encouraging landscape-based, mixed agro-sylvi-pastoral systems. The aim is to introduce trees and better pasture in grazing lands, provide improved fodder and shade, and reduce heat stress for animals and soil degradation. The results are impressive—including increased meat and milk yields as well as improved water infiltration, increased bird populations, reduced methane generation, and improved carbon capture (López 2012). This livestock policy is part of a broader land use policy intended to support sustainable intensification together with forest and landscape restoration. These approaches have helped achieve "triple wins" of increased productivity, enhanced resilience to climate variability, and reduced carbon emissions ("climate-smart agriculture").

Some agricultural subsidies exacerbate the negative effects of intensification. In land-scarce, intensely farmed agricultural systems with already high levels of inputs, subsidization of inorganic fertilizer encourages overuse, with deleterious effects on the environment (box 5.4). However, in countries with low-input/low-output systems, a fertilizer subsidy may initially be justified to increase yields and enhance vegetative growth and soil carbon.

BOX 5.4 The use and misuse of agricultural input subsidies in India

In India, fertilizer and other input subsidies contributed to rapid development of irrigation and more intensive farming methods, resulting in increases in yields and food security: by 2010, irrigated wheat yields in some provinces averaged 4.5 tons per hectare, up from 1.5 tons per hectare in 1975. However, subsidized energy is now contributing to excess groundwater withdrawals (about 75 percent of groundwater used in Punjab and Harayana originates from overexploited aquifers), requiring pumping water from ever-deeper aquifers and salinization of aquifers in some areas. In addition, the fertilizer subsidy—which cost the government $30 billion (2 percent of GDP) in 2008—is contributing to excessive use of nitrogen compared with phosphorus and potassium, exacerbating nitrate pollution of rivers and aquifers.

Source: Prince's Charities' International Sustainability Unit 2011.

Increasing efficiency and reducing waste. Reducing food waste involves some of the same issues encountered in increasing energy efficiency: even where the saving potential is huge, many barriers, including transactions costs, prevent efficiency-increasing investments from being made. The problem has been recognized for decades, but limited progress has been made. In both agriculture-dependent and OECD countries, up to one-third of food is lost or wasted. The reasons for this waste—and the solutions to the problem—vary with the settings (Foresight 2011).

In agriculture-dependent countries, where food accounts for a large share of household expenditure (46 percent in Pakistan), there is little household waste, despite lack of refrigeration at home. But 15–30 percent of food produced is lost before it reaches markets, because of postharvest losses caused by poor storage and inefficient transport systems. The problem is compounded by food quality and food safety issues, which may preclude poor farmers from participating in value chains (Gómez and others 2011). For low-income countries, the following strategies could reduce food waste:

- Diffusing existing knowledge and technology in storage and investing in transport infrastructure.
- Investing in new technologies to reduce postharvest waste.
- Using information and communication technology to improve market information, helping match supply and demand in local markets.
- Investing in capacity building, infrastructure, and regulatory improvements in food quality and food safety.

OECD countries have developed efficient supply chains from farm to market, with low spoilage rates and effective transport systems. But about one-third of food supplied is nevertheless wasted through losses in supermarkets (food thrown away because it is not sold by the sell-by date), losses in homes (food discarded before it is used), and plate waste (food that is served but not consumed). Because food accounts for a relatively small proportion of household expenditure in OECD countries (11 percent in Germany, 7 percent in the United States), there is little price incentive to avoid waste. However, new technologies, such as enhanced sensor technologies to monitor the edibility of food, could help reduce wastage. The main challenge is changing consumer behavior.

Harnessing technology. Technological innovation plays a key role in green growth strategies for agriculture. It can be used to increase input efficiency, as is the case in irrigation water management, where advances in the use of remote sensing technologies permit estimation of crop evapo-transpiration (the sum of evaporation and plant transpiration to the atmosphere) on farmers' fields and facilitate improvement of water accounting at the regional and basin-wide levels. China is adopting this approach with its Xinjiang Turpan Water Conservation Program, in an arid part of the country (World Bank 2010c). This program monitors basin-wide evapo-transpiration with remote sensing and supports a combination of engineering, agronomic, and irrigation management measures to increase agricultural productivity measured in terms of evapo-transpiration. Innovation includes developing agricultural products that feature improved characteristics, such as being drought resistant, requiring less fertilizer, and being resistant to common pests and diseases (which reduces the need for pesticides)—as India is doing with better backyard chickens (box 5.5).

Innovation can also be used to increase access to weather and climate information services for farmers, which improves resilience, increases efficiency, and raises income. In Florida, a timing tool helps farmers reduce the quantity of fungicide they use, reducing the harmful effects on the ecosystem and saving them money (Pavan and others 2010). But in many developing countries and transition economies, investment and expenditure in the classic public goods of weather and climate information generation and services is far too low (World Bank 2008a). A 2010 study by NetHope in Kenya indicates that farmers gain access to information through a

---

BOX 5.5   Producing a better backyard chicken in India

Kegg Farms in India has bred a robust and improved dual-purpose backyard chicken. The "Kuroiler" lays 100–150 eggs a year (many more than the 40 eggs a year the Desi chicken lays) and grows to 2.5 kilograms in about half the time a Desi chicken reaches 1 kilogram. The chickens typically command a premium of about Rs 60 per kilogram over other broiler chickens, because the meat is darker and more flavorsome.

Kegg Farms produces about 16 million day-old chicks a year, which it sells to 1,500 small enterprises that raise the chicks for about two weeks before inoculating them and selling them to about 6,500 bicycle salespeople, who sell them to some 800,000 farmers, most of them women, many located in some of the remotest parts of the country. The turnover in sales of chicks is about $5 million a year, with another $5 million turnover by the thousands of small, rurally based businesses that grow and sell the chicks.

An independent assessment indicates that the average gross revenue generated per Kuroiler chick (as eggs and meat) is $3.10. With some 16 million chicks distributed annually, total output is about $50 million, with a net profit of about $10 million. Profits from the Kuroiler are significantly higher than profits from the Desi bird. The Kuroiler birds contribute significantly to household cash flow. Women have maintained control over their chicken-growing enterprises as the business has become more commercial.

The success of Kegg Farms reflects several factors. Its chickens are more robust than other chickens, are better able to scavenge food, and have higher food conversion ratios. The company's business model features a devolved, rural-based distribution system with in-built incentives.

Source: Isenberg 2006.

---

range of methods, including SMS (cell phone messaging), radio, newspapers, and extension officers.[8]

Changing the structure of support policies. Changes in the structure of support policies can also help manage potential tradeoffs. In the European Union (EU)—and to a lesser extent the United States—the past 20 years have been characterized by a shift away from highly distortive price and quantity instruments (target prices, export subsidies, and quotas) toward lump-sum payments. The policy change has weakened the incentives for farmers to use polluting inputs, such as fertilizers and pesticides. Between 1991 and 2006 fertilizer use decreased in most EU member countries, though it increased in new member countries (Eurostat 2011). Moreover, as agricultural transfers became decoupled from production, they became increasingly subject to environmental provisions.[9]

Aquaculture

In 2009, humans consumed 117 million tons of fish—almost half of which was produced on farms (FAO 2010b). By 2030, this figure is expected to rise to 140 million tons. Capture fisheries are not expected to support the higher demand, leaving aquaculture to meet shortfalls in supply.

As in the livestock industry, competition, economies of scale, and economies of agglomeration have increased productivity but have pushed some systems into potentially damaging environmental practices. Farms tend to concentrate where there is expertise, good land, water resources, and marketing infrastructure. This crowding has sometimes led to overuse of ecosystems services, pollution, and massive fish kills. Agglomeration in the Norwegian salmon farming industry, for example, has reportedly improved the transfer of knowledge and increased the supply of specialized production factors, but it has also helped spread fish disease (Tveteras and Battese 2006).

There are two approaches to greening aquaculture. The first is zoning—that is, leaving adequate space between farms and interspersing a variety of aquaculture systems (including a mixture of species at the farm or watershed level) and water uses between major centers of production. This approach would hinder disease transmission, moderate negative impacts on wild fish populations, and reduce the contribution of aquaculture to water eutrophication.

The second approach is creating synergies with other economic activities in the watershed. The farming of aquatic plants (such as seaweed) and the filter feeding of detritivorous organisms (such as mussels, clams, and sea cucumbers, which together represent about 40 percent of total global aquaculture) reduce nutrient loading from livestock, agriculture, and other sources. Fish production in cages or culture-based fisheries can be conducted in reservoirs and irrigation systems to amortize costs, improve water quality, reduce weeds, and replace wild catch where dams have destroyed indigenous fish stocks. Mixed fish and rice production systems are widespread in low-lying areas and flood plains, taking advantage of synergies between the water and land management approaches.

Although dispersing fish farms is good for the environment, it does raise costs, in part because of the losses from agglomeration. Thus, green growth strategies will require practical financial and market incentives to support spatial dispersing, technical guidelines on green technology, and government policies that encourage investors to avoid the traditional practice of copying successful production/ market models and instead explore new partnerships at the watershed level.

Plantation forests

Afforestation—the planting of forests in areas that were not forested in recent times—is expected to meet an increasing share of the demand for wood and fiber, possibly reducing pressure on primary and natural forests. In 2010, the global area under plantation forests (forested areas artificially created by planting or seeding) accounted for 7 percent of total forest area and 40 percent of industrial timber production (FAO 2011). Plantation forests provide a growing share of industrial timber, both because the area

under plantation forests has increased and because productivity has risen. Areas under bamboo and rubber plantation are also increasingly being used to provide timber products, providing an important source of income for rural households. Reforestation and restoration of degraded woodlands also play a role in plantation forestry.

Whether plantation forests help or hurt the environment depends on the land use systems they replace. In China, for example, bamboo plantations have helped control soil erosion by replacing agriculture on steep slopes. But in some provinces, where plantations have replaced natural forests in areas not well suited to bamboo, soil erosion has increased. The Chinese government has tried to address these negative environmental effects by establishing environmental regulations, but these regulations have been resisted in some cases (Ruiz-Perez and others 2001). More recently, China has supported programs with species better adapted to local ecosystems (World Bank 2010c).

Agroforestry systems, in which trees are incorporated into the broader production landscape, are widespread in some areas. They can yield the "triple wins" of climate-smart agriculture by enhancing productivity, resilience, and carbon sequestration, as they have in Kenya and the Sahel (Liniger and others 2011).

Nonprovisioning services: Creating knowledge and markets for economic valuation

In addition to ecosystems that provide food and water ("provisioning services") are ecosystems that regulate, support, and offer cultural services ("nonprovisioning" services). This group includes nature-based tourism supported by biodiversity, watershed services, and climate-regulating services. The main challenge in this area is to create markets for these services so that they become part of the visible economy and are efficiently provided.

Another challenge is coping with the timing of benefits. Although efforts to reduce the loss of ecosystem services are likely to boost growth in the near term, efforts to restore these services take a long time and are unlikely to do so in the near term (Vincent 2012).

Biodiversity

Biodiversity refers to the degree of variation of life forms, including all animals, plants, habitats, and genes. It matters because genetic diversity provides the basis for new breeding programs, improved crops, enhanced agricultural production, and food security. When species become extinct or habitats are threatened, biodiversity is reduced; according to the International Union for Conservation of Nature, 875 species went extinct (or extinct in the wild) in 2008. Ecosystem fragmentation can contribute to species loss, especially for large predators, leading to a cycle of habitat degradation.

Tropical, temperate, and boreal forests (forests in northerly latitudes) are home to the vast majority of the world's terrestrial species. They play a major role in biodiversity and provide cultural, recreational, and other supporting services, such as soil and water conservation. For this reason, 12 percent of the world's forests are designated for the conservation of biodiversity—an increase of more than 20 percent since the 1990s (FAO 2010a).

A key reason why the world has experienced such a dramatic loss in biodiversity is the difficulty of valuing it, given knowledge, time, and spatial asymmetries. Building a road around, rather than through, a fragile ecosystem increases its cost by a known amount, payable immediately; the benefit of protecting the ecosystem and its inherent biodiversity is much more difficult to value and accrues only over time. At the global level, many efforts are under way to protect biodiversity, dating back to the 1992 Convention on Biological Diversity. At the local level, the incentive could come in part from the economic returns that biodiversity can generate through nature-based tourism and bioprospecting.

Nature-based tourism. Nature-based tourism (or ecotourism) is defined by the International Ecotourism Society as "responsible travel to natural areas that conserves the environment and sustains the well-being of local people." It is one of the fastest-growing sectors in the tourism industry, with annual growth rates of 10–12 percent (TIES 2006). Nature-based tourism aims to combine stringent environmental provisions with the generation of local economic revenues, thus concurrently triggering positive development impacts and incentives to conserve natural capital.

Nature-based tourism can be a significant source of employment, economic growth, and revenue (including foreign exchange) (Aylward and others 1996; Wunder 2000). A study of nature-based tourism in Zambia estimates that ecotourism generated 3.1 percent of GDP in 2005 (agriculture contributed 6.5 percent, mining 8.6 percent, and manufacturing 10.6 percent) (World Bank 2007d). Potential tradeoffs between rural livelihoods and nature-based tourism need to be managed by involving local communities. Indeed, the success of a nature-based tourism initiative is often linked to such involvement, which requires establishing incentives for local people to effectively protect their community's natural capital (box 5.6). Tourism revenues are only a partial solution, however, as many important ecosystems have only limited appeal for tourists.

Bioprospecting. Bioprospecting is the search for genetic material from plants or animal species that can be used to develop valuable pharmaceutical (or other) products. It represents a second example of how the creation of a market can provide incentives to protect biodiversity, although in practice it is hard to achieve (Polasky and others 2005). Returns to bioprospecting are often too low to provide sufficient incentives to conserve biodiversity, and disputes arise over the distribution of rents resulting from discoveries. The Access and Benefit Sharing provisions of the Convention on Biological Diversity may help alleviate this problem.[10]

BOX 5.6   Involving local communities in nature-based tourism in Indonesia

The Komodo National Park is a protected marine area in the Lesser Sunda Islands of Indonesia. This World Heritage Site was established in 1980 to protect the habitat of the Komodo dragon. Since then, its goals have expanded to include protection of the area's many coral species and nearly 1,000 fish species.

In 2005, a nonprofit joint venture, Putri Naga Komodo (PNK)—comprising The Nature Conservancy, a local tourism company, and the International Finance Corporation—was set up to run the area. The aim is to protect biodiversity and enable local communities to benefit from the park in a sustainable way—through carefully managed nature-based tourism, alternative livelihoods for local people, and collaborative protection strategies, such as antipoaching patrols. All proceeds go toward stewarding biodiversity and developing alternative and sustainable livelihoods for the local communities.

PNK, which is the exclusive manager of the venture, has invested $1 million in helping people in the park develop new activities, such as woodcarving and textile weaving. It has also provided them with technical assistance to develop sustainable seaweed farms, as well as facilitate the breeding of high-value reef fish to substitute for threatened wild fish. These efforts notwithstanding, a recent evaluation report (Agardy and others 2011), while acknowledging the project's positive impacts, raises concerns about the sustainability of the results, given the difficulties encountered in making this public-private partnership work.

Source: The Nature Conservancy website (http://www.nature.org/); Catherine Cruveillier-Cassagne (personal communication).

Watershed services

Watersheds—that is, the area of land where all of the water that is under it or drains off it goes into the same place—provide a range of ecosystem services, supplying water and hydroelectric power, regulating water flows and floods,[11] controlling soil erosion, and creating habitats for wildlife. Because of spatial trade-offs—and in some cases open access regimes—the market often underprovides these services, creating the need for public intervention. To correct this market failure, governments have been investing directly in the restoration and enhancement of watershed services through initiatives such as watershed development programs. Payments for such environmental services are a recent policy innovation to create markets and provide incentives to conserve or generate these services.

Support for investments in soil and water conservation. Investments in soil and water conservation normally include support for a mix of measures adapted to local conditions, including landscape restoration, erosion control, grazing management, water harvesting, and agricultural productivity support measures. At lower altitudes in irrigated landscapes, they often include support for improved irrigation water management, drainage, and salinity control. Such integrated programs have been supported to scale in a number of countries and include a mix of private and public investment measures.

In Turkey, better land management practices—promoted through investments in watershed rehabilitation and landscape restoration and reforestation programs, as well as profound changes in agricultural policy—have led to greening in the interior of the country, despite declining rainfall and increased temperatures in these areas. However, it is unclear whether this "regreening" also led to increases in rural incomes and employment.

In India, where several watershed development programs have been tried in semiarid rain-fed regions of the country, the verdict is still out. These programs seek to increase agricultural productivity by controlling soil erosion, preventing siltation of water bodies, and improving the reliability of water resources. They also hope to provide employment opportunities and improve the availability of drinking water, particularly during the summer. Between 1996 and 2004, the government of India spent more than $6 billion on watershed development (WRI 2005), but no systematic, large-scale assessment of the impact of these programs has been conducted (Joshi and others 2004).

There are nevertheless some positive results for integrated landscape approaches. In Kazakhstan, the Syr Darya/Northern Aral Sea Control program in the lower Syr Darya watershed supported innovations in water management, combining "soft" and "hard" infrastructure solutions and flood management, which helped restore river functions and the Northern Aral Sea, leading to recovery of grazing lands, ecosystems, and fisheries (World Bank 2011b). In Rwanda, the land husbandry, water harvesting, and hillside irrigation programs have already increased yields and incomes and have reduced soil losses (World Bank 2011a).

Payments for ecosystem services. The Pago por Servicios Ambientales (PSA) program, implemented in Costa Rica in 1997, was one of the first schemes to pay people to provide ecosystem services. Under this program, private landowners and communities receive payments for conserving the forest and helping protect water quality downstream. Financing for the scheme comes from donor grants, earmarked taxes, and buyers of ecosystem services, including municipal utilities. Other examples of payments for ecosystem services include schemes established to eliminate or reduce animal waste and agricultural chemical residues to protect water reservoirs, payments to landowners to encourage conservation, and REDD+ schemes, under which payments will be made for carbon sequestration services and to provide an incentive to reduce deforestation and forest degradation.[12]

In some developing countries, policy makers have tried to design payment for ecosystem services programs to benefit the poor, but the evidence on both the environmental and the poverty reduction effects of payment programs is thin (Pattanayak and others 2010). In China's Sloping Land Conversion Program, average household incomes remained unchanged, although incomes increased for some households and decreased for others. In addition, increased availability of fodder to improve income from livestock rearing, and extension services to improve agricultural productivity have helped compensate households for the loss of agricultural incomes from the conversion to forests. In Ecuador, Costa Rica, and Mexico, large-scale payment for ecosystem services schemes (table 5.2) may have benefited the poor, although assessments remain to be done.

Whether the poor are helped will no doubt depend on the scheme's design. Those based on land diversion (from current use to a use that is more oriented toward the provision of environmental services) are likely to benefit the landed, some of whom are poor—although they could also hurt poor households, especially the landless, by reducing access to key natural resources. Those based on working lands are likely to increase the demand for labor and may thereby benefit the poor. However, schemes expected to meet poverty reduction goals may be less effective in meeting environmental goals (Jack and others 2008). Where the poverty reduction impacts are likely to be small, it may be better to design schemes to be as effective as possible in achieving environmental goals and draw on other instruments to reduce poverty (Bond and Mayers 2009; Wunder 2008).

Climate-regulating services

Natural capital—including the oceans, land, and their living organisms—plays a key role in climate regulation.[13] However, the value of these key regulating services is not adequately captured through markets, and valuing them is difficult.

One of the most important services that forests, soils, and water provide is storing carbon. Indeed, out of the 9 gigatons (Gt), or billion tons, of CO_2 emissions released in 2007, the

TABLE 5.2 Impacts of payment for ecosystem services schemes on poverty reduction

Country/study	Scheme	Seller characteristics/results	Payment	Impact on income
China/Bennett (2008)	Sloping land conversion program	Tens of millions of rural households; 9 million ha of marginal sloping lands converted from agriculture to forests, 4.92 million ha of degraded lands reforested	Annual in-kind payment of grain (1,500–2,250 kg per ha), cash subsidy ($36 per ha), and free seedlings. Length of subsidy depends on type of forests. Income from forests and grasslands tax free	Mixed results: in Gansu, 50% of participants lost 8% of 1999 household net income; in Sichuan, 30% lost 11% of net income; in Shaanxi, 7% lost 33% of net income; estimates do not include net present value of future income from trees and grasses
Costa Rica/ Pagiola (2008)	Payments for environmental services	Private landowners, indigenous communities; 270,000 ha enrolled in 2005	$64 per ha per year for forest conservation and $816 per ha for 10 years for timber plantation (15% of which goes toward transactions fees)	Bulk of benefits goes to larger and better off farmers, but no assessment of impact on poverty reduction
Ecuador/Wunder and Albán (2008)	PROFAFOR	109 private landowners (50- ha minimum contract size), 43 communities.	$100–$200 per ha to cover plantation costs; 70–100% value of harvested wood, 100% of nontimber forest products	Upfront payment of $60–$635 per household (6–50% of household expenditure); income of $7–$2,481 per household from harvesting

oceans absorbed about 2Gt and terrestrial ecosystems about 2.7Gt. The remaining half remained in the atmosphere, increasing the concentration of CO_2 and contributing to global warming (World Bank 2010d). Maintaining and, where possible, increasing the sequestration capacity of terrestrial, coastal, and marine ecosystems thus plays an important role in mitigating climate change.

Healthy ecosystems that sequester carbon also function better in flood and erosion management, increasing the adaptive capacity of ecosystem services such as agriculture, forestry, and fisheries in the following ways:

- Coastal ecosystems (including mangroves and wetlands) reduce erosion and flooding and provide spawning grounds for marine species.
- Freshwater wetlands and floodplains maintain water flow and quality, acting as floodwater reservoirs and water storage facilities in times of drought; they also provide grazing land for livestock and aquatic habitats.
- Forests and vegetation stabilize slopes, control erosion and flash floods, and conserve soil fertility for agriculture.

- Integration of trees into agricultural production systems builds climate resilience.

However, ecosystem losses reduce their effectiveness as carbon sinks and their role in adaptation. Under current management regimes, land-based ecosystems in some countries contribute significantly to greenhouse gas emissions: emissions from agriculture, land use change, and forestry (deforestation, degradation, and fires) account for more than 30 percent of greenhouse gas emissions (forests account for about 17 percent and agriculture another 14 percent) (UNFCCC 2007).

Overall, more progress has been made in recognizing the importance of terrestrial ecosystems in climate regulation than in marine ecosystems, and more progress has been made in recognizing the role of forests in climate mitigation than of soils (UNEP and others 2009). Total carbon stocks in vegetation and in the top meter of soils are estimated at 466Gt (vegetation) and 2,011Gt (soil) (Ravindrah and Ostwald 2008; Watson and others 2000). The top meter of soil is important because annual crops depend on its quality and organic content for growth. For tropical forests, nearly half of the 428Gt of carbon stocks is from above-ground vegetation; in tropical savannahs, 80 percent of the 330Gt of carbon stocks is from soil.

Much work remains to be done to incorporate agricultural and grazing land and soils into climate change regimes. Only one pilot program in Africa, the Agricultural Soil Carbon Project, has benefited from financial support from carbon finance through the BioCarbon Fund.[14] The project supports increased agricultural productivity, agroforestry, and sustainable land management practices on more than 65,000 hectares in western Kenya; farmers benefit from selling carbon sequestered both in and above the soil as a result of improved farming practices (World Bank 2011a). The Clean Development Mechanism recognizes emissions from livestock and paddy rice as major sources of emission, especially in more intensive farming systems in East Asia and OECD countries.[15]

Lessons can be learned from the progress made on forests, including the work on REDD+. As countries prepare REDD+ strategies, they must address carbon monitoring, reporting, and verification as well as challenges regarding tenure rights to carbon stored or sequestered, potential tradeoffs between conservation and development, the rights of indigenous people and forest-dependent communities, and the tradeoffs between carbon sequestration and other ecosystem services, such as biodiversity.

Increasingly, countries are weighing co-benefits from adaptation and local income generation as they develop REDD+ strategies (box 5.7). However, given the modest development of international carbon markets, it is important to manage expectations regarding potential revenues from these sources over the next few years (FAO 2010a).

The role of marine ecosystems in adaptation and mitigation has received relatively little attention, partly because of their complexity, their status as an international common property resource, and the absence of robust mitigation metrics. Focusing first on coastal ecosystems in relatively shallow waters, where restoration approaches are well known, would be a low-risk, shorter-term strategy that could restore their capacity in oxygenating coastal waters, provide nurseries for fish stocks, and shelter coastal settlements

---

BOX 5.7   Scoring a triple win in Ethiopia by restoring the landscape

The overexploitation of forest resources in Ethiopia has left less than 3 percent of the country's native forests untouched. In Humbo, near Ethiopia's Great Rift Valley, deforestation threatens groundwater reserves that provide 65,000 people with potable water. It has caused severe erosion, resulting in floods and mudslides. With a population that depends heavily on agriculture, exacerbation of droughts and floods creates poverty traps for many households, thwarting efforts to build up their assets and invest in a better future.

Under the Humbo Assisted Natural Regeneration Project (implemented with the help of World Vision), farmer-managed regeneration of the natural forest encourages new growth from felled tree stumps that are still living. The regeneration of nearly 3,000 hectares has resulted in increased production of wood and tree products, such as honey and fruit, which has increased household revenues. Improved land management has also stimulated grass growth, providing fodder for livestock that can be sold as an additional source of income. Regeneration of the native forest is expected to provide an important habitat for many local species and reduce soil erosion and flooding.

The forest now acts as a carbon sink, absorbing and storing nearly 0.9 million tons of CO_2 over the project life. The project is the first large-scale reforestation project in Africa to be registered with the United Nations Framework Convention on Climate Change. The operation is regarded as a model for scaling up under a broader green growth and landscape restoration strategy for Ethiopia.

Source: Brown and others 2011.

from storms while additional scientific work is undertaken on assessing technical strategies for using oceans as potential carbon sinks (UNEP and others 2009).

Nonrenewable resources: Promoting rent recovery and reinvestment

Economic growth in countries with nonrenewable resources is a process of extracting resources efficiently and investing revenues from these resources in other forms of productive capital that can continue to produce income after the nonrenewable resources are depleted. Only in this way can these resources be used to promote sustainable development.

Some nonrenewable resources are essential for green growth. The generation of solar power uses silicon; devices that control vehicle exhaust and refining processes for cleaning fuels require precious metals to act as catalysts; wind turbines, semiconductors used in smart grids and other computer applications, and batteries for hybrid vehicles require rare earths; and almost all processes require steel, which is made from iron, carbon, and alloying elements. Natural gas is a relatively clean fuel; because it can readily generate power on demand, it complements solar and wind power well.

Avoiding the natural resource curse

One major problem for countries with abundant natural resources is what is known as the natural resource curse. This phenomenon refers to the economic observation that countries rich in natural assets—particularly oil, gas, and minerals—often fail to use these resources as a platform for sustainable growth and actually grow less rapidly than similar countries without such assets. These countries—such as the Democratic Republic of Congo, Guinea, Nigeria, and República Bolivariana de Venezuela—fail to transform natural capital into other types of capital, such as human capital and infrastructure.

Early explanations of the resource curse focused on economic factors, such as the difficulty of managing revenue volatility or the negative impact of exchange rate appreciation on the more technologically sophisticated manufacturing sector (Dutch disease). Such analysis left open the question of why some countries were able to overcome these economic hurdles.

The current consensus is that the resource curse is the result of weak governance (institutional capital) and human capital (Gelb and Grasmann 2010). Concentrated resources, coupled with very large investments, are easily subject to capture. Instead of directing their energies toward productive activities and the development of the institutions needed in a market-oriented economy, political and economic elites engage in "rent seeking," using their proceeds to reward their supporters and stifle dissent by potential reformers. During downturns, the government finds it difficult to adjust to lower levels of spending, because the survival of the regime may depend on rent allocation. In short, resource rents are used not to develop other forms of productive capital but to perpetuate the political regime and its inefficient economic policies. Once trapped in the resource curse, it is difficult to escape, because the elite have little incentive to do so. In the extreme case, the resource curse can lead to armed conflicts as a way to determine access to the rents.

Not all resource-rich countries get trapped by the resource curse. Some (like Australia, Botswana, Canada, Chile, and Kazakhstan) have managed to avoid it altogether. Others (like Ghana, Peru, and Zambia) suffered the resource curse earlier in their development but went on to enjoy steady growth in the past 10–15 years. Moreover, many of the fastest-growing countries in the world in the past decade have been mineral-rich countries, some of which were once victims of resource curse, although the sustainability of such growth has not been tested by a significant drop in resource prices or production.

Given that most of the fastest-growing countries in Africa since 2000 have large extractive industries—with major investments ongoing or planned—it is particularly important that these countries act now to avoid the resource curse. History shows that countries that have successfully managed concentrated natural resources for economic development have tended to have a cadre of strong technocrats, pointing to the importance of developing human capital. Countries that have recently become resource abundant, such as Mongolia and Mozambique, need to be as transparent with their rents as possible (through the Extractive Industries Transparency Initiative and other means); set up a means of smoothing volatile revenue, such as a fiscal stabilization fund; and focus on policies and programs to build human capital and competitive industries.

Even where growth has been rapid, the presence of nonrenewable resources can skew income distribution in undesirable ways. In Equatorial Guinea, for example, one of the richest and most resource-dependent countries in Africa, 77 percent of the population lives on less than $2 per day (Goldman 2011). Institutional innovations can help countries avoid this outcome. Botswana and Norway, which have strong institutional capacity, have managed their resource rents well. That even countries with a history of political instability—such as Chile, Indonesia, and Malaysia—have used resource rents effectively for economic development suggests what can be achieved (Gelb and Grasmann 2010).[16]

Managing resource revenues

How can policy makers promote efficient production, rent recovery, and rent reinvestment in ways that support broader economic growth? First, they can adopt saving mechanisms, such as fiscal stabilization funds and saving funds, which help smooth expenditure and ensure that funds are used only when the country has the capacity to absorb the new investment. Second, they can use the nonrenewable resource rents to help overcome market failures or deficiencies—such as inadequate skills, poor health and social protection, lack of infrastructure (especially electricity), and high business transactions costs. Third, they can avoid using these rents to promote industries in which their country has no or little comparative advantage.

The World Bank's comprehensive wealth accounts—notably, its adjusted net savings (ANS) indicator—assess whether countries rich in subsoil assets are using their natural capital to support sustainable development through rent capture and reinvestment (World Bank 2005b, 2010b). These accounts can help countries assess whether they are on a sustainable development path. Unlike national accounts, which measure gross savings and depreciation of produced capital but do not record changes in the stocks of human and natural capital, ANS measures the change in a country's national wealth. Since 2000, many low-income, resource-rich countries have failed to leverage their nonrenewable resources for broader development. In fact, their ANS indicators were negative for several years and were relatively low when positive, suggesting that they may be running down their total wealth (figure 5.2). High-income non-OECD countries are also exhausting their natural resource wealth. The Wealth and Valuation of Ecosystem Services Initiative is being used to pilot incorporation of natural resource depletion or restoration, including renewable natural resources, into national accounts in a number of OECD and developing countries.

Practicing sustainability in mining

The largest source of employment in nonrenewable industries comes from artisanal and small-scale mining. This sector contributes to livelihood development, creating tens of thousands of jobs in many countries and hundreds of thousands in several countries (including the Democratic Republic of

FIGURE 5.2   Not enough wealth creation from natural capital

(adjusted net savings of resource-rich countries, by income group, 2000–08)

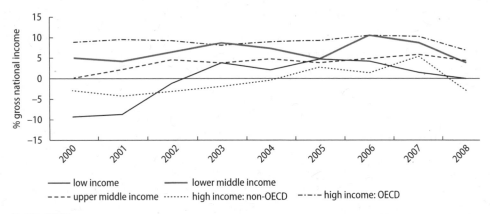

Source: World Bank 2010b.
Note: Adjusted net savings (ANS) measures the change in a country's national wealth. A positive ANS indicates that the country is adding to its wealth; a negative ANS indicates that the country is running down its capital stocks.

Congo and Ghana). But for the sector to be sustainable, there needs to be a long-term commitment by the government and strong local institutions.

Artisanal and small-scale mining is often a highly destructive industry that causes significant environmental damage, including mercury pollution and extensive riverbed destruction. The struggle to obtain control of the resources in remote, largely lawless areas also creates social tensions. Although continuation of the current mode of artisanal and small-scale mining is damaging, prohibiting it would immediately throw many miners and their families into poverty. For this reason, there is a consensus that the way forward is to recognize the role of this type of mining in development and to support improved management and livelihood development through formalization of the sector, registration of both miners and traders, adoption of technological good practice, strengthened health and safety standards and their enforcement, economic diversification, and adequate protection for female and child labor.

For medium- and large-scale mining projects, foundations and financial sureties are increasingly being used to deliver sustainable benefits to communities. These two instruments help mining contribute to broader economic development while providing environmental protection (box 5.8).

Sustainable management of natural capital underlies green growth in other sectors, including agriculture and manufacturing. It is also key to resilience and welfare gains. Well-managed, nonrenewable natural capital can provide both jobs and revenues for investment in human capital and infrastructure. Well-managed, renewable natural capital protects people and key infrastructure from floods and drought, provides key productive and cultural services, and is the basis for important tourism-based activities. Innovation, efficiency gains, and enhanced human and physical capital all play roles in achieving natural capital outcomes that are consistent with green growth. In turn, as the next chapter illustrates, the infrastructure agenda and investments in physical capital can support or undermine green growth, depending on management, policy, and investment choices.

BOX 5.8 How the mining sector is investing in communities

Medium- and large-scale mining projects typically leave a large environmental footprint, resulting in the destruction of land, loss of natural habitats, damage to ecosystems, and the reduction of water and air quality. To reduce these negative externalities and produce sustainable benefits for the community, mining companies are increasingly establishing foundations—there are now more than 60 worldwide—and financial sureties (a sum of money or a guarantee by a third party that a financial liability will be met).

Foundations

Mining companies often set up foundations for larger mining operations; a few countries, including Canada and South Africa, require that they be established. These entities increase the benefits of mining by developing skills (for mining-related jobs and alternative livelihoods) and providing funds that can provide a benefit stream once a mine is closed. They are usually funded by one or more mining operations, which contribute 0.25–1.0 percent of their gross revenues. The funds are used to deliver community investment programs for companies, facilitate the use of government payments to local areas, and manage compensation funds. A critical condition for success is adaptation to the local context, which should be subject to extensive social assessment to define the foundation's vision, beneficiaries, and project types. The foundation's com-

plexity should be proportionate to the funding and capacity of the operating environment, and its operations should be integrated with local and regional development plans.

Financial sureties

Over the past 20 years, it has become the norm for mining companies to be legally obligated to set up financial sureties. These instruments reduce the negative externalities associated with mining by ensuring that there will be sufficient funds to pay for site rehabilitation and postclosure monitoring and maintenance at any stage of a mining project, including early or temporary closure. Funding should be based on a cash accrual system or a financial guarantee provided by a reputable financial institution. Mine closure requirements should be reviewed annually and the closure funding arrangements adjusted to reflect any changes. Financial sureties should not be regarded as a surrogate for a company's legal liability for clean-up but rather as a buffer against the public having to shoulder costs for which the operator is liable. Closure costs vary enormously but tend to range from $5–$15 million for medium-size open pit mines to more than $50 million for large operations. Some sureties include socioeconomic obligations, making their goals similar to those of foundations.

Source: Sassoon 2009; Wall and Pelon 2011.

Notes

1. By and large, natural capital is the form of capital that is not created by deliberate investment, although investments may be needed to restore it (by removing pollutants or reversing soil erosion, for example) or enhance it (by building water storage structures to enhance the water retention services of watersheds, for example). This chapter considers the role of natural capital as a factor of production. Its role as a sink and the relationship to growth is covered in other chapters.

2. Following the Millenium Ecosystem Assessment (2003), ecosystem services can be classified into "provisioning services" (services that produce goods and services, such as water, food, fuel, fiber, and fodder) and "nonprovisioning services." Nonprovisioning services include services that provide regulating services (such as watershed management and climate regulation), supporting services (such as nutrient cycling and soil formation), and cultural services (including services that embody recreational and spiritual values). The report states that biodiversity and ecosystems are closely related concepts. Biodiversity is the

variability of living organisms from all types of ecosystems.

3. Landscape approaches integrate management of land, agriculture, forests, fisheries and water at local, watershed and regional scales to ensure that synergies are captured.

4. Exclusive economic zones—referred to in the preamble to the United Nations Convention on the Law of the Sea Treaty (1982)—are defined as waters that are 200 nautical miles or less from the coastline of a sovereign state. Within these areas, the state has exclusive economic rights concerning management of all natural resources.

5. Projections vary widely, depending on assumptions about recycling and the move from paper to electronic communication formats.

6. In the case of aquifers, in which the actual recharge rate is negligible, water can be considered as a nonrenewable resource. A study of China estimates the annual environmental cost of the depletion of nonrechargeable groundwater in deep freshwater aquifers to be on the order of 50 billion yuan (World Bank 2007b).

7. Dead zones are areas in which oxygen concentrations are less than 0.5 millimeters per liter of water. These conditions usually lead to mass mortality of sea organisms.

8. Nethope is a Kenya-based organization that brings together 33 nongovernmental organizations, with the mission of improving connectivity and access to information.

9. EU farmers receiving direct payments must respect mandatory cross-compliance provisions, which require them to fulfill the requirements of 19 European legislative acts related to the environment, public and animal health, pesticides, and animal welfare. Farmers who do not comply face partial or total withdrawal of their Single Farm Payment. Beneficiaries of direct payments must also keep their land in good agricultural and environmental condition.

10. The Nagoya Protocol on Access and Benefit-Sharing is an international treaty that aims to develop greater legal certainty as well as transparency for providers and users of genetic resources. The protocol covers the use of genetic resources (covered by the Convention on Biological Diversity) and the traditional knowledge that is associated with it. Its objective is for both parties to acknowledge and respect their reciprocal obligations.

11. The evidence on the role of forests in regulating water flows and floods is mixed, as Vincent (2012) notes. The evidence that forests mitigate large floods is scant, and it appears that their effect on low flows can go in either direction, depending on the balance between infiltration and evapo-transpiration.

12. REDD stands for "reducing emissions from deforestation and forest degradation." To this, REDD+ adds conservation, sustainable management of forests, and enhancement of forest carbon stocks.

13. This section does not address nonrenewable natural capital from subsoil assets (fossil fuels), which are dealt with in other chapters.

14. The BioCarbon Fund, housed within the World Bank's Carbon Finance Unit, is a public-private initiative mobilizing resources for pioneering projects that sequester or conserve carbon in forest and agro-ecosystems, mitigating climate change and improving rural livelihoods.

15. The mechanism, defined in Article 12 of the Kyoto Protocol on Climate Change, allows a country with an emission-reduction or emission-limitation commitment under the 1997 Kyoto Protocol (mostly high-income countries) to implement an emission-reduction project in developing countries. Such projects can earn saleable certified emission reduction credits, each equivalent to one tonne of CO_2, which can be counted toward meeting Kyoto targets.

16. Chile had the highest human development index of all South American countries in 2010 (UNDP 2010).

References

Agardy, T., Hicks, F., and A. Hooten. 2011. "Komodo Collaborative Management Initiative." Evaluation Report, International Finance Corporation, Washington, DC.

Ali, D. A., K. Deiniger, and M. Goldstein. 2011. "Environmental and Gender Impacts of Land Tenure Regularization in Africa: Pilot Evidence from Rwanda." Policy Research Working Paper, World Bank, Washington, DC.

Aylward, B., K. Allen, J. Echeverria, and J. Tosi. 1996. "Sustainable Nature-Based Tourism in

Costa Rica: The Monteverde Cloud Forest Preserve." *Biodiversity and Conservation* 5 (3): 315–44.

Bai, Z. G., D. L. Dent, L. Ollsen, and M. E. Schaffman. 2008. "Proxy Global Assessment of Land Degradation." *Journal of Soil Use and Management* 24 (September): 223–34.

Belcher, B., M. Ruiz-Perez, and R. Achdiawan. 2005. "Global Patterns and Trends in the Use and Management of Commercial NTFPs: Implications for Livelihoods and Conservation." *World Development* 33 (9): 1435–52.

Bennet, M. 2008. "China's Sloping Land Conversion Program: Institutional Innovation or Business as Usual?" *Ecological Economics* 65 (4): 699–711.

Bond, I., and J. Mayers. 2009. "Fair Deals for Watershed Services: Lessons from a Multi-Country Action Learning Project." *Natural Resource Issues* 13. London: International Institute for Environment and Development.

Bowler, D., L. Buyung-Ali, J. R. Healey, J. P. G. Jones, T. Knight, and A. S. Pullin. 2010. "The Evidence Base for Community Forest Management as a Mechanism for Supplying Global Environmental Benefits and Improving Local Welfare." CEE Review 08-011 (SR48).

Brown, D. P. Dettman, T. Rennado, H. Teferu, and A. Tofu. 2011. *Poverty Alleviation and Environmental Restoration Using the CDM (Clean Development Mechanism): A Case Study from Humbo Ethiopia.* Dakar: Africa Adapt World Vision.

Chinese National Census of Pollution. 2010. Ministry of Environmental Protection. Beijing.

Deininger, K., and G. Feder. 2001. "Land Institutions and Land Markets." In *Handbook of Agricultural Economics*, ed. B. L. Gardner and G. C. Rausser, vol. 1, 287–331. Amsterdam: North-Holland.

Dobermann, A., C. Witt, and R. J. Buresh. 2008. "Ecological Intensification of Irrigated Rice Systems in Asia." In Procedures of the 5th International Crop Science Congress, Jeju (CD).

Eurostat. 2011. "Agri-Environment Indicators." European Commission, Brussels.

Fang, X., T. L. Roe, and R. B. W. Smith. 2006. "Water Shortages, Water Allocation and Economic Growth: The Case of China." Paper presented at the 10th Joint Conference on Food, Agriculture and the Environment, Duluth, MN, August 27–30.

FAO (Food and Agricultural Organization). 2001. *Economics of Conservation Agriculture.* Rome: FAO Natural Resource Management and Environment Department.

———. 2010a. "Global Forest Resources Assessment 2010." Forestry Paper 163, FAO, Rome.

———. 2010b. *The State of World Fisheries and Aquaculture.* Rome: FAO.

———. 2011. *State of the World's Forests.* Rome: FAO.

Foresight. 2011. "The Future of Food and Farming." Final Project Report, Government Office for Science, London.

Gelb, A., and S. Grasmann. 2010. "How Should Oil Exporters Spend Their Rents?" Center for Global Development, Washington, DC. http://www.cgdev.org/files/1424356_file_Gelb_Grasmann_Oil_Rents_FINAL.pdf.

Goldman, A. 2011. "Poverty and Pro-Governance in the Land of the Plenty: Assessing an Oil Dividend in Equatorial Guinea." Background paper for the Oil-to-Cash Initiative, Center for Global Development, Washington, DC. http://www.cgdev.org/doc/Initiatives/Oil2Cash/EG_Goldman_Formatted_Version_Final.pdf.

Gómez, M. I., C. B. Barrett, L. E. Buck, H. De Groote, S. Ferris, H. O. Gao, E. McCullough, D. D. Miller, H. Outhred, A. N. Pell, T. Reardon, M. Retnanestri, R. Ruben, P. Struebi, J. Swinnen, M. A. Touesnard, K. Weinberger, J. D. H. Keatinge, M. B. Milstein, and R. Y. Yang. 2011. "Research Principles for Developing Country Food Value Chains." *Science* 332 (6034): 1154–5.

Hausmann, R., B. Klinger, and R. Lawrence. 2008. "Examining Beneficiation." CID Working Paper 162, Center for International Development, Harvard University, Cambridge, MA.

Isenberg, D. 2006. "Keggfarms (India): Which Came First, the Kuroiler™ or the KEGG™?" Harvard Business Review Case Study, Harvard University, Cambridge, MA.

Jack, B. K., Kousky, C., and Sims, K. R. E. 2008. "Designing Payments for Ecosystem Services: Lessons from Previous Experience with Incentive-Based Mechanisms." *Proceedings of the National Academies of Sciences* 105 (28): 9465–70.

Joshi, P. K., V. Pangare, B. Shiferaw, S. P. Wani, J. Bouma, and C. Scott. 2004. "Socioeconomic and Policy Research on Watershed Management in India: Synthesis of Past Experiences and Needs for Future Research." In *Global Theme on Agroecosystems*, Report 7, International Crops Research Institute for the Semi-Arid Tropics, Andhra Pradesh, India.

Khush, G. S., and P. S. Virk. 2005. *IR Varieties and Their Impact.* Manila: International Rice Research Institute.

Landers, John. 2005. *Zero Tillage Development in Tropical Brazil.* Wageningen, the Netherlands: Wageninen University.

Liniger, H. P., R. Mekdaschi Studer, C. Hauert, and M. Gurtner. 2011. *Sustainable Land Management in Practice: Guidelines and Best Practices for Sub-Saharan Africa.* Rome: TerrAfrica, World Overview of Conservation Approaches and Technologies (WOCAT), Berne, and Food and Agriculture Organization of the United Nations (FAO).

López, R. 2002. "The Economics of Agriculture in Developing Countries: The Role of the Environment." In *Handbook of Agricultural Economics*, ed. B. Gardner and G. Rausser, vol. 2, 1213–47. Amsterdam: Elsevier.

———. 2012. "Sustainable Agriculture and Animal Production in Colombia." Paper presented to the Ministry of Agriculture and Rural Development of Colombia during Sustainable Development Week, Bogota.

Millennium Ecosystem Assessment. 2003. *Ecosystems and Human Well-Being: A Framework for Assessment.* Washington, DC: Island Press.

Nkonya, E., N. Gerber, J. von Braun, and A. De Pinto. 2011. "Economics of Land Degradation: The Costs of Action versus Inaction." IFPRI Issue Brief 68, International Food Policy Research Institute, Washington, DC.

OECD (Organization for Economic Co-operation and Development). 2008. *Environmental Outlook to 2030.* Paris: OECD.

———. 2011. *Agricultural Policy Monitoring and Evaluation 2011.* Paris: OECD.

Pagiola, S. 2008. "Payments for Environmental Services in Costa Rica." *Ecological Economics* 65 (4): 712–72.

Pattanayak, S. K., S. Wunder, and P. J. Ferraro. 2010. "Show Me the Money: Do Payments Supply Environmental Services in Developing Countries?" *Review of Environmental Economics and Policy* 4 (2): 254–74.

Pavan, W., C. W. Fraisse, and N. A. Peres. 2010. *A Web-Based Decision Support Tool for Timing Fungicide Applications in Strawberry.* Tallahassee: Florida State University Cooperative State Extension Program.

Polasky, S., C. Costello, and A. Solow. 2005. "The Economics of Biodiversity." In *Handbook of Environmental Economics*, ed. K. G. Mäler and J. R. Vincent, vol. 3, 1517–60. Amsterdam: Elsevier.

Prince's Charities' International Sustainability Unit. 2011. "Towards Sustainable Agricultural Production Systems: What Price Resilience?" Clarence House, London. http://www.fcrn.org.uk/sites/default/files/ISU_Resilience_report_July11.pdf.

Ravindrah, N. H., and M. Ostwald. 2008. *Carbon Inventory Methods Handbook for Greenhouse Gas Inventory, Carbon Mitigation and Roundwood Production Projects: Advances in Global Research.* Berlin: Springer-Verlag.

Ruiz-Perez, M., M. Fu, X. Yang, and B. Belcher. 2001. "Towards a More Environmentally Friendly Bamboo Forestry in China". *Journal of Forestry* 99 (7): 14–20.

Sassoon, M. 2009. *Financial Surety: Guidelines for the Implementation of Financial Surety for Mine Closure.* Extractive Industries for Development Series 7. Washington, DC: World Bank.

Scheierling, S. M. 1996. "Overcoming Agricultural Water Pollution in the European Union." *Finance & Development* 33(3): 32–5.

Scherr, S. J., L. E. Buck, T. Majanen, J. C. Milder, and S. Shames. 2011. "Scaling-Up Landscape Investment Approaches in Africa: Where Do Private Market Incentives Converge with Landscape Restoration Goals?" Background paper for the Investment Forum on Mobilizing Investment in Trees and Landscape Restoration, EcoAgriculture Partners and Program on Forests (PROFOR), Washington, DC.

TIES (International Nature-Based Tourism Society). 2006. "TIES Global Nature-Based Tourism Fact Sheet." TIES, Washington, DC.

Tveteras, R., and G. E. Battese. 2006. "Agglomeration Externalities, Productivity, and Technical Inefficiency." *Journal of Regional Science* 46 (4): 605–25.

UNDP (United Nations Development Programme). 2010. *Human Development*

Report 2010. *The Real Wealth of Nations: Pathways to Human Development.* New York: UNDP.

UNEP (United Nations Environment Programme), FAO (Food and Agriculture Organization), IOC (Intergovernmental Oceanographic Commission), and UNESCO (United Nations Educational, Scientific and Cultural Organization). 2009. *Blue Carbon: The Role of Healthy Oceans in Binding Carbon.* New York: UNEP.

UNFCCC (United Nations Framework Convention on Climate Change). 2007. "Climate Change 2007." Fourth Assessment Report of the United Nations Intergovernmental Panel on Climate Change (IPCC), Bonn.

Vincent, J. R. 2012. "Ecosystem Services and Green Growth." Paper presented at the Green Growth Knowledge Platform inaugural conference, Mexico City, January 12–13.

Wall, L., and R. Pelon. 2011. *Sharing Mining Benefits in Developing Countries.* Extractive Industries for Development Series 21. Washington, DC: World Bank.

Watson, R. T., I. R. Noble, N. H. Bert Bolin, D. J. V. Ravindranath, and D. J. Dokken, eds. 2000. *Land Use, Land-Use Change, and Forestry.* Report of the Intergovernmental Panel on Climate Change. Cambridge: Cambridge University Press.

Weitzman, M. 1974. "Free Access vs. Private Ownership as Alternative Systems for Managing Common Property." *Journal of Economic Theory* 8 (2): 225–34.

World Bank. 2004. "Towards a Water-Secure Kenya: Water Resources Sector." Memorandum, World Bank, Africa Region, Water and Urban I, Washington, DC.

———. 2005a. "Arab Republic of Egypt Country Environmental Analysis, 1992–2002." Report 31993–EG, World Bank, Washington, DC.

———. 2005b. *Where Is the Wealth of Nations? Measuring Capital for the 21st Century.* Washington, DC: World Bank.

———. 2006a. "Pakistan Country Environmental Analysis." Report 36946–PK, World Bank, Washington, DC.

———. 2006b. "Republic of Colombia Mitigating Environmental Degradation to Foster Growth and Reduce Inequality." Report 36345–CO, World Bank, Washington, DC.

———. 2007a. "Agriculture for Development." In *World Development Report 2008: Agriculture and Development.* Washington, DC: World Bank.

———. 2007b. *Cost of Pollution in China: Economic Estimates of Physical Damages.* Conference ed. Washington, DC: World Bank.

———. 2007c. "Ghana Country Environmental Analysis." Report 36985–GH, World Bank, Washington, DC.

———. 2007d. "Zambia Economic and Poverty Impact of Nature-based Tourism." Report 43373-ZM, Africa Region, World Bank, Washington, DC.

———. 2008a. *Hydromet Services in Eastern Europe and Central Asia Region.* Washington DC: World Bank.

———. 2008b. "Tajikistan Country Environmental Analysis." Report 43465-TJ, World Bank, Washington, DC.

———. 2010a. *Central African Republic Country Environmental Analysis: Environmental Management for Sustainable Growth.* Washington, DC: World Bank.

———. 2010b. *The Changing Wealth of Nations: Measuring Sustainable Development in the New Millennium.* Washington, DC: World Bank.

———. 2010c. *China Forest Policy: Deepening the Transition.* Washington, DC: World Bank.

———. 2010d. *World Development Report 2010: Development and Climate Change.* Washington DC: World Bank.

———. 2011a. "Climate Smart Agriculture: A Call to Action." In collaboration with the African Union, CCAFS (Climate Change, Agriculture and Food Security), Department of Agriculture, Forestry and Fisheries of South Africa, IFAD (International Fund for Agricultural Development, PROFOR (Program on Forests), UNEP (United Nations Environment Programme), WBI (World Bank Institute), FAO (Food and Agriculture Organization), WFP (World Food Programme), Washington DC.

———. 2011b. "Kazakhstan: Syr Darya Northern Aral Sea Control Project." Implementation Completion Report, World Bank, Washington, DC.

———. 2012. "India National Dairy Support Program." Project Appraisal Report, World Bank, Washington, DC.

World Bank and FAO(Food and Agriculture Organization). 2009. *The Sunken Billions: The*

Economic Justification for Fisheries Reform. Washington, DC: World Bank; Rome: Food and Agricultural Organization.

WRI (World Resources Institute). 2005. *Millennium Ecosystem Assessment: Ecosystems and Human Well-Being Biodiversity Synthesis.* Washington, DC: WRI.

Wunder, S. 2000. "Nature-Based Tourism and Economic Incentives: An Empirical Approach." *Ecological Economics* 32: 465–79.

Wunder, S., and M. Albán. 2008. "Decentralized Payments for Environmental Services: The Cases of Pimampiro and PROFAFOR in Ecuador." *Ecological Economics* 65 (4): 685–98.

Physical Capital: The Role of Infrastructure in Green Growth Strategies | 6

Key Messages

- Infrastructure policies are central to green growth strategies, because of the huge potential for regret (given the massive infrastructure investments required and the inertia they create) and substantial potential for co-benefits (given the current gap in infrastructure service provision).
- The infrastructure gap offers opportunities to "build right" and leapfrog; but huge unmet needs also can imply difficult trade-offs between "building right" and "building more," particularly given financing and fiscal constraints.
- A framework for green infrastructure must build on efforts to address overall constraints on infrastructure finance (including cost recovery issues) and must develop strategies to both minimize the potential for regrets and maximize short-term co-benefits to address social and political acceptability constraints.

Getting infrastructure "right" is at the heart of green growth. It is critical because infrastructure choices have long-lived and difficult-to-reverse impacts on the carbon, land, and water intensity of future patterns of development. Infrastructure also offers substantial co-benefits: many investments needed for growth and improved living conditions are also good for the environment.

The challenges and opportunities of greening infrastructure in developing countries must be understood in the context of the huge unsatisfied needs that remain: the fact that much remains to be built creates an opportunity to build right; the fact that needs are so large implies important trade-offs between "building right" and "building more." While the additional costs of building green are relatively modest, they occur in a context of frequently binding financing and fiscal constraints. Complicating matters is the dramatic rise in population and growing urbanization. As such, a framework for green infrastructure needs to offer strategies to minimize the potential for regrets and maximize short-term local benefits; and it must build on efforts to address overall constraints on infrastructure finance.

This chapter focuses on long-lived infrastructure systems such as energy, water, sanitation and transport infrastructure, although it recognizes other infrastructure—for example, buildings—also play a key role in driving the demand for infrastructure services (irrigation is covered in chapter 5).

Infrastructure as the heart of green growth

Infrastructure policies are central to green growth strategies because of their unique characteristics, namely the large potential for regret (linked with the large inertia embodied in infrastructure investments) and the substantial potential for co-benefits (linked to the current gap in infrastructure service provision).

A massive potential for regret

Infrastructure decisions are long-lived (table 6.1). They influence the purchase of consumer durables and the location choices of households and firms. As such, they create substantial inertia in socioeconomic systems. Because the economic system reorganizes itself around infrastructure, this inertia can even exceed the physical lifetime of specific infrastructure investments. A delay in greening investments may therefore prove

extremely costly if it results in a lock-in into technologies that turn out to no longer be appropriate (because of their excessive carbon, land, or water intensity) or settlement patterns that prove vulnerable to changing climatic conditions. The infrastructure already in place now will raise global temperatures by 1.3°C–1.7°C unless it is retrofitted or retired before the end of its useful life (Davis and others 2010; Guivarch and Hallegatte 2011).

Inertia is particularly evident in urban policies and the transport-related decisions that shape cities. The consequences of these decisions are illustrated by the contrast between Atlanta and Barcelona, two cities with roughly the same population and income but dramatically different densities and, hence, dramatically different options in terms of urban transportation and housing (figure 6.1). Once a city is developed, it is difficult to change its form. This irreversibility makes the idea of "growing dirty and cleaning up later" inapplicable in this domain (box 6.1).

The consequence of the inertia in infrastructure development is an enormous potential for regret if decisions are made without adequate consideration of how conditions—socioeconomic, environmental, and technological—will change over time. The potential for regret has always been a challenge for infrastructure policy; it is made much more complex by climate change, which introduces deep uncertainty about future climatic conditions, technologies, and environmental standards and prices.

Uncertainty about future climatic conditions. This complicates decision making, given the importance of weather and climate conditions for infrastructure design and performance (Hallegatte 2009). In the energy sector, weather directly affects demand (which varies with temperature) and supply. Water availability affects electricity production from hydropower and thermal plants (because of cooling needs), and wind and nebulosity determine wind and solar power. Electricity networks are also highly vulnerable to extreme events

TABLE 6.1 Sectors in which inertia and sensitivity to climate conditions are great

Sector	Example	Time scale (years)
Water	Dams, reservoirs	30–200
Land-use planning	New development in flood plain or coastal areas	>100
Coastal and flood defenses	Dikes, sea walls	>50
Building and housing	Insulation, windows	30–150
Transportation	Port infrastructure, bridge, roads, railways	30–200
Urbanism	Urban density, parks	>100
Energy production	Coal-fire plants	20–70

Source: Hallegatte 2009.

FIGURE 6.1   Urban densities determine cities' options for greening

(built-up areas of Atlanta and Barcelona, represented at the same scale)

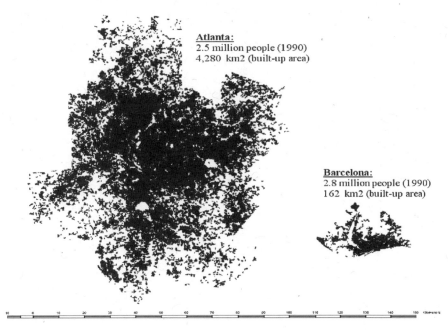

Atlanta:
2.5 million people (1990)
4,280 km2 (built-up area)

Barcelona:
2.8 million people (1990)
162 km2 (built-up area)

Source: Bertaud 2003.

(such as strong winds and snowstorms, as illustrated by the January 2008 snowstorm that left millions of people stranded across China or the repeated power outages caused by heavy snow in the United States). Transport infrastructure, which affects urban development and land use, including in flood-prone areas, must also account for long-term climate changes.

Uncertainty about how technologies evolve. This has a particularly important effect on cities. With current technologies, low-density single-home suburban developments lead to high carbon emissions. But they may become sustainable in terms of emissions (albeit maybe not in terms of water and land consumption) with efficient electric vehicles, decarbonized electricity production and low-energy-consumption houses (box 6.2). Uncertainty about the evolution of energy technology costs complicates the design of energy policy (Kalkuhl and others 2011). Anecdotal evidence suggests that uncertainty is also leading investors to postpone investments for

fear of being stuck with an older and uncompetitive technology.

Uncertainty about environmental policies and prices for energy, oil, or carbon. Energy-intensive development may create deep vulnerabilities and loss of competitiveness in a future with high carbon or energy prices (Rozenberg and others 2010; World Bank 2010). Dense cities are less vulnerable to shocks in energy—hence transportation—prices (Gusdorf and Hallegatte 2007).

The combination of sensitivity to uncertain parameters and the high level of inertia creates a high risk of lock-ins into situations that will be undesirable in the future. Avoiding these lock-ins—and the corresponding regret or retrofitting costs—should be a priority for decision making on infrastructure (see chapter 7).

The vast potential for co-benefits

The second reason why infrastructure will play a key role in green growth strategy is that

BOX 6.1   The case for immediate action in the transport sector

Transport is a major contributor to CO_2 emissions. It is also one of the fastest-growing sources of emissions. Not surprisingly given the 1 billion cars already on the road, road transport accounts for about two-thirds of total transport emissions.

Developing countries, which still face a huge transport infrastructure gap, have the opportunity to choose their transport development path: low-emission transport or car-dependent transport (box figure B6.1.1). Experience suggests that demand for car ownership increases dramatically at annual household incomes of $6,000–$8,000. If history repeats itself, an additional 2.3 billion cars will be added by 2050, mostly in developing countries,

given expected economic growth and past patterns of motorization (Chamon and others 2008). Without policies to encourage high-density urbanization and public transport, high reliance on individual car transport will ensue.

If public transport is included as a major part of modal structure in urban transport, there is no conflict between a low emission transport sector and rapid growth or high income. In fact, economies with some of the lowest ratios of energy consumption to gross domestic product (GDP) in the world—including Japan, Singapore, and Hong Kong SAR, China—have experienced extraordinary development over the past few decades.

FIGURE B6.1.1   As income rises, will countries choose low energy consumption in road transport?

(relationship between per capita income and energy consumption from the road sector)

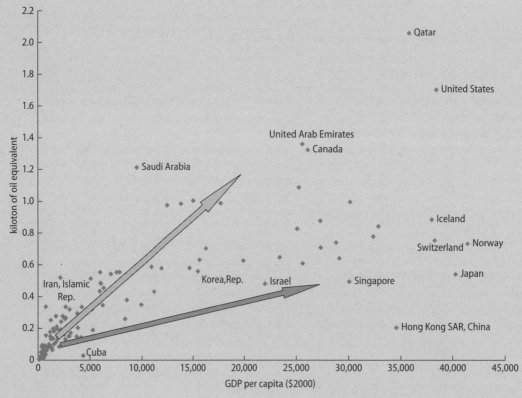

Source: World Bank 2011d.

BOX 6.2 The impact of technologies on transport policies—not enough?

Given the significance of emissions from road transport, the green growth path of transport depends on how rapidly vehicle technologies develop. If low- or zero-emission vehicles become available in the near future, relatively small changes in existing transport infrastructure stock would be required. People could continue relying on individual cars without harming the climate. But this may not be realistic.

Technical standards in transport can also help reduce emissions in the sector. Emissions per kilometer of new cars have historically been reduced through better gasoline and diesel internal combustion engines, better lighting and air conditioning, and better tires. The aviation fleet has also reduced emissions in accord with international efficiency agreements. There is also an opportunity to reduce emissions levels through Intelligent Transport Systems—for instance, by allowing drivers to access timely traffic reports, identify available parking spots, and optimize routing.

But technical standards are unlikely to lead to massive reductions in emissions, so barring the rapid emergence and global adoption of low-carbon engine technologies, modal shifts will be needed. An

average bus emits only half as much CO_2 equivalent per passenger kilometer as a small car. For travel between distant cities, railways are even more eco-friendly than buses: emissions from light-rail transit can be as much as half of average bus emissions. But the efficiency and feasibility of modal shifts depend on urban forms, with mass transit requiring minimum levels of density, and on tackling market structure and coordination failures.

Modal shifts will also imply addressing consumer preferences, and here the "nudging" and social marketing campaigns discussed in chapter 2 are an important complement to price incentives and supply-side interventions. In a world in which major automobile companies spent some $21 billion worldwide on advertising in 2009—an increasing percentage of which is aimed at emerging markets—public transport agencies across Africa, Europe, and North and South America are beginning to apply to public transportation the same marketing approaches used by the auto industry to bolster sales to shift demand for public transportation (Weber and others 2011).

---

infrastructure is a domain in which substantial synergies exist between economic growth and the environment. Infrastructure systems are indeed designed to provide welfare-improving and productivity-enhancing services, which are critical for development, but they also often provide environmental benefits.

Providing service to the unserved—who usually pay a higher price for water and energy than connected households—provides both social and environmental benefits (box 6.3). Universal access to water and sanitation is good not only for welfare and economic growth—with impacts on health and human capital, especially for the poor—but also for the environment. (For instance, providing sanitation services to the slums surrounding the Guarapiranga Lake helped slum dwellers but also preserved the water source of 25 percent of São Paulo's 18 million inhabitants in the early 1990s.) This is also

true for energy. When reliable network electricity is available, pollution is reduced and competitiveness increases, as firms no longer need to rely on expensive back-up diesel generators. Photovoltaic (PV) solar systems are optimal solutions for isolated, low-density areas; hydroelectricity is the cheapest and most reliable energy source for some countries (box 6.4). Better public urban transport reduces congestion and air pollution, with large economic and health impacts.[1]

An additional source of co-benefits is linked to distributional effects. Infrastructure consumption subsidies are both regressive and bad for the environment (Komives and others 2005). Subsidies not only distort demand, with financial and environmental consequences, they also often fail to reach the very poor they are supposed to help (see chapter 2). The poor do not own cars and often are not served by utilities; if they do, they consume

---

BOX 6.3   Benefits from using photovoltaic electricity in rural areas

Power grids in Africa are available only in cities and high-density areas. In most rural areas, kerosene and candles are the main source of lighting, while dry cell batteries are used to power radios. All are expensive (1 liter of kerosene can cost more than $0.80 and provides about 20 hours of light). PV systems are superior solutions. For example, a solar home system may be sized to power a refrigerator and television (costing $1,000); a large television and three lamps (for $250); a small television, three lamps, and a radio (for $100); or a lamp, radio, and cell phone charger (for as low as $50—about the same cost as a cell phone).

Africa offers a huge market for modern, energy-efficient lighting products. Although the market has a low profit margin, its strength is in the high number of clients (if the right product for the right price can be offered). The GTZ-sponsored pico-PV program and the World Bank Group's Lighting Africa are examples of two initiatives that aim to transform the lighting market from fuel-based products to clean, safe, and efficient modern lighting appliances.

Source: ESMAP 2009.

BOX 6.4   Hydropower as a green choice for lower-income countries

For lower-income countries, sustainable hydropower represents an important clean energy source—and one that will assume a larger share of the world's energy production as these countries develop further. Africa is exploiting only 7 percent of its hydropower potential; if the region developed it to the same extent that Canada has, its electricity supply would be multiplied by a factor of 8.

The reality, however, is that hydropower projects are complex—with impacts on agriculture, water management, irrigation, food production, climate change, and the sustainability of communities. They require detailed planning and studies before a shovel breaks the ground. Social and environmental impacts have to be assessed and addressed, consultations must be held, and regulations need to be developed. In some cases, new institutions have to be created

and made viable. None of this is easy or cheap, but it is essential, because well-managed hydro projects can generate an array of benefits, including flood control, drought management, provision of water supply, and environmental benefits.

Storage facilities for hydropower are essential to adapt to changes in the hydrological cycle that are expected to occur as a result of climate change. With increasing water scarcity in some regions, there is a need to develop multiyear storage that is economically, environmentally, and socially feasible. Where the intensity and frequency of floods increases, storage is required to manage flows. Multipurpose storage facilities can also provide water services to agriculture, water supply, and environmental flows.

Box text contributed by Diego Rodriguez.

---

small quantities of water and electricity or transport fuel. The lion's share of consumption subsidies benefits wealthier segments of the population (Arze del Granado and others 2010). The urban poor may enjoy some spillovers, but the rural poor seldom do.

There are also trade-offs between infrastructure development and the environment. A first trade-off is related to infrastructure's

direct environmental footprint. Building the infrastructure that is needed for development will have detrimental impacts on natural areas, biodiversity, and the environment (Geneletti 2003). Another trade-off is linked to the fact that building better (cleaner, more resilient, or both) can be more expensive. This trade-off raises the fear that countries faced with severe financing constraints may need to choose between "building right" (which may make both economic and environmental sense) and "building more" (which may be what is required socially).

But the additional cost of building greener infrastructure should not be overstated. In some sectors, green infrastructure is more expensive—where electricity grids are present, solar or wind energy is more expensive than electricity produced from coal, for example. But thanks to innovation and economies of scale, the difference in cost is narrowing rapidly, and green energies are now competitive in some contexts (where the hydropower endowment is large, where electricity is produced off-grid, or where carbon is priced). In the transport sector, providing public transport is more expensive than building roads, but public and individual transports are imperfect substitutes: in highly congested cities, public transportation becomes necessary for economic reasons, and the environmental benefits can be reaped with no or little additional cost. In the construction sector, the additional cost to build lower-energy buildings—thanks to better insulation and more efficient heating systems—may not exceed 5 percent, and this additional investment cost is rapidly recouped by reduced energy bills.

One case in which additional costs may create trade-offs is the retrofit of existing buildings. Indeed, retrofitting the lowest-efficiency buildings into average-efficiency buildings costs €500 per square meter in France (Giraudet and others 2011). However, energy savings can pay back upfront costs in many instances. The main constraint is thus one of access to capital rather than financial or economic viability, as many green investments pay for themselves over the medium to long term.

Recognizing the need for efficiency: Meeting large unsatisfied infrastructure needs within tight fiscal constraints

Developing countries are characterized by large unsatisfied needs, including needs met by infrastructure such as drinking water and reliable electricity (table 6.2). The scale

TABLE 6.2   Gaps in access to infrastructure in developing countries remain large, particularly in Africa

	All developing countries	Africa
Percentage of households with access to electricity	75	31
Improved water source	89	61
Improved sanitation facilities	63	31
Percentage of rural population with access to an all-weather road	70	33
Telecom: mobile and fixed lines per 100 inhabitants	85	46

Source: Roberts and others 2006 for roads; World Bank 2011d for telecom; IEA 2011 for electricity; and WHO-UNICEF 2012.
Note: Road access data are for 2005 or the latest year available up to that date; telecoms, for 2010; water and sanitation data are for 2010. Averages are weighted by country population. The road access indicator measures the share of the rural population that lives within 2 kilometers of an all-season road.

of unmet needs is particularly great in Sub-Saharan Africa, where less than a third of households have access to electricity. Connectivity also remains low in the developing world, particularly in rural areas, where only 70 percent of the population has access to an all-weather road (33 percent in Africa). Access to water has increased, but 780 million people still lack access to an improved water source (WHO-UNICEF 2012).

Globally, the challenge is greater for sanitation than for water supply. The percentage of the population with adequate access to potable water increased from 74 percent in 1990 to 89 percent in 2010. Sanitation figures are much lower, having increased from 44 percent in 1990 to just 63 percent in 2010 (WHO-UNICEF 2012). The difference partly reflects the greater "public good" and "externality" element of sanitation and sewerage— that is, individuals feel the welfare impacts of inadequate access to water, whereas other sectors and members of society feel the effects of inadequate sanitation (through impacts on water quality and corresponding health and productivity impacts). Estimates of the costs of inadequate water and sanitation in the Middle East and North Africa are about 1 percent of GDP in the Arab Republic of Egypt and 2.8 percent in the Islamic Republic of Iran (Hussein 2007). With 2.5 billion people lacking access to improved sanitation, the achievement of the Millennium Development Goal (MDG) on sanitation is unlikely.[2]

Filling the infrastructure gaps in developing countries—to address household needs and expanding infrastructure so that firms have access to the kind of energy and transport services they need to compete—will cost an estimated $1.0–$1.5 trillion a year, or 7 percent of developing-country GDP (Fay and others 2010).[3] Developing countries are currently investing about half that amount, although the amount varies dramatically by region and income level. In Africa, infrastructure needs were projected to reach 15 percent of the region's GDP in 2008, about twice the level actually spent (Foster and Briceño-Garmendia 2010). Moreover, given the constraints on poor households' budgets, increases in infrastructure services need to be provided in a way that is affordable.

In the energy sector, the challenge is to provide all people with modern energy to meet their basic needs at affordable costs while ensuring the sustainable growth path of energy consumption (through conservation and greater energy efficiency) and making energy sources more environmentally sustainable (box 6.5). Thus, the goals of the

---

BOX 6.5   The energy challenge: Expanding access and increasing supply in an efficient, clean, and cost-effective manner

How will countries meet the goal of the United Nations Sustainable Energy for All initiative of providing universal energy access at affordable costs while ensuring environmental sustainability through improved efficiency and an increased role for renewables? The answer is through a portfolio of technologies (World Bank 2010).

To achieve universal access to electricity by 2030, countries need to develop not only grid systems but also off- and mini-grid power systems, at least as a transition solution. The International Energy Agency estimates that about 45 percent of electricity will come from national grids, 36 percent from mini-grid solutions, and the remaining 20 percent from isolated off-grid solutions serving remote and low-density areas. Off- and mini-grid technologies can be complemented by other solutions at the end-user level. For instance, the Lighting Africa initiative lowers entry barriers to the off-grid lighting market by establishing quality standards, developing a good investment climate, and supporting product development while educating consumers on the benefits of solar lighting products. In 2010, more than 134,000 solar portable lamps that had passed Lighting Africa quality tests were sold in Africa, providing more than 672,000 people with cleaner, safer, better lighting and improved energy access.

Energy-efficiency policies could potentially contribute a quarter to a third of averted greenhouse gas emissions by 2050 (World Bank 2010). Technologies that increase energy efficiency are typically not costly or innovative: existing technologies alone could reduce energy consumption 30–40 percent across many sectors and countries. For instance, 70 percent of lighting (which consumes 20 percent of total global electricity consumption) can save 50 percent of energy use just by using current technologies alone. A problem is that the transaction costs for energy-efficiency projects tend to be high, compared with their relatively small amount of investment. Relatively long pay-back periods may still be a considerable barrier to financing these projects (World Bank forthcoming).

Among renewable sources of energy, large-scale hydropower tends to be the least expensive. It can be competitive with conventional thermal generation. Geothermal energy can also be cost competitive, making it another suitable candidate. Both types of energy involve large upfront costs and long lead-times for development, however. At the opposite end of the spectrum, solar energy is more expensive, but it may still be the least-cost option in remote, isolated areas.

One challenge in developing renewables is the temporal variation in the availability of electricity. Demand for electricity varies continuously, with large fluctuations during the day and even larger variation from season to season. Rapid variability of some renewables can add to the challenge of maintaining a balance between supply and demand at all times. A proper mix of generation technologies with varied output control characteristics (for example, hydropower with storage and fast-responding gas units), well-developed transmission systems, and improved forecast and grid operations capacity will help cushion the effects of variability.

United Nations Sustainable Energy for All (UN SE4ALL) initiative are to achieve universal access to modern energy, doubling the global rate of improvement of energy efficiency, and doubling the global share of renewable energy.

And providing modern energy services to all does not need to be done at the expense of the environment—in fact, the environmental impacts are likely to be modest to positive, even when using brown technologies. This is because the poor consume little even when they are connected to modern infrastructure services, particularly in comparison to the rich. For instance, the additional emissions produced by providing electricity using standard technologies to the 1.3 billion people who currently lack service could be offset by a switch of the U.S. vehicle fleet to European standards (World Bank 2010). Greening, infrastructure does not need to come at the expense of universal access—in fact, universal access is likely to be good for the environment.

In the water sector, developing countries will need to invest an estimated $72 billion a year to reach the MDG targets on improved water supply and sanitation, 75 percent of which is needed just to maintain existing facilities (Hutton and Bartram 2008).

Meeting infrastructure needs, protecting the environment

Even with significant synergies between infrastructure service development and environmental consideration, greening growth will increase investment needs in the infrastructure sector. As an illustration, an analysis of mitigation scenarios from four models suggests that the global energy investment needed to achieve a greenhouse gas concentration of 450 ppm CO_2-eq (parts per million CO_2 equivalent) could amount to $350 billion–$1.1 trillion a year by 2030 (figure 6.2). A 550 ppm target appears much easier to achieve, requiring $50–$200 billion of additional annual investments. (These figures are gross investment costs; they do not take into account the benefits from higher

energy efficiency and reduced operating costs.) These additional investment needs are significant, but they remain a small share of total world investments, at least for the 550 ppm target. They do not include the cost of adapting infrastructure to a changed climate, which could cost developing countries an additional $15–$30 billion a year by 2050 (World Bank 2010).

Financing infrastructure: Efficiency and cost recovery to improve access and sustainability

Investment in infrastructure in the developing world is inadequate partly because infrastructure is expensive and "lumpy"—capacity can be increased only in large increments, not through a continuous process. In addition, when investments require public funding, the financing gap is linked to limits to the borrowing capacity. Even when a project is economically beneficial and will generate sufficient tax revenues to pay back the upfront cost, it is difficult to mobilize private finance because of information asymmetry, long return on investments, and political risks. Doing so would require shifting the risk-adjusted return upward, by increasing returns or reducing risks, so that proposed projects can compete with other categories of investment.

Another reason for the insufficiency of investment in infrastructure is that economic and fiscal sustainability has long been a major challenge in the infrastructure sector. Full-cost pricing continues to be an elusive goal, and infrastructure often involves significant technical and nontechnical inefficiency. Colombia grappled with both issues successfully (box 6.6). In Africa, quasi-fiscal deficits caused by underpricing, technical losses, and nonpayment amount to about 2 percent of GDP. Eliminating these problems could offset about a third of the financing gap (Briceño-Garmendia and others 2008). In South Asia, more than 20 percent of electricity produced is lost because of technical and nontechnical reasons, including illegal connections (World Bank 2011d); 30–45 percent of water

FIGURE 6.2   Upfront investment costs for energy supply and greater energy efficiency could be substantial

(additional investment needs in the energy sector projected by four global models and for two climate objectives)

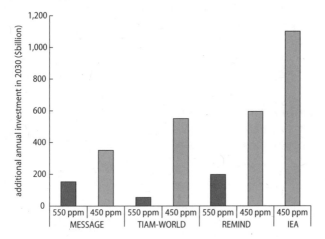

Source: Authors' compilation based on following sources: MESSAGE: van Vliet and others 2012; REMIND: Luderer and others forthcoming; TIAM-World: Loulou and Labriet 2008; IEA: IEA 2011.
Note: The targets 450 ppm and 550 ppm are in CO_2-eq (parts per million CO_2 equivalent) which measures the concentration of all greenhouse gases using the functionally equivalent amount or concentration of CO_2 as the reference; 450 ppm CO_2-eq is the concentration is needed to maintain a 50 percent chance of not exceeding global warming of more than 2°C above preindustrial temperatures. IEA 2011 does not provide estimates for a 550 ppm scenario.

is leaked from the network or not accounted for (IBNET 2011).

What can be done? Addressing these inefficiencies would help improve both infrastructure coverage and the greening of infrastructure. Strengthening cost recovery would not only contribute to the financial sustainability of energy sector development, it would also encourage consumers to use energy wisely. Efficient management of metering, billing, and collection would improve the financial performance of service providers. New metering technologies based on information and communications technology are facilitating this activity in many places, including small, off-grid private service providers and large publicly owned distribution utilities. And more efficient management of utilities would eliminate waste and reduce environmental impacts.

In addition, incentive mechanisms should be tightened at the utility and end-user levels. The biggest hurdles to doing so are accountability and enforceability in implementing

tariff setting and collection. The cost of energy imports and power generation can be volatile; it needs to be passed on to consumer prices, although smoothing mechanisms may be required. Adjusting tariffs will greatly improve the financial sustainability of utilities. But utilities will also have to take measures against illegal connections and nonpayers.

Chapter 2 discusses the difficulties in eliminating subsidies to infrastructure services. It suggests complementary actions to mitigate undesirable distributive impacts of these measures (such as connection subsidies or targeted cash transfers).

Another measure in the arsenal may be cross-country collaboration. Because infrastructure exhibits significant economies of scale and scope, cross-country collaboration—for instance, through regional power pools—is generally helpful, particularly for small countries.

In Africa, where many countries are too small to build national power plants at an efficient scale, $2 billion of energy investment could be saved if trade in power trade was fully exploited (Foster and Briceño-Garmendia 2010). Regional power pools (for example, in West and East Africa) can help capture benefits from economies of scale and smooth the intermittency of solar and wind energy. Trade and cross-country coordination also help countries manage natural resources (such as shared water resources) and improve reliability.

Hydro-meteorological services also benefit from cross-country collaboration. An analysis of South Eastern Europe estimates that the financing needed to strengthen national hydro-meteorological services in seven countries without regional cooperation and coordination would be about €90 million (ISDR and others 2011). With deeper cooperation, the cost would be 30 percent lower.

Managing demand

Improving the delivery of infrastructure services is critical. But in infrastructure, increased supply often translates into

BOX 6.6   Pairing cost recovery with deregulation in Colombia

In 1964, only 50 percent of people in Bogota and other large cities had access to electricity, water, and sanitation. And coverage rates were even worse in smaller cities (about 40 percent for water and electricity and 20 percent for sanitation). Today, Colombia has almost universal access to basic services in cities of all sizes. But achieving convergence took more than 40 years (box figure B6.6.1).

How did Colombia achieve near universal coverage? The key was a series of policy reforms in the 1990s that brought tariffs toward cost recovery levels. In the water sector, average residential tariffs per cubic meter were increased from $0.33 in 1990 to $0.78 in 2001 (World Bank 2004). With almost 90 percent of households having metered connections, the price increase triggered a decrease in household water consumption from 34 to 19 cubic meters per month over the same period—in the process reducing the need for major new infrastructure. But even with higher prices, water remains relatively affordable for the average household. The tariff structure allows the Colombian government to cross-subsidize the poorest consumers from richer households and industrial users. As a result, the average poor household spends less than 5 percent of its income on utility services.

In the electricity sector, in the 1990s the rules on who gets to generate and sell electricity were changed. After two major blackout periods (1983 and 1992/93), the government grappled with increasing capacity or increasing efficiency. Given severe financial constraints, increasing capacity was not an option. Deregulation was therefore undertaken to improve the efficiency of existing capacity (Larsen and others 2004). As part of the reforms, electricity was unbundled into generation, transmission, distribution, and commercialization. In the 1990s, the electricity sector represented a third of Colombia's public debt stock. By 2004, this had fallen to less than 5 percent and Colombia had become a net exporter of electricity.

Box text contributed by Somik Lall.

FIGURE B6.6.1   Access to basic infrastructure services has risen dramatically in Colombia

(access to services, by city size, 1964–2005)

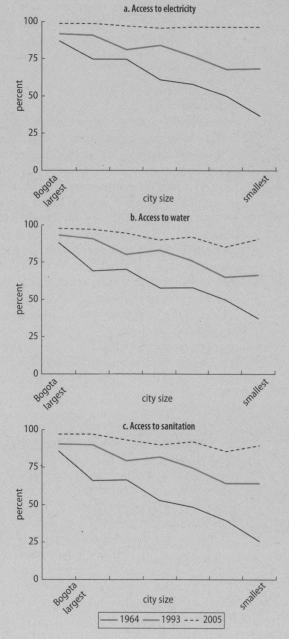

Source: Based on data from the Colombia's National Administrative Department of Statistics (DANE) census 1964, 1993, and 2005.

increased demand, making a supply-side-only approach both costly and ineffective. For instance, building new roads is often ineffective in reducing congestion because it incentivizes the use of individual vehicles, leaving congestion unchanged. For this reason, action is also needed to manage demand. Policy makers can chose from an array of tools that includes price instruments, regulation, and integrated planning of supply and demand.

Prices: Important but hampered by low elasticity

Price elasticity—that is, the percentage change in quantity demanded in response to a change in price—is relatively low in the transportation sector, at least in the short term. This is, in part, because consumers may be slow in responding to price signals. But it is also because the real cost of transport (sometimes referred to as the generalized cost) includes both the monetary cost of transport and the cost of the time spent in transportation. And sometimes the cost of time is larger than the monetary cost of transportation. Elasticity is greater in the long run, because individuals can adjust their choice of where to live, means of transportation, or lifestyle. For instance, the price elasticity of automobile fuel demand ranges from −0.1 to −0.4 in the short run and −0.6 to −1.1 in the long run (Chamon and others 2008).

This low elasticity explains why the rebound effect (whereby people may increase their driving when the cost of car use decreases as a result of improved efficiency) is relatively limited, even though it may be greater at lower income levels. Sorrel (2007) finds that this effect should remain below 30 percent (that is, less than 30 percent of the gain in efficiency will be "taken back" by the increase in demand). Greene and others (1999) find that the rebound effect for individual transport in the United States is about 20 percent.

Various price instruments have proven efficient. Singapore's Area Licensing Scheme—the first-ever comprehensive road pricing scheme in the world—required drivers to pay an area license fee of S\$3 (\$1.25) a day to enter the central business district during peak hours. The number of vehicles entering the restricted zone declined by 73 percent, and average speeds increased by an estimated 10–20 percent (Federal Highway Administration 2008). Modal shift can improve the efficiency of such price-based transport policies and help mitigate their negative consequences (such as the significant spatial inequality they can create) (see Gusdorf and others 2008). But it requires investments in public transport multimodal coordination (such as creating parking lots next to train stations), and urban planning (to maximize access to public transit and ensure that passenger density is high enough to justify the required investments).

In the water sector, different uses have different elasticities. Residential use has a low price elasticity, estimated at about −0.1 to −0.3 (Nauges and van den Berg 2009; Nieswiadomy and Molina 1989). Agricultural use has a higher elasticity, and subsidies (whether to water or to the electricity needed for pumping) in this sector can thus create distorted incentives, favoring activities with high water consumption. And disincentives to water conservation are greatest where the resource is scarcest (Frederick and Schwarz 2000). Removing subsidies and raising prices can thus be efficient in this sector.

Demand-side actions, standards, and regulations: Critical complements to prices

Price-based instruments can be made more efficient if complemented with appropriate demand-management actions. Large quantities of water can be saved in India through better irrigation technologies, obviating the need to exploit new raw water sources. In China, industrial water reuse systems can save water, reducing the need to build expensive water conveyance systems. Many of the technologies that can make a difference already exist and are in use in developed countries. Further application needs to be supported by institutions and promoted by sector leaders. India's Total Sanitation campaign is a successful example of using noneconomic incentives to promote greener options (box 6.7).

Standards and regulations may also be useful where price elasticity is limited or the political economy of price reform is complex. Examples of such instruments include renewable portfolio standards, in which regulators require utilities to include a given percentage or an absolute quantity of renewable energy capacity in their energy mix.

In transport, fuel economy standards are common for new vehicles (see chapter 2). In 1995, Japan introduced fuel economy standards to reduce new car fuel consumption by 19 percent, achieving the target by 2004. A new target, set in 2006, aims for another 23.5 percent reduction (An and others 2007). In Europe, improvements in fuel economy occurred largely as a side effect of air pollutant regulations, although automobile manufacturers agreed with the European Commission on a voluntary fleet average emission target of 140 grams of CO_2 per kilometer for new passenger cars. Governments can also create automobile restricted zones to limit passenger car traffic in urban areas, as Denmark did in the city of Aalborg.

Promoting clean cooking and heating solutions is another case in which standards and public investments are likely to be more helpful than pricing instruments. Replacing traditional three-stone cooking fires with advanced stoves could significantly reduce emissions and health risks (World Bank 2011b). Without drastic interventions, 2.7 billion people may still lack clean cooking facilities in 2030 (IEA 2011).

Integrated market development, including technology standards, is needed to promote the use of clean and efficient solutions at the household level. The Global Alliance for Clean Cookstoves, launched in September 2010, aims to enable 100 million households to adopt clean and efficient stoves and fuels by 2020. The alliance works with public, private, and nonprofit partners to help overcome the market barriers that impede the production, deployment, and use of clean cookstoves in the developing world.

Green infrastructure requires planning and strong institutions

Because infrastructure is lumpy, infrastructure systems cannot be grown incrementally and continuously, and they need to be planned in a holistic manner. A road or train line cannot be designed without considering other parts of the transport system, land use regulations, and urban planning.

Moreover, different infrastructure systems interact across sectors and cannot be designed in isolation. Water availability affects electricity generation, and electricity is critical in water management (for groundwater pumping, for example). Transportation and energy interact closely: energy production often requires transport infrastructure, and different transport modes have different energy needs (from liquid fuel transport to electricity grids for electrified cars). Smart use of information and communication technologies can green the urban environment and improve the efficiency of other infrastructure systems (box 6.8). Thus, much can be gained from

---

BOX 6.7   Using noneconomic incentives to reduce the demand for water and sanitation

India's Total Sanitation Campaign, launched in 1999, focused on communication, education, community mobilization, and the provision of toilets in government schools, mother/child centers, and low-income households (World Bank 2011c). There was little government contribution to the capital cost of sanitation facilities. Instead, the focus was on private investment and private behavior change.

Part of the effort involved the Clean Village Award Program—awards to local councils that achieved the status of "Open-Defecation Free and Fully Sanitized Uni." The awards—inspired by a program initially introduced in Maharastra (the "Sant Gadge Baba")—helped increase reported sanitation coverage from 21 percent in 2001 to 57 percent in 2008.

BOX 6.8   Harnessing smart information and communication technologies to shape a green future

The smart application of information and communication technologies can facilitate green growth, both by reducing emissions of greenhouse gases and by creating new market opportunities, such as smart grids and Intelligent Transport Systems (ITS). To date, most of these mitigation opportunities have been applied in high- and middle-income countries. But it is arguably in the megacities of the developing world where the impact could be greatest. Application of ITS in Bangkok or Manila, where there are few substitution opportunities for private road traffic in the form of mass-transit system, would have a much more beneficial impact than in, say Hong Kong SAR, China, or Singapore. Asian countries committed to introducing ITS—such as electronic fare and road-user charging systems, transport control centers, and real-time user information—in Goal 11 of the Bangkok Declaration on Sustainable Transport Goals for 2010–20.

---

a planning system that can integrate various objectives and infrastructure systems at both the country and regional level to significantly reduce infrastructure costs.

Developing cities: Managing rapid expansion to tap the potential for efficiency gains

Rapid urbanization is both a driver and a feature of economic development, with serious consequences for infrastructure design (World Bank 2009). In many developing countries—particularly countries transitioning from low- to middle-income status—the next few decades will see a dramatic increase in the share of people living in cities. In fact, the number of people living in urban areas in developing countries is expected to double, from 2 billion to 4 billion, between 2000 and 2030. And this massive increase is expected to triple the physical footprint of urbanized areas from 200,000 to 600,000 square kilometers. The public policy and investment challenges of managing the social and environmental implications while promoting cities that are economic drivers of the economy are substantial. Fortunately, practical options exist to efficiently green the urbanization process.

The first priority is designing policies and institutions that can help anticipate future urbanization. These policies should enable existing urban areas to be redeveloped and should prepare the peri-urban fringe to accommodate new settlements. For this to work, land markets need to be functional. Urban land markets mediate demand and supply and enable the efficient use of land and optimal development of constructed floor area, both of which shape a city's spatial structure. Developed countries typically rely on market data from transactions and property attributes to reveal land and property prices. In contrast, most developing countries lack the basic institutional machinery to value and price land.

Higher land prices routinely lead to higher density—which enhances productivity spillovers, potentially increases the supply of affordable housing, and helps manage the demand for transport. But this mechanism is sometimes impaired by land regulations—in many Indian cities the floor-space index is limited to 1 (as opposed to 5–15 in other Asian cities). As a result, high land prices coexist with low density and sprawl, creating both housing affordability and transportation issues.

Also, when "official" land prices do not reflect demand and are depressed at the urban periphery, it is likely that sprawl or suburbanization will be excessive. How the peri-urban expansion is managed will be a critical determinant of whether cities can harness agglomeration economies and induce efficient resource allocation. The absence of a functioning land market creates a major urban governance challenge, as the scale at which urban and metropolitan economies now operate often does not coincide with their physical and administrative boundaries. The institutional arrangements that can enhance coordination across these entities is likely to be context specific, but significant efforts are needed to make them emerge.

The second priority is redeveloping older, obsolescent areas to promote more efficient development and achieve higher densities. Older areas typically share several common traits. Their network of streets and alleys is often irregular and highly granular—limiting the ability of developers to build modern high-rise buildings. An alternative is to redesign these areas to accommodate higher densities. Doing so typically requires assembling small plots into larger and more efficient parcels and ensuring that the redeveloped area has adequate infrastructure (particularly transport, water, electricity, broadband Internet, and public services) to support higher population densities. These actions should be designed using consultations with the local population, to make sure they benefit. For instance, rehabilitation projects need to account for the fact that slum dwellers often gain more from slum upgrading than from relocation (World Bank 2006).

The third priority is integrating land policy with urban mobility and transportation (Viguié and Hallegatte 2012). Options for urban transportation are closely tied to

urban land development and can create both positive and negative externalities as cities grow. Problems arise when there are inconsistencies between new developments and mass transit investment—as in Hanoi, where new dense urban development projects are not being located near the planned transit network. This kind of planning creates a double risk of having too few users of a public transit system, threatening the financial and social return on investment, and increasing the number of cars on the roads, with consequences on congestion and air pollution.

Urban transport is best addressed as part of integrated urban strategies that can address the interests of multiple user groups and anticipate long-term needs for which no one is yet advocating but that will become critical in the future. Although public transport tends to be more sustainable than personal motor vehicles, it is often unviable in low-density agglomerations (table 6.3).

Although planning and developing public transit is likely to generate co-benefits for economic integration and manage demand for private modes of motorized transport, these strategies should not come at the expense of allowing a wider range of transport options that can enhance the poor's mobility. Surveys show that many people cannot afford public transport. In Sub-Saharan African cities, walking represents between 5 percent (in Kigali) and 80 percent (in Conakry) of all urban trips, with public transportation ranging from 10 percent to 90 percent (World Bank 2008). A significant share of households

TABLE 6.3   Effect of land use and density on use of public transport

Population density	Typical region	Modal model split (%)			Automobile use (km/person/yr)	Public transport use (trips/person/yr)	Petrol consumption for transport (MJ/person/yr)
		Motorized private	Public transport	Non-motorized			
Low (25 people per ha)	North America and Australia	80	10	10	>10,000	<50	>55,000
Medium (50–100 people per ha)	Europe	50	25	25	—	—	—
High (more than 250 people per ha)	Asia	25	50	25	<5,000	>250	<15,000

Source: Gomez-Ibañez 2012.
Note: —=not available.

reports no public transport expenditure, but the average share of income spent in public transport ranges from 3 percent (in Addis Ababa) to 14 percent (in Lagos), reaching about $12–$16 a month in most cities. This implies that at low-income levels, the wider availability of different service levels and modes at different prices is a necessary strategy for providing urban transport services. In particular, improving sidewalks, streetlights, and other measures to protect pedestrian users should be parts of an urban transport strategy.

Urban transport also plays a key role in spatially integrating urban labor markets. As cities around the world expand their spatial footprints, the limited reach of walking trips may exacerbate slum formation, as many people trade off housing quality to be close to jobs. It can also severely limit labor market opportunities for people who live farther away from economic centers. Bovenberg and Goulder (1996) suggest that higher commuting costs can decrease labor supply. Graham (2005) finds that productive firms are located in accessible and densely populated places.

A fourth priority is integrating urban planning with natural risk management— still rare, especially in low-income countries. In 2005, the global community adopted the Hyogo Framework for Action, a 10-year plan to make the world safe from natural disasters. To date, 70 percent of high-income countries are carrying out urban and land-use planning under the framework, but only about 15 percent of low-income countries are doing so (figure 6.3). This low participation matters because cities are increasingly vulnerable to natural hazards, including floods that are becoming more destructive in many parts of the world. And considering the limited protection offered by dikes and sea walls, only risk-sensitive land-use planning can mitigate flood losses over the long term (Hallegatte 2011).

Given the role of urbanization in development, a green policy able to develop cities without increasing risks and negative environmental outcomes would help maintain or increase cities' attractiveness and produce economic benefits (World Bank 2009). It is an open question as to how cities can

FIGURE 6.3   Too few countries are implementing plans to mitigate against natural disasters

(percentage of countries that implemented risk management policies under the 2005 UN Hyogo Framework for Action)

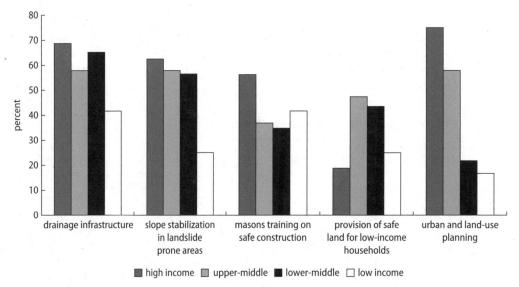

Source: UN 2011.

accommodate the huge increase in urban population that is expected in many regions without experiencing a hike in disaster losses (World Bank 2010). That said, a recent World Bank study uses Alexandria, Casablanca, Rabat, and Tunis to illustrate how flood risks and climate change can be integrated in urban planning (World Bank 2011a). Transportation infrastructure has a key role to play to make it possible for the population to live in safe locations while retaining access to jobs and services (Hallegatte 2011).

Infrastructure robustness and redundancy are critical to maintaining the functions of the economic system after disasters, especially in urban environments, where the failure of one component (such as electricity, transport, water, or sanitation) can paralyze activity. In many cases, indirect disaster impacts caused by the loss of lifeline and essential infrastructure services are of similar magnitude to direct disaster losses (Hallegatte 2008; Tierney 1997). However, increasing robustness and redundancy is costly, creating trade-offs between the resilience of the economic system and its efficiency in normal conditions (Henriet and others 2012).

Minimizing the potential for regrets and maximizing short-term benefits

Some infrastructure investments that are required from a development and economic perspective and useful from an environmental point of view cannot be implemented because of financial, institutional, or planning constraints. Given these constraints, a green growth policy should seek to minimize the risk from regret and maximize short-term benefits.

To do so, one needs first to identify what investments made today can lead to irreversibility that will cause regret in the future. An example is urban planning and urban form, which are being decided on now in many countries and cannot be easily reversed in the future. Next, one needs to identify what policies (such as

removing subsidies or imposing an environmental tax) or additional investments in infrastructure (such as sanitation systems) can yield large co-benefits and synergies between economic and environmental objectives. An example is the provision of urban public transport in crowded cities with high congestion and air pollution levels, where public transport can increase economic efficiency and improve environmental conditions. Sometimes the synergy is between the environment and welfare, without being uniquely mediated by economic efficiency (an example is sanitation infrastructure, which improves water quality and thus population health).

Previous chapters have shown that many actions and policies can green growth and capture synergies between environmental protection and development. Designing a green growth strategy requires policy makers to choose among these options, based on what is most important and urgent. The next chapter proposes a methodology to identify priority actions, as a function of the inertia and irreversibility they imply and of the trade-offs and synergies they create.

Notes

1. Transport externalities in the United States are estimated at $0.11 per mile (Parry and others 2007). Traffic congestion not only increases emissions, it also increases local pollutants and noise.

2. WHO-UNICEF (2012) projects that by 2015 the share of people without improved water will have fallen to 8 percent, exceeding the target of 12 percent. In contrast, about 33 percent of the world's population is projected to lack access to improved sanitation, far from the 23 percent target.

3. Investment needs is a relative concept, as it depends on what the target level of coverage and quality is. No firm data exist on how much countries invest in infrastructure, although efforts have been made to collect information for Africa and for private investments in infrastructure (see Fay and others 2010; MDB Working Group on Infrastructure 2011).

References

An, F., D. Gordon, H. He, D. Kodjak, and D. Rutherford. 2007. *Passenger Vehicle Greenhouse Gas and Fuel Economy, Standards: A Global Update*. Washington, DC: International Council on Clean Transportation.

Arze del Granado, J. D. Coady, and R. Gillingham. 2010. "The Unequal Benefits of Fuel Subsidies: A Review of Evidence for Developing Countries." IMF working paper WP/10/02, International Monetary Fund, Washington, DC.

Bertaud, A. 2003. "Clearing the Air in Atlanta: Transit and Smart Growth or Conventional Economics?" *Journal of Urban Economics* 54 (3): 379–400.

Bovenberg, A. L., and L. H. Goulder. 1996. "Optimal Environmental Taxation in the Presence of Other Taxes: General Equilibrium Analysis." *American Economic Review* 86 (4): 985–1000.

Briceño-Garmendia, C., K. Smits, V. Foster. 2008. "Financing Public Infrastructure in Sub-Saharan Africa: Patterns and Emerging Issues." Background Paper 15. Africa Infrastructure Country Diagnostic, World Bank, Washington, DC.

Chamon, M., P. Mauro, and Y. Okawa. 2008. "Mass Car Ownership in the Emerging Market Giants." *Economic Policy* 23 (54): 243–96.

Davis, S. J., K. Caldeira, and H. D. Matthews. 2010. "Future CO_2 Emissions and Climate Change from Existing Energy Infrastructure." *Science* 329 (5997): 1330–3.

ESMAP (Energy Sector Assistance Management Program). 2009. "Offgrid Technology and Lighting Africa". Session 6 of the Africa Electrification Initiative Workshop. Maputo, Mozambique, May 9–12. http://www.esmap. org/esmap/sites/esmap.org/files/Rpt_Senegal_ Morocco_Ecuador_AEI6.pdf.

Fay, M., M. Toman, D. Benitez, and S. Csordas. 2010. "Infrastructure and Sustainable Development." In *Postcrisis Growth and Development: A Development Agenda for the G20*, ed. S. Fardoust, Y. Kim, and C. Sepulveda. Washington, DC: World Bank.

Federal Highway Administration. 2008. "Lessons Learned from International Experience in Congestion Pricing." Publication FHWA-HOP-08-047. Federal Highway Administration, Washington, DC.

Foster, V., and C. Briceño-Garmendia. 2010. *Africa's Infrastructure: A Time for Transformation*. Paris: Agence Française de Dévelopment; Washington, DC: World Bank.

Frederick, K. D., and G. E. Schwarz. 2000. "Socioeconomic Impacts of Climate Variability and Change on U.S. Water Resources." RFF Discussion Paper 00–21, Resources for the Future, Washington, DC.

Geneletti, D. 2003. "Biodiversity Impact Assessment of Roads: An Approach Based on Ecosystem Rarity." *Environmental Impact Assessment Review* 23 (3): 343–65.

Giraudet, L.-G., C. Givarch, and P. Quirion. 2011. "Exploring the Potential for Energy Conservation in French Households through Hybrid Modeling." *Energy Economics* 34 (2): 426–45.

Gomez-Ibañez, J. A. 2012. "Urban Transportation and Green Growth." Paper prepared for the Green Growth Knowledge Platform inaugural conference, Mexico City, January 12–13.

Graham, D. 2005. "Wider Economic Benefits of Transport Improvements: Link between Agglomeration and Productivity". Report to Department of Transport, London.

Greene, D. L., J. R. Kahn, and R. C. Gibson. 1999. "Fuel Economy Rebound Effect for US Household Vehicles." *Energy Journal* 20 (3): 1–31.

Guivarch C., and S. Hallegatte. 2011. "Existing Infrastructure and the 2°C Target." *Climatic Change Letters* 109 (3): 801–5.

Gusdorf, F., and S. Hallegatte. 2007. "Compact or Spread-Out Cities: Urban Planning, Taxation, and the Vulnerability to Transportation Shocks." *Energy Policy* 35 (10): 4826–38. doi:10.1016/j.enpol.2007.04.017.

Gusdorf, F., S. Hallegatte, and A. Lahellec. 2008. "Time and Space Matter: How Urban Transitions Create Inequality." *Global Environment Change* 18 (4): 708–19. doi:10.1016/j.gloenvcha.2008.06.005.

Hallegatte, S. 2008. "An Adaptive Regional Input-Output Model and Its Application to the Assessment of the Economic Cost of Katrina." *Risk Analysis* 28 (3): 779–99.

———. 2009. "Strategies to Adapt to an Uncertain Climate Change." *Global Environmental Change* 19 (2): 240–7.

———. 2011. "How Economic Growth and Rational Decisions Can Make Disaster Losses Grow Faster than Wealth." Policy Research

Working Paper 5617, World Bank, Washington, DC.

Henriet F., S. Hallegatte, and L. Tabourier. 2012. "Firm-Network Characteristics and Economic Robustness to Natural Disasters." *Journal of Economic Dynamics and Control* 36 (1): 150–67.

Hussein, M. A. 2007. "Cost of Environmental Degradation: An Analysis in the Middle East and North Africa Region." *Management of Environmental Quality* 19 (3): 305–7.

Hutton, G., J. Bartram. 2008. "Global Costs of Attaining the Millennium Development Goal for Water Supply and Sanitation." *Bulletin of the World Health Organization* 86 (1): 13–19.

IBNET. 2011. *The IBNET Water Supply and Sanitation Performance Blue Book.* Washington, DC: World Bank.

IEA (International Energy Agency). 2011. *World Energy Outlook 2011.* Paris: IEA.

ISDR (International Strategy for Disaster Reduction), World Bank, World Meteorological Organization, International Monetary Fund. 2011. *Strengthening the Hydro-Meteorological Services in South Eastern Europe.* http://www.unisdr.org/we/inform/publications/7650.

Kalkuhl, M., O. Edenhofer, and K. Lessmann. 2011. "Learning or Lock-In: Optimal Technology Policies to Support Mitigation." *Resource and Energy Economics* 34 (1): 1–23.

Komives, K., V. Foster, J. Halpern, and Q. Wodon. 2005. *Water, Electricity, and the Poor: Who Benefits from Utility Subsidies?* Washington, DC: World Bank.

Larsen, E. R., I. Dyner, L. Bedoya V, and C. J. Franco. 2004. "Lessons from Deregulation in Colombia: Successes, Failures and the Way Ahead." *Energy Policy* 32 (15): 1767–80.

Loulou, R., and M. Labriet. 2008. "ETSAP-TIAM: The TIMES Integrated Assessment Model Part I: Model Structure." *Computational Management Science, Special Issue on Managing Energy and the Environment* 5 (1): 7–40.

Luderer, G., R. Pietzcker, E. Kriegler, M. Haller, and N. Bauer. Forthcoming. "Asia's Role in Mitigating Climate Change: A Technology and Sector Specific Analysis with ReMIND-R." Preprint.

MDB Working Group on Infrastructure. 2011. Infrastructure Action Plan, submission to the G20.

Nauges, C., and C. Van Den Berg. 2009. "Demand for Piped and Non-Piped Water Supply Services: Evidence from Southwest Sri Lanka." *Environmental and Resource Economics* 42 (4): 535–49.

Nieswiadomy, M. L., and D. J. Molina. 1989. "Comparing Residential Water Demand Estimates under Decreasing and Increasing Block Rates Using Household Data." *Land Economics* 65 (3): 280–9.

Parry, I.W.H., M. Walls, W. Harrington. 2007. "Automobile Externalities and Policies." *Journal of Economic Literature* 45: 373–399.

Roberts, P, K. C. Shyam, and C. Rastogi. 2006. "Rural Access Index: A Key Development Indicator." Transport Sector Board Technical Paper 10, World Bank, Washington DC.

Rozenberg, J., S. Hallegatte, A. Vogt-Schilb, O. Sassi, C. Guivarch, H. Waisman, and J. C. Hourcade. 2010. "Climate Policies as a Hedge against the Uncertainty on Future Oil Supply." *Climatic Change* 101 (3–4): 663–8.

Sorrel, S. 2007. *The Rebound Effect: An Assessment of the Evidence for Economy-Wide Energy Savings from Improved Energy Efficiency.* London, UK: UK Energy Research Centre.

Tierney, K. J. 1997. "Business Impacts of the Northridge Earthquake." *Journal of Contingencies and Crisis Management* 5 (2): 87–97.

UN (United Nations). 2011. *United Nations Global Assessment Report on Disaster Risk Reduction.* New York: United Nations.

van Vliet, O., V. Krey, D. McCollum, S. Pachauri, Y. Nagai, S. Rao, and K. Riahi. 2012. "Synergies in the Asian Energy System: Climate Change, Energy Security, Energy Access and Air Pollution." *Energy Economics.*

Viguie, V., and S. Hallegatte. 2012. "Trade-Offs and Synergies in Urban Climate Policies." *Nature Climate Change* 2:334–7. doi: 10.1038/nclimate 1434.

Weber, E., E. Arpi, A. Carrigan. 2011. "From Here to There: A Creative Guide to Make Public Transport the Way to Go." Embarq, the WRI Center for Sustainable Transport, World Resource Institute, Washington, DC. http://www.embarq.org/sites/default/files/EMB2011_From_Here_to_There_web.pdf.

WHO-UNICEF (World Health Organization; United Nations Children's Fund) Joint Monitoring Programme for Water Supply and Sanitation. 2012. *Progress on Drinking Water and Sanitation: 2012 Update.* New York: UNICEF.

World Bank. 2004. *Colombia: Recent Economic Developments in Infrastructure (REDI):*

Balancing Social and Productive Needs for Infrastructure. Washington, DC: World Bank.

———. 2006. *Morocco, Poverty and Social Impact Analysis of the National Slum Upgrading Program*. Washington, DC: World Bank.

———. 2008. *Stuck in Traffic: Urban Transport in Africa*. Africa Infrastructure Country Diagnostic Report, World Bank, Washington, DC.

———. 2009. *World Development Report 2009: Reshaping Economic Geography*. Washington, DC: World Bank.

———. 2010. *World Development Report 2010: Development and Climate Change*. Washington, DC: World Bank.

———. 2011a. *Climate Change Adaptation and Natural Disasters Preparedness in the Coastal Cities of North Africa*. Washington DC: World Bank.

———. 2011b. *Household Cookstoves, Environment, Health, and Climate Change: A New Look at an Old Problem*. Washington, DC: World Bank.

———. 2011c. *The Political Economy of Sanitation: How Can We Increase Investment and Improve Service for the Poor?* Washington, DC: World Bank.

———. 2011d. *World Development Indicators*. Washington, DC: World Bank.

———. Forthcoming. *Maximizing Leverage of Public Funds to Unlock Commercial Financing for Clean Energy in East Asia*. Washington, DC: World Bank.

Crafting a Green Growth Strategy | 7

Key Messages

- The design of green growth policies must balance predictability against flexibility and relevance against enforceability.
- Step-by-step guidelines, including a checklist, can help analysts and decision makers structure the process of crafting green growth strategies.
- The suggested approach identifies priorities along two dimensions: synergy (the existence of local and immediate co-benefits) and urgency (inertia and the risk of irreversibility and lock-in).
- A green growth strategy needs to be designed before individual projects are assessed and selected. Project assessments need to account for uncertainty and diverging world views.

A good green growth strategy can increase welfare by providing both environmental and economic benefits. It is not a panacea to a country's economic ills: if economic growth is insufficient because of institutional or policy problems, green growth will not boost it in the absence of other structural changes.

Many green policies impose economic costs in the short term, such as higher investment or operational costs. But over the longer term, they are designed to yield economic benefits and contribute to long-term sustainable growth. Even so, short-term costs can create trade-offs between environmental protection and short-term economic growth.

For this reason, political and social acceptability require that green growth policies be designed with the specific goals of mitigating trade-offs across both space and time and offsetting costs by maximizing synergies and short-term economic benefits (such as job creation, poverty alleviation, and increased efficiency).

Traditional economic analysis of policies and projects can be complemented with a screening exercise that helps design policies that provide short-term economic benefits and are thus easier to implement. Not all green growth policies can yield such synergies, and trade-offs will be unavoidable. It is nevertheless useful to scrutinize policy designs for opportunities to achieve more co-benefits, if necessary by combining several policy interventions.

This chapter does not provide a one-size-fits-all green strategy, because the appropriate measures and policies are highly dependent on the context, especially on the most pressing environmental and economic issues. Countries at different income levels will necessarily have different priorities; the lowest-income countries are more likely to delay the implementation of environmental policies that imply trade-offs with short-term productivity. Instead, this chapter provides a step-by-step approach to designing a strategy that is appropriate in a given context.

The challenges of developing a green growth strategy

Much can be gained from framing environmental policies as national strategies with positive long-term goals. Doing so increases the acceptability of immediate costs by the population and the private sector. It also improves consistency among policies and fosters policy certainty—which creates a friendlier climate for investments, making it more likely that private resources will be invested in long-term projects. But building a national strategy creates some challenges of its own, including the need for interagency coordination, private sector engagement, and the definition of relevant long-term goals and indicators.

Balancing predictability and flexibility

Promoting a transition toward a more environment-friendly growth pathway requires balancing the credibility and predictability of long-term objectives on the one hand and the flexibility of the selected strategy on the other. Credible and predictable long-term objectives are necessary to help coordinate economic actors and promote

investments: businesses will not invest heavily in research on low-energy or water-saving technologies if they cannot be sure that a market will exist over the long term for innovations in these domains. Their willingness to invest in green technologies and infrastructure depends on their trust in and projections of future environmental goals.

But environmental policies themselves need to evolve over time, in response to new information (such as technology or scientific facts) and to the actions undertaken by other countries or regions. Thus, the ability to adjust course is essential—even if it can occur only at the expense of predictability.

Getting around the commitment problem. What factors might reduce predictability? Certainly, changes in the political landscape, scientific uncertainty, and differences in interpretations of scientific results or future technological potentials will arise—as will questions about the government's ability to commit (Dixit and Lambertini 2003; Kydland and Prescott 1977). The fact that governments lack the ability (or credibility) to make long-term commitments has led to the transfer of monetary policy to independent central banks in many countries. On the fiscal front, independent fiscal councils (such as the Office of Management and Budget in the United States) have been created to monitor government policies and inform policy makers from a technical and nonpartisan perspective.

This commitment problem exists in the environmental domain as well. Innovative solutions will have to be found to combine political legitimacy with the ability to commit. A process needs to be established that allows long-term objectives to be monitored by a body other than the government in place at a given point in time. There may be a role for an "independent environmental council" that monitors environmental policies for consistency with agreed-upon long-term objectives.

Building consensus. How a national strategy is developed and implemented strongly influences its sustainability, credibility, and predictability. National strategies help bring together diverse groups of stakeholders (businesses, worker unions, and civil society) to build connections, exchange viewpoints, raise awareness, and build a sustained political commitment. This approach signals to society that significant and durable efforts will be dedicated to environmental protection.

Local authorities play a vital role, given that it is at the local level that citizens experience the destructive impact of environmental degradation (such as atmospheric pollution) and government is often empowered to take corrective action (through land-use planning or the regulation of economic activity). Local authorities have proved to be willing innovators, offering opportunities to test policies and build consensus before scaling up.

Some countries, such as Brazil and France, have tried to build consensus through open and participatory approaches involving political parties and civil society. Ahead of the preparation of its National Plan on Climate Change, Brazil created the Brazilian Forum on Climate Change, which brought together representatives from government, civil society, business, universities, and nongovernmental organizations to mobilize society around a climate plan of action. Public participation took the form of a national conference on the environment and sector dialogues.

Approaches that feature iterative, multistakeholder involvement and extensive consultation with the private sector and civil society create the transparency and political buy-in to make commitments to green growth sustainable. Extensive consultation can also help address some of the governance risks inherent in climate change—which is characterized by complexity, uncertainty, and asymmetries in information. It is particularly important to ensure opportunities for the indigenous and poor communities to voice their concerns and priorities (Transparency International 2011).

Jointly setting economic and environmental goals. At the strategic level, integrating environmental concerns with broader government activity involves systematically evaluating government policies through an environmental lens and creating new coordinating mechanisms to ensure that environmental concerns are mainstreamed in government activity. Poverty reduction strategies, economic development plans, disaster risk reduction strategies, and climate strategies provide opportunities for this to happen.

Consider the case of climate strategies. One way for countries to balance climate policy and development objectives is through national climate plans and low-emission development strategies. Already, more than 47 countries have low-emission development strategies supported by bilateral or multilateral bodies; many more have issued climate change–related strategies on their own (World Bank 2011b).

For instance, India's National Action Plan on Climate Change defines eight national "missions," including policy programs for energy efficiency, a sustainable habitat, and sustainable agriculture. Bangladesh's 2009 Climate Change Strategy and Action Plan requires reviewing and revising existing government policies to ensure that they take climate change impacts into account. Climate change "focal points" within all line ministries are to work in coordination with a climate change unit housed within the Ministry of Environment and Forests (Government of Bangladesh 2009). Other country strategies outline a central interministerial body to coordinate climate activities, including with key economic ministries (table 7.1).

Another way to integrate economic and environmental goals is to require that the environment be brought into core government operations. A logical place for this to occur is through the budget, as the budget process is the central means of ensuring that expenditures are aligned with policy goals and that proper consideration is given to the trade-offs involved when climate-related concerns and growth objectives clash. For example, carbon pricing schemes, subsidy reform, and energy and infrastructure investment decisions all affect the fiscal balance (as discussed in chapter 2). As a result, finance ministries and other core government and development planning actors must be key players

TABLE 7.1 Inter-ministerial arrangements for coordinating on climate change strategy in selected countries

Country	Arrangement
Bangladesh	National Steering Committee on Climate Change headed by the Minister of Environment and Forests oversees the work of the Ministry of Environment and Forests' climate change unit, which works with climate change focal points in each line ministry.
Brazil	Inter-ministerial Commission on Climate Change is chaired by Ministry of Science and Technology and includes the Ministry of Planning, Budget, and Management, and the Ministry of Finance, among others.
India	Advisory Council on Climate Change, led by the prime minister, oversees climate policy. Coordinating unit within the Ministry of Environment and Forests implements the National Action Plan on Climate Change. Ad hoc inter-ministerial commissions will address the eight national "missions" identified in the National Action Plan.
Indonesia	National Committee for Climate Change includes representatives of all departments with responsibilities related to mitigation or adaptation.
Mexico	Inter-secretarial Commission on Climate Change, led by the Secretary of Environment and Natural Resources and including the Secretary of the Economy as well as other line ministries and agencies, is charged with promoting and coordinating the national plan and associated activities.
South Africa	Inter-ministerial Committee on Climate Change coordinates government climate change actions and aligns climate policy with existing legislation and policy.
Vietnam	National Steering Committee headed by the prime minister and representing all major line ministries oversees the work of a unit within the Ministry of Natural Resources and Environment that is to coordinate implementation of the National Target Program to Respond to Climate Change.

Source: Governments of Bangladesh 2009; Brazil 2010; India 2008; Indonesia 2009; Mexico 2009; South Africa 2010; and Vietnam 2008.

in developing and implementing green policies. The Republic of Korea's national green growth strategy (box 7.1) and many national climate strategies have already begun to reflect this reality.

- The Indonesian Ministry of Finance has taken a leading role in national climate policy. In 2009, it issued a green paper outlining actions to support the country's agenda on climate change (Government of Indonesia 2009). It was the lead national partner for a World Bank country study on low-carbon growth.

- Ministries of finance in Morocco and the Philippines, among others, are undertaking climate change public expenditure reviews to help align spending with climate change and development objectives.

- As part of Niger's participation in the Pilot Program for Climate Resilience—which provides assistance for integrating climate resilience into national development planning—the Ministry of Economy and Finance will house a strategic unit to coordinate actions taken under the country's climate resilience program (PPCR 2010).

Balancing relevance and enforceability

Key dimensions of the needed balancing act between relevance and enforceability of environmental objectives include the choice of indicators with which to measure progress toward objectives; the time horizon over which environmental objectives should be selected; and the scale (national, local, or sectoral) at which environmental objectives are set.[1]

The choice of indicators. Potentially accurate indicators may be difficult to set or enforce, and easier-to-implement indicators may be less relevant. For climate change, a natural indicator for measuring mitigation is a "long-term carbon budget," which measures global carbon emissions over the course of a given period of time, say, a century (Matthews and others 2009; Meinshausen and others 2009). But carbon budget commitments are difficult to introduce and enforce. Indeed, there is an incentive for decision makers to delay investments and efforts beyond their mandate.

Another possibility is to define emission targets at one or several points in time—such as the European objective of reducing

BOX 7.1   Implementing a green growth strategy in the Republic of Korea

Korea has moved assertively to become a leader in implementing green growth policies and defining a global green growth agenda. Its two-tier strategy focuses on a short-term response to the current global economic crisis and a long-term transition toward green growth through export-focused green-tech research and development. In acting as a resolute first mover, Korea has exposed itself to both risks and potentially high payoffs.

Policy makers in Korea are seeking transformation, not marginal adjustment, of the economy, seeking to move it away from its current heavy reliance on energy-intensive industries (which doubled its greenhouse gas emissions during the 1990s) and massive energy imports (which account for two-thirds of imports). In pursuing green growth, they are combining three complementary and mutually reinforcing objectives: responding to the economic crisis, reducing the country's energy dependency, and rebalancing the economy toward green sectors over the long term.

Korea's $30.7 billion stimulus package, adopted in 2009, was the greenest of any country, with 80 percent of all funds going toward environment-friendly projects (World Bank 2010). Investments initially targeted infrastructure as a short-term response to the crisis. Projects funded included the development of renewable energy sources, energy-efficient buildings, and low-carbon vehicles; the expansion of railways; and the management of water and waste. Most of the green investment funded three initiatives: river restoration, expansion of mass transit and railroads, and energy conservation in villages and schools. Together, the three projects were projected to create 500,000 jobs (World Bank 2010).

Source: http://www.greengrowth.go.kr.

greenhouse gas emissions by 20 percent by 2020. This type of objective is easier to enforce, but setting an objective for a particular point in time removes some flexibility as to when and how to act, leading to higher costs.

The time horizon over which environmental objectives are set. Relevance would favor setting very long-term objectives, but doing so risks encouraging policy makers and economic actors to delay action. Shorter-term goals are needed to ensure that action is taken. Shorter-term milestones are also useful because there is less uncertainty surrounding technologies and economic conditions over the short term, making it easier to define relevant targets. It thus makes sense to combine a long-term objective (such as limiting global warming to less than 2°C) with shorter-term objectives (such as reducing emissions by 20 percent by 2020).

Short-term goals complement rather than replace long-term goals. If a short-term goal is an end in itself, it may make sense to implement the least expensive solution. But in this case, there is a risk that the solutions selected to meet the short-term goal may lock in technology and infrastructure, making it impossible to reach longer-term objectives (Vogt-Shilb and Hallegatte 2011). To meet an ambitious long-term objective, a short-term target may need to be achieved by implementing options that have greater potential (or suffer from greater risks of lock-in or irreversibility). Urban policies such as land use planning or mass transportation may not be required to reach short-term targets (for instance, in terms of emissions by 2020). But considering the timescale of such policies, they need to be implemented without delay if longer-term (2050), more ambitious targets are to be met.

The scale (national, local, or sectoral) at which environmental objectives are set. Where objectives are economy wide (such as a carbon tax), the economic system has full flexibility to reach the objective by taking action where it is least expensive to do so. Given the information asymmetry between governments and economic agents, it makes sense to let market-based mechanisms determine where it is most cost-effective to act

(Laffont 1999). But the government cannot set credible and predictable signals over the very long term, and economic agents do not anticipate changes that occur over decades. As a result, there is underinvestment in land-use planning, resilient infrastructure, research, and other interventions critical to greening growth but whose benefits take time to materialize.

Given these constraints, action at the sector level may make sense in sectors with significant potential for both lock-in and green impacts (Vogt-Schilb and Hallegatte 2011; chapter 3). Overlapping sectoral objectives—such as the 20 percent renewable energy target in Europe, fuel-economy standards in the automobile industry, and changes in urban planning, building norms, and infrastructure design—may thus be part of an efficient mitigation policy.

However, sectoral policies are vulnerable to regulation capture, rent seeking, and inefficient micromanagement (Laffont 1996; Rodrik 2005). Rent-seeking behavior is likely to affect policies even in countries with strong institutional capacity and appropriate checks and balances (Anthoff and Hahn 2010; Helm 2010). Systematic appraisal of policies, using cost-benefit analysis where feasible, can mitigate these risks (see a discussion on such analysis below). It is also important for national authorities to ensure that sector policies are developed through a transparent process that provides opportunities for all stakeholders to contribute.

A step-by-step process for crafting a green growth strategy

How should policy makers design a green growth strategy that fits the country's requirements? This section proposes a series of steps to follow. A key principle is that individual projects need to be assessed with respect to a strategy rather than in an abstract and isolated way. For instance, building coal-powered electricity plants can be a useful short-term component of a strategy to green electricity over the long term, if doing so helps reduce reliance on diesel generators and is combined with demand-side action and measures to transition to cleaner sources of energy. Similarly, building coastal dikes can be part of a long-term land-use strategy to manage risks—although if it is not combined with appropriate maintenance and land use regulations, it can increase vulnerability. Given these kinds of consequences, a green growth strategy needs to be designed before individual projects are evaluated and selected.

Step 1: Identify economic and social objectives and key obstacles

Step 1 is to identify the key economic and social objectives in terms of the growth and welfare channels noted in the green growth framework presented in chapter 1 (the first three bullets relate to growth; the last two, to welfare):

- Increase production factors (human, natural, and physical capital).
- Enhance efficiency, by correcting market failures to move closer to the production function (the maximum production level possible with the available technology, physical capital, labor, and environment, assuming maximum efficiency).
- Push out the production frontier, by correcting innovation and dissemination market failures in order to be able to produce more with less.
- Increase economic resilience and reduce vulnerability to natural hazards and commodity price volatility.
- Increase the job content and poverty reduction of growth (that is, move toward "inclusive growth").

In addition, policy makers need to take other important policy goals—such as maintaining a balance in regional and local development, which may also offer a potential source of synergy—into account.

Once the objectives have been identified, the next step is to identify the market or institutional failures that retard growth and limit well-being (table 7.2). Hausmann and others (2008) claim that different countries

TABLE 7.2   Channels through which green policies could contribute to growth

Channel	Questions	Possible priorities
Increase in production factors (human, natural, and physical capital)	Which categories of capital (physical, natural, human) are important in limiting economic growth or in reducing population welfare?	Increasing transportation (and export) capacity, improving secondary education and population health
Enhanced efficiency (correcting market failures to move closer to the production frontier)	What are the greatest inefficiencies in the economic systems?	Reducing urban congestion and energy costs, increasing energy supply reliability, increasing employment of young qualified workers
Outward movement in the production frontier (correcting innovation and dissemination market failures to be able to produce more with less)	What are the obstacles to innovation and to innovation adaptation and dissemination?	Improving worker skills and property right protection, reducing entry costs for innovative firms, improving access to capital
Increases in economic resilience	Is the economy particularly vulnerable to exogenous shocks such as commodity price volatility, natural disasters, or competitor innovations?	Diversifying the economy, reducing energy intensity and dependency on imported energy, reducing vulnerability to large-scale disasters, improving food security
Increases in the job content and poverty reduction of growth (moving toward "inclusive growth")	What are the major problems in the labor market and poverty reduction, and why have they persisted up to now?	Reducing rural or urban poverty, mitigating ethnic segregation, fighting poverty traps, improving access to capital for the poor

face different obstacles to growth and that growth-enhancing policies need to be targeted to address the specific obstacles. A study by the Organisation for Economic Co-operation and Development (OECD 2011a) proposes that green growth strategies be developed by first identifying specific obstacles to growth.

Step 2: Identify environmental objectives and lock-in risks

Step 2 is to identify (1) the environmental improvements that are most likely to increase welfare and (2) the risks of irreversibility in both the environmental and economic domains. The idea is to focus on welfare-improving environmental objectives that preclude a "grow dirty, clean up later" pathway. Examples include improving water quality, reducing air pollution and flood losses, protecting soils, and avoiding irreversible destruction of coral reefs. Here (as in Step 1), the analysis should combine scientific and economic information from reports, local knowledge, and widely agreed priorities. It should rely on broad consultations to ensure consistency with population goals,

objectives, and preferences and to avoid conflicts between the green growth strategy and other planning initiatives.

Step 3: Consider six types of interventions and identify synergies

Step 3 is to determine which types of policy interventions would help a country reach its environmental goals while also improving economic growth and social welfare. This report singles out six types of interventions.

Pricing and fiscal policies: taxes, subsidies, or subsidy removal (chapter 2). Fiscal policies can be used to guide economic behavior and create environmental and economic benefits. Governments need to assess fiscal policies as a whole, taking account of the trade-offs between alternative ways to source and apply funds. Reallocating resources from fuel subsidies to spending on education, health, and infrastructure will help reach environmental objectives and increase economic growth. Reallocating these funds to services that are accessible to the poor will also help reduce poverty. Oil dependency, and thus vulnerability to oil price volatility, can be mitigated by imposing an energy tax, to favor energy-efficient technologies and equipments. Such policies would provide environmental benefits and enhance economic resilience.

Political economy considerations will play an important part in determining the feasibility of a realignment of fiscal policies with green growth objectives. Interest groups will resist the withdrawal of subsidies and tax incentives. Nonetheless, as recent efforts by the Islamic Republic of Iran to reduce fuel subsidies illustrate, progress can be made. A phased approach supported by communication and complementary policies that reallocate resources to the poor can help build constituencies for reforms. In some cases, resources may need to be allocated temporarily to compensate losers, even if they are not the poor or needy. Building in sunset clauses to such compensatory programs may help prevent temporary relief becoming another permanent subsidy.

Institutions, norms and regulations, and behavior-based policies (chapter 2). Economic incentives can be usefully complemented with other types of instruments. For instance, where low building energy efficiency contributes to high energy imports, introducing regulations or creating new mechanisms to make dwelling owners invest in insulation and efficient appliances could yield a double dividend, strengthening the economy and protecting the environment.

Policy makers must consider how environmental policies affect businesses and individuals, taking into account their decision-making biases and the noneconomic incentives that affect behaviors. A strategy that takes these aspects into account—by, for instance, framing policy changes within a positive collective project and providing individuals with feedback on how they behave with respect to the project—will be more efficient than one based on an economic argument alone. Information disclosure programs that require firms to publish their level of pollutant emissions can be as efficient as and less costly than a norm.

Innovation and industrial policies (chapter 3). The greening of the economy requires growing new industries, along with developing and disseminating new technologies. This process can be eased with specific policies that target (1) the development and dissemination of technologies and innovations, by correcting the effect of a knowledge spillover, and (2) the development of new industries and sectors, by correcting the effect of nonenvironmental market failures (such as coordination failures and capital market imperfections).

Green industrial policies can help disseminate new technologies (especially when they have been tested and demonstrated in developed countries) and develop new competitive sectors. Examples of green industrial policies that have been used include feed-in tariffs for solar electricity, or subsidies to research and development (R&D) in renewable energy. Countries with a latent competitive advantage in renewable energy (such as North Africa with solar energy) may want to pursue this advantage with the hope of creating a viable and competitive industry. However, support must carefully balance market failures and government failures given the risks of policy capture and rent-seeking, especially where institutions and civil society are weak (chapter 3).

Education and labor markets policies (chapter 4). Green transitions are likely to involve structural change away from some industries and toward new ones. Experience with trade liberalization offers valuable lessons as to how to reduce the cost and length of such structural changes. In particular, policies that facilitate the movement of workers from one sector to another can accelerate the transition and reduce adjustment costs. Where such movement is impeded by skill issues, training programs can help—for example by training construction employees to efficiently retrofit buildings.

Natural capital, agriculture, and ecosystem services management (chapter 5). An excellent way of greening agricultural production is through conservation agriculture, which simultaneously yields environmental benefits (by reducing pollution of waterways from nutrients and increasing carbon seques-tration in soils); increases the efficiency of production (by reducing the use of energy inputs); increases resilience (by frequently rotating crops); and increases agricultural productivity in the long run (by reducing ero-sion and enhancing soil structure).

But for this to work, there needs to be bet-ter information underlying decision making and better access to this information. For example, greater access to weather and cli-mate information services for farmers can improve resilience in the agricultural system and the overall value chain, including pro-duction, post-harvesting, storage, and market access. It can also help innovations to succeed (such as in weather-based risk products).

Infrastructure, building, urbanism, trans-port, and energy (chapter 6). Green sectoral interventions can help increase factors of production, push out the production fron-tier, enhance efficiency, improve resilience, create jobs, and reduce poverty. In some countries, urban congestion and the lack of efficient transportation reduce well-being and hold back economic growth, on top of causing negative environmental effects. Investments in public transit and changes in land-use plans to favor a more compact

urban area could reduce air pollution and spur growth (thanks to the benefits from urbanization and concentration). Multiple benefits can also be reaped from multipur-pose infrastructure such as water reser-voirs that produce hydroelectricity, mitigate floods, and ensure minimum river flow dur-ing drought. And regional integration in infrastructure design and investments can improve the efficiency of the system, for instance by increasing the reliability of elec-tricity generation and allowing for a greater penetration of renewable energy.

Step 4: Define priorities

Policy makers face limitations in terms of the capacity and resources to design and imple-ment reforms and the political and social capital to launch several reforms simultane-ously. They therefore need to define priori-ties based on urgency (to avoid lock-in and irreversibility) and synergies (the existence of local and immediate benefits that will help diminish political and social resistance).

Priorities can be defined by examining the policy options identified in step 3 through the lens of political and social acceptability and lock-in risk, as done in table 7.3. Columns

TABLE 7.3   Some guiding principles for establishing green growth strategies

		Local and immediate benefits	
		LOWER (Trade-offs exist between short-and long-term or local and global benefits)	**HIGHER** (Policies provide local and immediate benefits)
Inertia and/or risk of lock-in and irreversibility	**LOWER** (action is less urgent)	• Lower-carbon, higher-cost energy supply • Carbon pricing • Stricter wastewater regulation	• Drinking water and sanitation, solid waste management • Lower-carbon, lower-cost energy supply • Loss reduction in electricity supply • Energy demand management • Small-scale multipurpose water reservoirs
	HIGHER (action is urgent)	• Reduced deforestation • Coastal zone and natural area protection • Fisheries catch management	• Land use planning • Public urban transport • Family planning • Sustainable intensification in agriculture • Large-scale multipurpose water reservoirs

organize policies for the extent of local and immediate benefits they offer. Some policies provide immediate synergies between the economy and the environment (such as reducing leaks in water networks), whereas others involve trade-offs, at least in the short term (restricting development in coastal areas, for example). Rows classify interventions for the extent to which they prevent irreversibility and lock-in. Policies may need to be implemented more urgently even where they imply trade-offs, simply because acting later would be more costly or even impossible. Other policies can be postponed because they do not involve significant inertia.

In designing a green growth strategy, priority should go to policies that are high in terms of local and immediate benefits and more urgent (such as public urban transport and sustainable intensification in agriculture). Policies that provide local and immediate benefits, even if they are not urgent, can be implemented at any level of income.

It is more difficult to implement policies that are urgent but involve significant trade-offs (such as reduced deforestation). But these policies would be more costly—or even impossible—to implement later. For this reason, these policies require international cooperation, especially when they affect global challenges, such as climate change.

Developing countries (especially low-income countries) should focus on environmental policies that have a negative or zero economic cost thanks to synergies with development (such as developing hydropower where appropriate, or implementing specific urban plans); have a positive economic cost but large direct welfare impacts, that is, when they target *local* environment goods such as local air pollution or natural risks; and whose cost can be offset with external resources (such as carbon trading).

Step 5: Conduct a systematic analysis of the policies and projects included in the green growth strategy

Step 5 is to thoroughly review each policy and project as a function of the selected

priorities and strategic choices. Such a review should rely on a multicriteria analysis, given the limitations of cost-benefit analysis.

The limitations of cost-benefit analysis. The standard cost-benefit analysis—which is commonly used to evaluate public policies or investment projects—is necessary but needs to be supplemented by other approaches for green growth policies. The reason is that cost-benefit analysis encounters three major difficulties when applied to environmental or green growth policies.

First, some of the benefits (or costs) are difficult to assess and measure. Environmental benefits are often problematic to quantify and value, beyond the assessment of health impacts. But some economic benefits, like innovation-related or resilience-related ones, are also difficult to assess and are thus often left out of the analysis. For instance, the innovation benefit of a demonstration project cannot usually be quantified. More generally, benefit-cost ratios consider only one project at a time and often cannot take into account the integration within a broader, longer-term strategy and the consistency with priorities and strategic choices.

Second, different stakeholders often assign very different weights to different types of consequences, and differences in world views and priorities translate into different preferences for design and targets of policies. Cost-benefit analysis requires agreeing on values—something that can be very difficult to achieve.

Third, many of the tools and policies that can be part of a green growth strategy involve significant uncertainties. For instance, reducing vulnerability to oil shocks is a clear economic benefit, but is difficult to quantify in the absence of reliable probabilistic estimates of future oil volatility. This uncertainty arises from many sources, including technological change, climate change, and policy efficiency and enforcement. Cost-benefit analysis can capture uncertainty when it can be translated into probabilities for different outcomes. Where policies and projects involve deep uncertainty, however—as green growth policies often do—it is very difficult to estimate probabilities or reconcile different stakeholders' world views.

Differing world views, diverging priorities, and the use of multicriteria analysis. A green/wealth accounting system would allow the consequences of green policies to be aggregated and policies compared. However, as noted in chapter 2, aggregation is difficult, because many prices are missing; aggregation also raises ethical and philosophical issues on which there is little consensus. In the absence of such an accounting system, many policies will involve difficult trade-offs between improving the environment and traditionally measured growth.[2] Thus, it is useful to complement the cost-benefit analysis with decision-making methods that facilitate capturing—if only qualitatively—the full costs and benefits and the corresponding uncertainty.

For these reasons, multicriteria analysis can be useful, at least as a first screening tool. It does not provide an objective ranking of all possible actions, but it allows decision makers to include a full range of social, environmental, technical, and economic criteria and policy goals in a balanced manner—mainly by quantifying and highlighting trade-offs between conflicting objectives that are difficult to compare directly and agree on.

Multicriteria analysis is widely applied to environmental issues, including disaster risk reduction and climate change adaptation assessments. In the past several years, it has been applied to urban flood risk in France (Viguie and Hallegatte 2012) and Germany (Kubal and others 2009); to adaptation options for climate change in the Netherlands (Brouwer and van Ek 2004; De Bruin and others 2009); to climate change–related health risks (Ebi and Burton 2008); and to adaptation planning in Canada (Qin and others 2008). Older examples include identifying vulnerability in the agricultural sector and assessing alternative crop options (Julius and Scheraga 2000), and prioritizing climate change adaptation options in Africa (Smith and Lenhart 1996).

In 2002, the United Nations Framework Convention on Climate Change developed guidelines for using the adaptation assessment process in low-income countries. The guidelines suggest using multicriteria analysis to prioritize adaptation measures (UNFCCC 2002).[3] In 2011, the United Nations Environment Programme proposed a multicriteria decision-making tool for climate policies in its Multi-Criteria Analysis for Climate (MCA4Climate) project (box 7.2). The project lists the various benefits, co-benefits, costs, and co-costs of a set of environmental policies to ensure that coeffects are included.

This multicriteria approach is particularly appropriate for green growth, because it allows analysts to identify trade-offs and synergies and present decision makers with the information they need to capture the potential for co-benefits from green policies. A variety of indicators can be used to measure the potential benefits from green growth policies. Each of the channels shown in table 7.4 could be further broken down (for example, improved environment could be split into biodiversity, air pollution, and climate). Many institutions—including the OECD (2011b), World Bank (2011a), and the United Nations Statistical Division that created the System of Environmental and Economic Accounting—have proposed indicators for this purpose.

Applying such a process would ensure that the real motives for implementing a project are taken into account. For example, a demonstration of new technology that depends on economies of scale to be efficient would not be expected to pass a cost-benefit analysis (or to reach the classically required return on investment) that does not take this demonstrator status into account. These benefits can be made explicit by simply identifying the projects' contribution to a set of policy objectives, as Morocco did for a solar power project (box 7.3).

Of course, no methodology provides a purely objective way of making decisions; it can communicate only trade-offs

BOX 7.2 MCA4Climate: A practical framework for planning pro-development climate policies

Climate change is a pervasive and complex problem, with uncertainty surrounding its multifaceted impacts. Setting priorities is hampered by the lack of a systematic and comprehensive description of the issues concerned, the links among them, and the trade-offs involved. Structured guidance is needed to underpin long-term policy planning in this area—guidance that systematically considers the direct and indirect economic, social, environmental, and institutional costs and impacts.

The goal of the MCA4Climate initiative is to help fill this gap by developing practical guidance that enables governments to identify low-cost, environmentally effective, and pro-poor climate mitigation and adaptation policy choices. The multicriteria framework offers a useful planning tool for prioritizing and populating with concrete measures, including Nationally Appropriate Mitigation Actions,

National Adaptation Programs of Action, and other broad, economy-wide climate strategies.

MCA4Climate rests on three main principles:

- Climate change policy has multidimensional implications for human societies and the environment, affecting multiple interests and a wide range of values and priorities.
- If formulated appropriately, policy responses to climate change can help meet country-specific development objectives.
- Nonmonetary values, uncertainty, and the long-term dynamics of environmental, socioeconomic, and technological systems are inherent to climate change. They should be considered in the development of any policy response to it.

Source: UNEP 2011.

TABLE 7.4   Framework for measuring potential benefits from green growth policies

Type of benefit	Channels	Examples of indicators
Environmental	Improved environment	Indicators specifically developed for the domain in question (for example, reduction in greenhouse gas emissions, natural area protected from development, air or water quality)
Economic	Increase in factors of production (physical capital, human capital, and natural capital)	Measured by the additional production from increased capital (potentially measured by the value of ecosystems or renewable resources), or by the value of additional capital
	Accelerated innovation, through correction of market failures in knowledge	Measured by productivity indicators (for example, efficiency of photovoltaic panels used to produce electricity) or dissemination indicators (for example, the fraction of the population with access to photovoltaic electricity)
	Enhanced efficiency, through correction of non-environmental market failures	Measured by indicators for resource efficiency (for example, the material or energy intensity of production, reduction in the value of time lost from congestion), or by additional production
Social	Increased resilience to natural disasters, commodity price volatility, and economic crises	Measured by metrics related to the project, from avoided disaster losses (in monetary terms) or number of people at risk from floods to a measure of the vulnerability to oil price volatility
	Job creation and poverty reduction	Measured by the number of jobs created or an indicator of the impact on the poor (for example, reduction in the number of people without access to drinking water and sanitation)

BOX 7.3   Using a policy framework to analyze the benefits of Morocco's Ouarzazate concentrated solar power project

Through a public-private partnership, the World Bank is helping finance the first phase of a 500 megawatt Ouarzazate solar power plant in Morocco. The project's goal is to increase power generation from solar power, along with mitigating greenhouse gas emissions and the deleterious effects of power production on the local environment.

The project illustrates the limits of a cost-benefit analysis when a project has nonmonetary objectives and is part of a broader national strategy. Both cost-effectiveness analysis and cost-benefit analysis indicate that the project is not economically justified under prevailing economic conditions. However, a simple listing of policy objectives and the project's contributions to these goals can help identify co-benefits that would otherwise be ignored.

- The project seeks to help develop a globally available noncarbon power generation technology and to reduce the cost of concentrated solar power worldwide (a global public goods benefit).

- It will contribute to Morocco's energy and climate change objectives of security of supply, energy diversification, and reductions in CO_2 emissions, as well as other economic and social objectives, such as helping start a new green industry, developing interior regions of the country, and creating jobs.

- It will test the use of storage technology in concentrated solar plants, create a precedent for the use of the public-private partnership business model to develop concentrated solar power plants in Morocco and elsewhere, and contribute to regional integration of the electricity market in the Mediterranean.

These co-benefits can be identified using the six rubrics shown in table B7.3.1. The multicriteria analysis is thus useful for decision makers, even though it should not replace the cost-benefit analysis, which provides invaluable information.

TABLE B7.3.1   Co-benefits of the Ouarzazate concentrated solar power project

Type of benefit	Channels	Examples of indicators
Environmental	Climate change mitigation	Reduced greenhouse gas emissions
Economic	Increase in factors of production (physical capital, human capital, and natural capital)	Added electricity production capacity
		Local learning on solar technologies
	Accelerated innovation, through correction of market failures in knowledge	Demonstrate technology that has market potential in region, given likely latent competitive advantage and capacity to export solar resources to Europe
		Institutional innovation through the development of PPP. Reduce cost of concentrated solar power globally
	Enhanced efficiency, through correction of non-environmental market failures	None
Social	Increased resilience to natural disasters, commodity price volatility, and economic crises	Diversifying energy in Morocco
	Job creation and poverty reduction	Creating jobs and new industries
		Spurring economic activity in interior regions of the country

Source: Based on the "Ouarzazate Concentrated Solar Power Project for Morocco" Project Appraisal Document.

to decision makers. For instance, a cost-benefit analysis will provide different answers if different aggregation methods are used (how to aggregate losers and winners) or if different valuation methods are used (how to measure ecosystem losses in monetary terms).

Uncertainty and the need for robust decision making

Assessing the costs and benefits of a green growth strategy is extremely difficult, especially when the future is difficult to project or even describe using probabilities.[4]

Uncertainty surrounding green growth strategies stems from at least three sources:

- Many factors of success are not controlled by national decision makers. Such factors include the availability of technologies from abroad; the price of internationally traded goods such as oil, minerals, and food; economic growth and imports and exports from other countries; and green or trade policies in other countries.
- There are many implementation obstacles, and it is difficult to predict how efficient innovation policies will be or how quickly production costs will fall when production volumes increase.
- Scientific uncertainty is high. No one can project future changes in local climates with certainty, complicating decisions about land-use planning, water management, and electricity production.

Green growth strategies need to be robust with respect to these uncertainties. Kalkulh and others (2012) highlight how the optimal policy in the presence of perfect knowledge on technology potentials and market failures differs from the optimal policy in the presence of deep uncertainty. Disregarding uncertainty and basing actions on the most likely scenario is dangerous and may lead to undesirable outcomes (box 7.4).

Cost-benefit analyses can be extended to consider multiple states, each with a probability of occurrence. These probabilities are sometimes determined by a frequency-based method (How often did the event occur in the past?) or by belief-based analysis, such as

---

BOX 7.4   Incorporating uncertainty in protecting Ho Chi Minh City

Ho Chi Minh City already experiences extensive routine flooding; increased precipitation and rising sea levels in the coming decades could permanently inundate a large portion of the city, placing the poor at particular risk and threatening new economic development in low-lying areas.

In response to these challenges, Ho Chi Minh City has developed plans for, and started implementing numerous infrastructure projects to mitigate flood risks. Over the years, its multibillion dollar investment plans in sewerage and drainage infrastructure have included 6,000 kilometers of canals and pipes covering 650 square kilometers in the city to upgrade the discharge capacity of the storm sewer system and address land up-filling; roughly 172 kilometers of dikes and river barriers, mainly to control tides; and a tide control plan that uses at least 12 gates and 170 kilometers of dikes to create a polder system.

These plans were based on the best predictions of future climate and development available at the time they were made. Recent analysis suggests, however, that climate change and urbanization will be greater than expected. In fact, some variables already exceed the maximum values considered in the design phase. These surprises require significant revisions to the plans. The canals and pipes built principally to upgrade the discharge capacity of the storm sewer system and address land up-filling may not be able to handle increased flows. Increases in precipitation and tide levels observed over the past decade already exceed those projected and may top dikes and barriers. Future saline intrusion and rainfall intensity may be more severe than anticipated, potentially rendering the poldering plans obsolete before they are approved.

In addition, unforeseen effects may cause significant harm and increase risk in Ho Chi Minh City. Since the plan was created, the city has experienced unprojected urbanization in low-density areas, perhaps because of the illusion of safety associated with the presence of flood prevention infrastructure there. The city's Steering Committee for Flood Control is concerned that the insufficiency of the planned infrastructure may exacerbate flooding in some areas. If it does, the legacy of the intervention will have been to increase vulnerability.

The Steering Committee is now preparing an integrated flood management strategy to harmonize

(continued next page)

BOX 7.4   (continued)

the master plans for the storm sewer system, flood control system, and urban development. Aware of the consequences of underestimating uncertainty, they have chosen a robust approach to address concerns that their earlier approaches to planning consistently under- or misestimated uncertainties; that plans proved brittle to assumptions that proved inaccurate, leading to costly realignment; and that it was often difficult to reach consensus among diverse actors and agendas. Through an integrated, robust approach, the Steering Committee is accepting the role of persistent, deep uncertainties as a new component in its planning process.

Maximizing the robustness of strategies may require changes in decision-making approaches. Traditional decision-making processes address quantifiable uncertainty (risk) by predicting a future state and designing a plan or project for the conditions of that state. This approach produces optimal results for the intended future, but its application may be increasingly limited when faced with larger uncertainties.

Source: Hallegatte and others 2012.

Bayesian analysis (What are the odds of the event? How much do I trust my model?).

But as uncertainty grows, it becomes more difficult to characterize the probability of an event's occurrence, particularly when multiple stakeholders with differing values and expectations are involved. In such a situation, the optimal solution may be designed for a world whose existence is uncertain; that solution may perform poorly in other plausible, yet unanalyzed, worlds. In such a context, solutions should be adopted that are more robust—often achieved by making them flexible and allowing for adjustment over time, as new information becomes available. Learning and action are thus conducted in parallel, in an iterative process that includes learning and monitoring as a major component (figure 7.1). "Waiting for more information" is never an option: information has to be created, through experimentation, monitoring, and analysis. If information is not sufficient to make an investment decision, a learning plan is required.

The robust decision-making approach helps design strategies able to cope with deep uncertainty (Lempert and others 2003). It starts with analyzing a candidate strategy to determine its vulnerability to surprise and uncertainty. It then tries to reduce this vulnerability, thereby increasing the overall resilience of the strategy. In practice, this

FIGURE 7.1   Schematic for crafting solutions in the presence of deep uncertainty

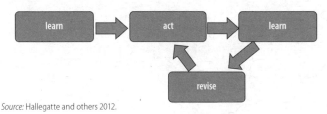

Source: Hallegatte and others 2012.

is done through a stakeholder consultation process that identifies the available strategies or "policy levers," then determines the criteria for appraising these strategies and the range of uncertainties to consider. Next, decision makers proceed through an iterative process, identifying the vulnerabilities that different scenarios expose and how these can be addressed until the vulnerabilities are reduced to an appropriate level. This robust decision-making approach can be managed through a consultative process or supported by sophisticated modeling (box 7.5).

This approach is particularly relevant when multiple policy goals and world views coexist, because it allows for a flexible definition of success and failure. A cost-benefit analysis requires a consensual objective function that is able to rank all potential outcomes. In contrast, the robust decision-

---

BOX 7.5   Using robust decision making in water planning in southern California water

Planners have traditionally used historical stream flow data and weather patterns to develop seasonal water forecasts. But because climate change is expected to change weather patterns, air temperature, and precipitation patterns in an as yet unpredictable fashion at the local scale, planners are now seeking methods to incorporate the impacts of climate change into their planning processes.

In 2006, the RAND Corporation worked with the Inland Empire Utility Agency (IEUA), in Chino Hills, California, to test its robust decision-making framework. In 2005, IEUA released its Regional Urban Water Management Plan (UWMP), in response to a projected population increase of 800,000 to 1.2 million people by 2030. The document outlined a plan to meet future water demands by improving water use efficiency and developing local resources.

The robust decision-making analysis took the UWMP as its initial strategy, used climate information from the National Center for Atmospheric Research, and employed a planning system from the Stockholm Environment Institute to assess how different policy levers would perform under a variety of possible futures.

The first run of the model evaluated the proposed management plan under four climate scenarios. Its findings generally indicated that if the impacts of climate change were minimal, the UWMP would meet its supply goals for 2030. However, if climate change were to cause significant warming and drying, the UWMP could perform poorly and miss many of its goals, causing economic losses.

Additional runs of the model, using more than 200 scenarios and 8 additional management strategies, were then performed. In 120 of the scenarios, cost was 20 percent higher than expected. The analysis revealed that UWMP was particularly vulnerable when future conditions were drier, access to imported water more limited, and natural percolation of the groundwater basin lower. Strategies ranged from increasing water use efficiency, recycling storm water to replenish groundwater, and developing the region's water recycling program. In all cases, augmenting the UWMP with additional management strategies reduced both costs and vulnerability.

The analysis concluded that local solutions should not be overlooked when developing ways to mitigate the impacts of climate change. Local policies and management opportunities may be more cost effective, reliable, and feasible than other options.

Under the robust decision-making analysis, the best management plan was found to be adaptive and to include near-term implementation of more water use efficiency techniques. Presented with these results, water managers expressed increased confidence that they could plan for the effects of climate change despite the uncertainty of forecasts.

Source: For more information, see http://www.cakex.org/case-studies/1029.

---

making approach makes it possible to combine different performance criteria. It is thus useful for the design of green growth policies, which are based largely on the identification of synergies across policy goals.

Both robust and optimal techniques are necessary elements in a decision-making process involving significant uncertainties. Analyses focused on optimality are vulnerable to overconfidence bias. Robust approaches dwell on consequences and eschew risky behavior. Managed risk-taking, however, is an essential part of development and inseparable from innovation.

One critique of robust approaches is their sensitivity to the worst-case scenario. This tendency is not an artifact of the methodology; rather, it reflects the reality of some choices; in other cases, decision makers can judge that hedging about a worst-case scenario is too expensive and not worth it. Robust processes deal with this issue through stakeholder participation and exchanges with experts. The choice of the worst-case scenario is thus a negotiated, participatory process that plays a key role in determining which policy options will eventually be implemented.

This type of approach is particularly appropriate in the context of green growth, because it allows analysts to identify the policies and measures that are necessary to avoid getting locked into patterns that will be extremely difficult to change in the future. Robust decision making thus helps identify measures that are needed over both the short and medium terms.

Moreover, the deep uncertainty surrounding environmental issues affects the type of solutions that need to be implemented. As any good solution must be context specific, the application of "best practices" is difficult. Two general rules can be proffered, however. First, solutions that allow greater flexibility should be favored over those that create lock-in; and where choices that could lead to irreversible consequences must be considered, they should be evaluated very carefully (Hallegatte 2009). Second, given the difficulty in projecting the consequences of all policies, implementation should be based on experimentation, monitoring, and generalization of successful methods.

Developing green growth strategies and responding to climate change entail an investment in planning. One option is for governments to develop specific green growth strategies alongside their core planning instruments. An alternative—possibly more in line with the goals of integrating climate change, growth, and poverty reduction policy objectives—is to incorporate green growth strategies in core planning instruments (such as national development plans). This approach highlights the trade-offs that governments will have to weigh: between predictability and flexibility, between relevance and enforceability, and among the various policy objectives. The step-by-step process proposed here helps them resolve these trade-offs, identify synergies and co-benefits, and formulate a comprehensive green growth strategy that incorporates the range of policies available, while taking into account the deep uncertainty that characterizes climate change. The process is equally applicable at the national, local, and sectoral levels.

Notes

1. This section draws heavily on Vogt-Schilb and Hallegatte (2011).
2. With widely accepted prices (and an agreed upon discount rate), all the components of future welfare can be summarized in a single number (which can be referred to as "wealth"). In this case, a policy is "good" (it increases wealth) or "bad" (it decreases wealth).
3. For an example of standardized multicriteria analysis scoring for a variety of adaptation actions, see Republic of Burundi (2007).
4. This section relies extensively on Hallegatte and others (2012).

References

Anthoff, D., and R. W. Hahn. 2010. "Government Failure and Market Failure: On the Inefficiency of Environmental and Energy Policy." *Oxford Review of Economic Policy* 26 (2): 197–224.

Brouwer, R., and R. van Ek. 2004. "Integrated Ecological, Economic and Social Impact Assessment of Alternative Flood Protection Measures in the Netherlands." *Ecological Economics* 50 (1–2): 1–21.

De Bruin, K., R. Dellink, A. Ruijs, L. Bolwidt, A. Van Buuren, J. Graveland, R. De Groot, P. Kuikman, S. Reinhard, R. Roetter, V. C. Tassone, A. Verhagen, and E. C. van Ierland. 2009. "Adapting to Climate Change in the Netherlands: An Inventory of Climate Adaptation Options and Ranking of Alternatives." *Climatic Change* 95: 23–45.

Dixit, A., and L. Lambertini. 2003. "Interactions of Commitment and Discretion in Monetary and Fiscal Policies." *American Economic Review* 93 (5): 1522–42.

Ebi, K., and I. Burton. 2008. "Identifying Practical Adaptation Options: An Approach to Address Climate Change–Related Health Risks." *Environmental Science & Policy* 11(4): 359–69.

Government of Bangladesh. 2009. *Bangladesh Climate Change Strategy and Action Plan.* Dhaka.

Government of Brazil. 2010. *Second National Communication to the UNFCCC.* Brasilia.

Government of India. 2008. *National Action Plan on Climate Change.* Delhi.

Government of Indonesia. 2009. *Ministry of Finance Green Paper: Economic and Fiscal Policy Strategies for Climate Change*

Mitigation in Indonesia. Jakarta: Ministry of Finance and Australia-Indonesia Partnership.

Government of Mexico. 2009. *Programa especial de cambio climático 2009–2012.* Mexico City: Comisión Intersecretarial de Cambio Climático. http://dof.gob.mx/PDF/280809-VES.pdf.

Government of South Africa. 2010. *National Climate Change Response Green Paper.* Capetown: Department of Environmental Affairs.

Government of Vietnam. 2008. "Decisions on Approval of the National Target Program to Respond to Climate Change". Document 158/2008/QĐ-TTg, Ho Chi Minh City.

Hallegatte, S. 2009. "Strategies to Adapt to an Uncertain Climate Change." *Global Environmental Change* 19 (2): 240–7.

Hallegatte, S., A. Shah, S. Gill, and R. Lempert. 2012. "Investment Decision-Making under Deep Uncertainty." Background paper prepared for this report. World Bank, Washington, DC.

Hausmann, R., D. Rodrik, and A. Velasco. 2008. "Growth Diagnostics." In *The Washington Consensus Reconsidered: Towards a New Global Governance*, ed. J. Stiglitz and N. Serra New York: Oxford University Press.

Helm, D. 2010. "Government Failure, Rent-Seeking, and Capture: The Design of Climate Change Policy." *Oxford Review of Economic Policy* 26 (2): 182–96.

Julius, S. H., and J. D. Scheraga. 2000. "The TEAM Model for Evaluating Alternative Adaptation Strategies." In *Research and Practice in Multiple Criteria Decision Making*, ed. Y. Y. Haimes and R. E. Steuer, 319–30. New York: Springer-Verlag.

Kalkuhl, M., O. Edenhofer, and K. Lessmann. 2012. "Learning or Lock-In: Optimal Technology Policies to Support Mitigation." *Resource and Energy Economics* 34: 1–23.

Kubal, C., D. Haase, V. Meyer, and S. Scheuer. 2009. "Integrated Urban Flood Risk Assessment: Adapting a Multicriteria Approach to a City." *Natural Hazards and Earth System Sciences* 9 (6): 1881–95.

Kydland, F. E., and E. C. Prescott. 1977. "Rules Rather Than Discretion: The Inconsistency of Optimal Plans." *Journal of Political Economy* 85 (3): 473–91.

Laffont, J.-J. 1996. "Industrial Policy and Politics." *International Journal of Industrial Organization* 14 (1): 1–27.

———. 1999. "Political Economy, Information, and Incentives." *European Economic Review* 43: 649–69.

Lempert, R. J., S. W. Popper, and S. C. Bankes. 2003. *Shaping the Next One Hundred Years: New Methods for Quantitative, Long-Term Policy Analysis.* Santa Monica, CA: RAND Corporation.

Matthews, H. D., N. P. Gillett, P. A. Stott, and K. Zickfeld. 2009. "The Proportionality of Global Warming to Cumulative Carbon Emissions." *Nature* 459 (7248): 829–32.

Meinshausen, M., N. Meinshausen, W. Hare, S. C. B. Raper, K. Frieler, R. Knutti, D. J. Frame, and M. R. Allen. 2009. "Greenhouse-Gas Emission Targets for Limiting Global Warming to 2C." *Nature* 458 (7242): 1158–62.

OECD (Organisation for Economic Co-operation and Development). 2011a. *Tools for Delivering on Green Growth.* Paris: OECD.

———. 2011b. *Towards Green Growth: Monitoring Progress: OECD Indicators.* Paris: OECD.

PPCR (Pilot Program for Climate Resilience) Subcommittee. 2010. *Strategic Program for Climate Resilience: Niger.* Tunis: African Development Bank Group.

Qin, X. S., G. H. Huang, A. Chakma, X. H. Nie, and Q. G. Lin. 2008. "A MCDM–Based Expert System for Climate-Change Impact Assessment and Adaptation Planning: A Case Study for the Georgia Basin, Canada." *Expert Systems with Applications* 34 (3): 2164–79.

Republic of Burundi. 2007. *National Adaptation Plan of Action (NAPA), Ministry for Land Management, Tourism and Environment.*

Rodrik, D.. 2005. "Growth Strategies." In *Handbook of Economic Growth.* vol. 1, Part A, chapter 14, 967–1014. Elsevier.

Smith, J. B., S. S. Lenhart. 1996. "Climate Change Adaptation Policy Options." *Climate Research* 6: 193–201.

Transparency Transparency International. 2011. *Global Corruption Report: Climate Change.* London: Earthscan.

UNEP (United Nations Environment Programme). 2011. "MCA4Climate: A Practical Framework for Planning Pro-Development Climate Policies." New York. http://www.mca4climate.info/_assets/files/MCA4climate_Summary.pdf.

UNFCCC (United Nations Framework Convention on Climate Change). 2002.

Annotated Guidelines for the Preparation of National Adaptation Programmes of Action. Least Developed Countries Expert Group. http://unfccc.int/files/cooperation_and_support/ldc/application/pdf/annguide.pdf.

Viguie, V., S. Hallegatte. 2012. "Trade-Offs and Synergies in Urban Climate Policies." *Nature Climate Change.* doi:10.1038/nclimate1434.

Vogt-Schilb, A., and S. Hallegatte. 2011. "When Starting with the Most Expensive Option Makes Sense: Use and Misuse of Marginal Abatement Cost Curves." Policy Research Working Paper 5803, World Bank, Washington, DC.

World Bank. 2010. *World Development Report 2010: Development and Climate Change.* Washington, DC: World Bank.

———. 2011a. *The Changing Wealth of the Nations.* Washington, DC: World Bank.

———. 2011b. "International Support for Low-Emissions Policy Implementation: Toward Greater Coherence." Background Note for Low Emissions Development Policy Implementation Conference, Washington, DC, July 13.